The Complete Kincaid of the Rifles

The Complete Kincaid of the Rifles

With the 95th (Rifles) during the Napoleonic Wars

Adventures in the Rifle Brigade

Random Shots from a Rifleman

John Kincaid

Unabridged & Unedited

The Complete Kincaid of the Rifles
*With the 95th (Rifles) during
the Napoleonic Wars*
Adventures in the Rifle Brigade
&
Random Shots from a Rifleman
by John Kincaid

First published under the titles
Adventures in the Rifle Brigade
and
Random Shots from a Rifleman

Leonaur is an imprint
of Oakpast Ltd

Copyright in this form © 2009 Oakpast Ltd

ISBN: 978-1-84677-906-0 (hardcover)
ISBN: 978-1-84677-905-3 (softcover)

http://www.leonaur.com

Publisher's Notes

In the interests of authenticity, the spellings, grammar and place names used have been retained from the original editions.

The opinions of the authors represent a view of events in which he was a participant related from his own perspective, as such the text is relevant as an historical document.

The views expressed in this book are not necessarily those of the publisher.

Contents

Adventures in the Rifle Brigade   7

Random Shots from a Rifleman   187

Adventures in the Rifle Brigade

Contents

Advertisement	12
Join the Rifles	13
Embark for the Peninsula	15
Myself, and My Regiment	21
Campaign of 1811 Opens	32
Passage of the Mondego	43
End of the Campaign of 1811	54
Death of General Crawford	62
March again for the North	72
Affairs on the 18th and 19th of July	83
Enter Madrid	94
End of the Campaign of 1812	103
March to Salamanca	111
Defeat of the Enemy	118
Soult's Advance	127
Returns after an Action	134
An Enemy's Gratitude	143
Passage of the Garonne	152
Join the Regiment at Brussels	162

| Battle of Quatre Bras | 165 |
| The End | 175 |

To Major-Gen Sir Andrew Barnard K.C.B.
Colonel of the First Battalion
Rifle Brigade and its leader
during a long and brilliant period
of its history
This volume is respectfully inscribed
by his very obedient
and very obliged servant
J. Kincaid

Advertisement

In tracing the following scenes, I have chiefly drawn on the reminiscences of my military life, and endeavoured faithfully to convey to the mind of the reader the impression which they made on my own at the time of their occurrence. Should any errors, as to dates or trifling circumstances, have inadvertently crept into my narrative, I hope they will be ascribed to want of memory, rather than to any wilful intention to mislead. I am aware that some objections may be taken to my style; for

> *Rude am I in my speech,*
> *And little bless'd with the set phrase of peace;*
> *For, since these arms of mine had seven years' pith,*
> *Till now, some nine moons wasted, they have used*
> *Their dearest action in the tented field;*
> *And little of this great world can I speak,*
> *More than pertains to feats of broil and battle;*
> *And therefore little shall I grace my cause*
> *In speaking for myself; yet, by your gracious patience,*
> *I will a round unvarnish'd tale deliver.*

Chapter 1

Join the Rifles

I joined the Second battalion Rifle Brigade, (then the Ninety-Fifth,) at Hythe Barracks, in the spring of 1809, and, in a month after, we proceeded to form a part of the expedition to Holland, under the Earl of Chatham.

With the usual Quixotic feeling of a youngster, I remember how very desirous I was, on the march to Deal, to impress the minds of the natives with a suitable notion of the magnitude of my importance, by carrying a donkey-load of pistols In my belt, and screwing my naturally placid countenance up to a pitch of ferocity beyond what it was calculated to bear.

We embarked in the Downs, on board the *Hussar* frigate, and afterwards removed to the *Namur*, a seventy-four, in which we were conveyed to our destination.

I had never before been in a ship of war, and it appeared to me, the first night, as if the sailors and marines did not pull well together, excepting by the ears; for my hammock was slung over the descent into the cockpit, and I had scarcely turned in when an officer of marines came and abused his sentry for not seeing the lights out below, according to orders. The sentry was proceeding to explain, that the middies would not put them out for him, when the naked shoulders and the head of one (illuminated with a red nightcap) made its appearance above the hatchway, and began to take a lively share in the argument.

The marine officer, looking down, with some astonishment demanded, "D—n you, sir, who are you?" to which the head and shoulders immediately rejoined, "And d——n and b——t you, sir, who are you?"

We landed on the island of South Beeveland, where we remained about three weeks, playing at soldiers, smoking *mynheer's* long clay pipes, and drinking his *vrow's* butter-milk, for which I paid liberally with my precious blood to their infernal mosquitoes; not to mention that I had all the extra valour shaken out of me by a horrible ague, which commenced a campaign on my carcass, and compelled me to retire upon Scotland, for the aid of my native air, by virtue of which it was ultimately routed.

I shall not carry my first chapter beyond my first campaign, as I am anxious that my reader should not expend more than his first breath upon an event which cost too many their last.

Chapter 2

Embark for the Peninsula

I rejoined the battalion at Hythe, in the spring of 1810, and, finding that the company to which I belonged had embarked, to join the first battalion in the Peninsula, and that they were waiting at Spithead for a fair wind, I immediately applied, and obtained permission to join them.

We were about the usual time at sea, and indulged in the usual amusements, beginning with keeping journals, in which I succeeded in inserting two remarks on the state of the weather, when I found my inclination for book-making superseded by the more disagreeable study of appearing eminently happy under an irresistible inclination towards sea-sickness. We anchored in the Tagus in September; no thanks to the ship, for she was a leaky one, and wishing foul winds to the skipper, for he was a bad one.

To look at Lisbon from the Tagus, there are few cities in the universe that can promise so much, and none, I hope, that can keep it so badly.

I only got on shore one day for a few hours, and, as I never again had an opportunity of correcting the impression, I have no objection to its being considered an uncharitable one; but I wandered for a time amid the abominations of its streets and squares, in the vain hope that I had got involved among a congregation of stables and outhouses; but when I was, at length, compelled to admit it as the miserable apology for the fair city that I had seen from the harbour I began to contemplate, with astonishment, and no little amusement, the very appropriate appearance of its inhabitants.

The church, I concluded, had, on that occasion, indulged her numerous offspring with a holiday, for they occupied a much larger portion of the streets than all the world besides. Some of them were languidly strolling about, and looking the sworn foes of time, while others crowded the doors of the different coffee-houses; the fat jolly-looking friars cooling themselves with lemonade, and the lean mustard-pot-faced ones, sipping coffee out of thimble-sized cups, with as much caution as if it had been physic.

The next class that attracted my attention was the numerous collection of well-starved dogs, who were indulging in all the luxury of extreme poverty on the endless dung-heaps.

There, too, sat the industrious citizen, basking in the sunshine of his shop-door, and gathering in the flock which is so bountifully reared on his withered tribe of children. There strutted the spruce cavalier, with his upper man furnished at the expense of his lower, and looking ridiculously imposing; and there—but sacred be their daughters, for the sake of one, who shed a lustre over her squalid sisterhood, sufficient to redeem their whole nation from the odious sin of ugliness.

I was looking for an official person, living somewhere near the Convent D'Estrella, and was endeavouring to express my wishes to a boy, when I heard a female voice, in broken English, from a balcony above, giving the information I desired. I looked up, and saw a young girl, dressed in white, who was loveliness itself! In the few words which passed between us, of lively unconstrained civility on her part, and pure confounded gratitude on mine, she seemed so perfectly after my own heart, that she lit a torch in it which burnt for two years and a half.

It must not detract from her merits that she was almost the only one that I saw during that period in which it was my fate to tread war's roughest, rudest path,—daily staring his grim majesty out of countenance, and nightly slumbering on the cold earth, or in the tenantless mansion, for I felt as if she would have been the chosen companion of my waking dreams in rosier walks, as I never recalled the fair vision to my aid, even in the worst of times, that it did not act upon my drooping spirits like a glass of brandy.

It pleased the great disposer of naval events to remove us to another and a better ship, and to send us off for Figuera, next day, with a foul wind.

Sailing at the rate of one mile in two hours, we reached Figuera's Bay at the end of eight days, and were welcomed by about an hundred hideous-looking Portuguese women, whose joy was so excessive that they waded up to their waists through the heavy surf, and insisted on carrying us on shore on their backs! I never clearly ascertained whether they had been actuated by the purity of love or gold.

Our men were lodged for the night in a large barn, and the officers billeted in town. Mine chanced to be on the house of a mad-woman, whose extraordinary appearance I never shall forget. Her petticoats scarcely reached to the knee, and all above the lower part of the bosom was bare; and though she looked not more than middle aged, her skin seemed as if it had been regularly prepared to receive the impression of her last will and testament; her head was defended by a *chevaux-de-frise* of black wiry hair, which pointed fiercely in every direction, while her eyes looked like two burnt holes in a blanket. I had no sooner opened the door than she stuck her arms akimbo, and, opening a mouth which stretched from ear to ear, began vociferating, "*Bravo, bravissimo!*"

Being a stranger alike to the appearance and manners of the natives, I thought it possible that the former might have been nothing out of the common run; and concluding that she was overjoyed at seeing her country reinforced, at that perilous moment, by a fellow upwards of six feet high, and thinking it necessary to sympathize in some degree in her patriotic feelings, I began to "*bravo*" too; but as her second shout ascended ten degrees, and kept increasing in that ratio, until it amounted to absolute frenzy, I faced to the right-about, and before our *tête-à-tête* had lasted the brief space of three quarters of a minute, I disappeared with all possible haste, her terrific yells vibrating in my astonished ears, long after I had turned the corner of the street; nor did I feel perfectly at ease until I found myself stretched on a bundle of straw in a corner of the barn occupied by the men.

We proceeded, next morning, to join the army; and as our route lay through the city of Coimbra, we came to the magnanimous resolution of providing ourselves with all manner of comforts and equipments for the campaign on our arrival there; but, when we entered it, at the end of the second day, our disappointment was quite eclipsed by astonishment at finding ourselves the only living things in a city, which ought to have been furnished with ten thousand souls.

Lord Wellington was then in the course of his retreat from the frontiers of Spain, to the lines of Torres Vedras, and had compelled the inhabitants on the line of march to abandon their houses, and to destroy or carry away everything that could be of service to the enemy.

It was a measure that ultimately saved their country, though ruinous and distressing to those concerned; and on no class of individuals did it bear harder, for the moment, than our own little detachment, a company of rosy-cheeked, chubbed youths, who, after three months' feeding on ship's dumplings, were thus thrust at a moment of extreme activity, in the face of an advancing foe, supported by a pound of fresh beef, drawn every day fresh from the bullock, and a mouldy biscuit.

The difficulties we encountered were nothing out of the usual course of old campaigners; but, untrained and unprovided as I was, I still looked back upon the twelve or fourteen days following the battle of Busaco as the most trying I have ever experienced, for we were on our legs from daylight until dark, in daily contact with the enemy; and to satisfy the stomach of an ostrich, I had, as already stated, only a pound of beef, a pound of biscuit, and one glass of rum.

A brother officer was kind enough to strap my boat-cloak and portmanteau on the mule carrying his heavy baggage, which, on account of the proximity of the foe, was never permitted to be within a day's march of us; so that, in addition to my simple uniform, my only covering every night was the canopy of heaven, from whence the dews descended so refreshingly, that I generally awoke, at the end of an hour, chilled, and wet to the skin; and I could only purchase an equal length of additional repose by jumping up and running about, until I acquired a sleeping quantity of warmth.

Nothing in life can be more ridiculous than seeing a lean, lank fellow, start from a profound sleep, at midnight, and begin lashing away at the Highland fling, as if St. Andrew himself had been playing the bagpipes; but it was a measure that I very often had recourse to, as the cleverest method of producing heat. In short, though the prudent general may preach the propriety of light baggage in the enemy's presence, I will ever maintain that there is marvellous small personal comfort in travelling so fast and so lightly as I did.

The Portuguese farmers will tell you, that the beauty of their climate consists in their crops receiving from the nightly dews the refreshing influence of a summer's shower, and that they ripen in the daily sun. But they are a sordid set of rascals! Whereas I speak with the enlightened views of a man of war, and say, that it is poor consolation to me, after having been deprived of my needful repose, and kept all night in a fever, dancing wet and cold, to be told that I shall be warm enough in the morning! It is like frying a person after he has been boiled; and I insisted upon it, that if their sun had been milder, and their dews lighter, I should have found it much more pleasant.

THE DUKE OF WELLINGTON

From the moment that I joined the army, so intense was my desire to get a look at this illustrious chief, that I never should have forgiven the Frenchman that had killed me before I effected it. My curiosity did not remain long ungratified; for, as our post was next the enemy, I found, when anything was to be done, that it was his also. He was just such a man as I had figured in my mind's eye; and I thought that the stranger would betray a grievous want of penetration who could not select the Duke of Wellington from amid five hundred in the same uniform.

CHAPTER 3

Myself, and My Regiment

Having now brought myself regularly into the field, under the renowned Wellington, should this narrative, by any accident, fall into the hands of others who served there, and who may be un-reasonable enough to expect their names to be mentioned in it, let me tell them that they are most confoundedly mistaken!—Every man may write a book for himself if he likes, but this is mine; and, as I borrow no man's story, neither will I give any man a particle of credit for his deeds, as I have got so little for my own that I have none to spare.

Neither will I mention any regiment but my own, if I can possibly avoid it, for there is none other that I like so much, and none else so much deserves it; for we were the light regiment of the Light Division, and fired the first and last shot in almost every battle, siege, and skirmish, in which the army was engaged during the war.

In stating the foregoing resolution, however, with regard to regiments, I beg to be understood as identifying our old and gallant associates, the Forty-Third and Fifty-Second, as a part of ourselves; for they bore their share in everything, and I love them as I hope to do my better half, (when I come to be divided,) wherever we were, they were; and although the nature of our arm generally gave us more employment in the way of skirmishing, yet, whenever it came to a pinch, independent of a suitable mixture of them among us, we had only to look behind to see a line, in which we might place a degree of confidence, almost equal to our hopes in Heaven; nor were we ever disappointed. There never was a corps of riflemen in the hands of such supporters!

October 1st, 1810.—We stood to our arms at daylight this morning, on a hill in front of Coimbra; and, as the enemy soon after came on in force, we retired before them through the city. The civil authorities, in making their own hurried escape, had totally forgotten that they had left a gaol full of rogues unprovided for, and who, as we were passing near them, made the most hideous screaming for relief. Our quarter-master-general very humanely took some men, who broke open the doors, and the whole of them were soon seen howling along the bridge into the wide world, in the most delightful delirium, with the French dragoons at their heels.

We retired, the same night, through Condacia, where the commissariat were destroying quantities of stores which they were unable to carry off. They handed out shoes and shirts to anyone who would take them, and the streets were literally running ankle deep with rum, in which the soldiers were dipping their cups and helping themselves as they marched along. They some years afterwards called for a return of the men who had received shirts and shoes on that occasion, with a view of making us pay for them; but we very briefly replied, that the one half were dead, and the other half would be d—d before they would pay anything.

We retired next day to Leiria, and, at the entrance of the city, saw an English and a Portuguese soldier dangling by the bough of a tree—the first summary example I had ever seen of martial law.

A provost-marshal, on active service, is a character of considerable pretensions, as he can flog at pleasure, always moves about with a guard of honour, and though he cannot altogether stop a man's breath without an order, yet, when he is ordered to hang a given number out of a crowd of plunderers, his friends are not particularly designated, so that he can invite any one that he takes a fancy to, to follow him to the nearest tree, where, without further ceremony, he relieves him from the cares and troubles of this wicked world.

There was only one furnished shop remaining in the town, and I went in to see what they had got to sell; but had scarcely passed the threshold when I heard a tremendous clatter at my heels, as if the opposite house had been pitched in at the door after me; and, on wheeling round to ascertain the cause, I found, when the dust cleared away, that a huge stone balcony, with iron railings, which had been over the door, overcharged with women reconnoitring the troops, had tumbled down; and in spite of their vociferations for the aid of their patron saints, some of them were considerably damaged.

We halted one night near the convent of Batalha, one of the finest buildings in Portugal. It has, I believe, been clearly established, that a living man in ever so bad health is better than two dead ones; but it appears that the latter will vary in value according to circumstances; for we found here, in very high preservation, the body of King John of Portugal, who founded the edifice in commemoration of some victory, God knows how long ago; and though he would have been reckoned a highly valuable antique, within a glass case, in an apothecary's hall in England, yet he was held so cheap in his own house, that the very finger which most probably pointed the way to the victory alluded to, is now in the baggage of the Rifle Brigade! Reader, point not thy finger at me, for I am not the man.

Retired on the morning of a very wet, stormy day to Allenquer, a small town on the top of a mountain, surrounded by still higher ones; and, as the enemy had not shown themselves the evening before, we took possession of the houses, with a tolerable prospect of being permitted the unusual treat of eating a dinner under cover. But by the time that the pound of beef was parboiled, and while an officer of dragoons was in the act of reporting that he had just patrolled six leagues to the front, without seeing any signs of an enemy, we saw the indefatigable rascals, on the mountain opposite our windows, just beginning to wind round us, with a mixture of cavalry and infantry; the wind blowing so strong, that the long tail of each particular horse stuck as stiffly out in the face of the one behind, as if the whole had been strung upon a cable and dragged by the leaders. We turned out a few companies, and kept them in check while the division was getting under arms, spilt the soup as usual, and transferring the smoking solids to the haversack, for future mastication, we continued our retreat.

We passed through the town of Sobral, soon after dark, the same night; and by the aid of some rush-lights in a window, saw two apothecaries, the very counterparts of Romeo's, who were the only remnants of the place, and for the sake of the gallipots had braved the horrors of war in the hopes that their profession would be held sacred. They were both on the same side of the counter, looking each other point blank in the face, their sharp noses not three inches apart, neither daring to utter a syllable, but both listening intensely to the noise outside. Whatever their courage might have been screwed to before, it was evident that we were now indebted for their presence to their fears; and their appearance altogether was so ludicrous, that they excited universal shouts of laughter as they came within view of the successive divisions.

Our long retreat ended at midnight, on our arrival at the handsome little town of Arruda, which was destined to be the piquet post of our division, in front of the fortified lines. The quartering of our divisions, whether by night or by day, was an affair of about five minutes. The quarter-master-general preceded the troops, accompanied by the brigade-majors and the quarter-masters of regiments; and after marking off certain houses for his general and staff, he split the remainder of the town between the majors of brigades: they in their turn provided for their generals and staff, and then made a wholesale division of streets among the quarter-masters of regiments, who after providing for their commanding officers and staff, retailed the remaining houses, in equal proportions, among the companies; so that, by the time that the regiment arrived, there was nothing to be done beyond the quarter-master's simply telling each captain, "Here's a certain number of houses for you."

Like all other places on the line of march, we found Arruda totally deserted, but with this difference, that its inhabitants had fled in such a hurry, that the keys of their house doors were the only things they carried away; so that when we got admission, through our usual key,[1] we were not a little gratified to find that the houses were not only regularly furnished, but most of them had some food in the larder, and a plentiful supply of good wines in the cellar; and, in short, that they only required a few lodgers capable of appreciating the good things which the gods had provided; and the deuce is in it if we were not the very folks who could!

Unfortunately for ourselves, and still more so for the proprietors, we never dreamt of the possibility of being able to keep possession of the town: we thought it a matter of course that the enemy would attack the lines, and, as this was only an outpost, that it must fall into their hands; so that, in conformity with the system upon which we had all along been retreating, we destroyed everything that we could not use ourselves, to prevent their benefiting thereby. But, when we continued to hold the place beyond the expected period, our indiscretion was visited on our own heads, as we had destroyed in a day what would have made us luxurious for months.

We were afterwards in hopes that the enemy would have forced the post, if only for an hour, that we might have saddled them with the mischief; but, as they never even made the attempt, it left it in the power of ill-natured people to say, that we had plundered one of our own towns. This was the only instance during the war in which the Light Division had reason to blush for their conduct; and even in that we had the law martial on our side, whatever gospel law might have said against it.

The day after our arrival, Captain Simmons and myself had the curiosity to look into the church, which was in nowise injured, and was fitted up in a style of magnificence becoming such a town. The body of a poor old woman was there, lying

---
1. Transmitting a rifle-ball through the keyhole; it opens every lock.

dead before the altar. It seemed as if she had been too infirm to join in the general flight, and had just dragged herself to that spot by a last effort of nature, and expired. We immediately determined, as her's was the only body we had found in the town, either alive or dead, that she should have more glory in the grave than she appeared to have enjoyed on this side of it; and, with our united exertions, having succeeded in raising a marble slab, which surmounted a monumental vault, beautifully embellished with armorial blazonry, we deposited the body inside, and replaced it again carefully. If the personage to whom it belonged happened to have a tenant of his own for it soon afterwards, he must have been rather astonished at the manner in which the apartment was occupied.

Those who wish a description of the lines of Torres Vedras, must read *Napier*, or someone else who knows all about them; for my part, I know nothing, excepting that I was told that one end of them rested on the Tagus, and the other somewhere on the sea; and I saw, with my own eyes, a variety of redoubts and field-works on the various hills which stand between. This, however, I do know, that we have since kicked the French out of more formidable looking and stronger places; and, with all due deference be it spoken, I think that the Prince of Essling ought to have tried his luck against them, as he could only have been beaten by fighting, as he afterwards was without it! And if he thinks that he would have lost as many men by trying, as he did by not trying, he must allow me to differ in opinion "with him!!!".

In very warm or very wet weather it was customary to put us under cover in the town during the day, but we were always moved back to our bivouac, on the heights, during the night; and it was rather amusing to observe the different notions of individual comfort, in the selection of furniture, which officers transferred from their town house to their no house on the heights. A sofa, or a mattress, one would have thought most likely to be put in requisition; but it was not unusual to see a full-length looking-glass preferred to either.

The post of the company to which I belonged, on the heights, was near a redoubt, immediately behind Arruda; there was a cattle-shed near it, which we cleaned out, and used as a sort of quarter. On turning out from breakfast one morning, we found that the butcher had been about to offer up the usual sacrifice of a bullock to the wants of the day; but it had broken loose, and, in trying to regain his victim, had caught it by the tail, which he twisted round his hand; and, when we made our appearance, they were performing a variety of evolutions at a gallop, to the great amusement of the soldiers, until an unlucky turn brought them down upon our house, which had been excavated out of the face of the hill, on which the upper part of the roof rested, and in they went, heels over head, butcher, bullock, tail and all, bearing down the whole fabric with a tremendous crash.

N.B.—It was very fortunate that we happened to be outside; and very unfortunate, as we were now obliged to remain out.

We certainly lived in clover while we remained there: everything we saw was our own, seeing no one who had a more legitimate claim; and every field was a vineyard. Ultimately it was considered too much trouble to pluck the grapes, as there were a number of poor native thieves in the habit of coming from the rear, every day, to steal them; so that a soldier had nothing to do but to watch one until he was marching off with his basket full, when he would very deliberately place his back against that of the Portuguese, and relieve him of his load, without wasting any words about the bargain. The poor wretch would follow the soldier to the camp, in the hope of having his basket returned, as it generally was, when emptied.

Massena conceiving any attack upon our lines to be hopeless, and as his troops were rapidly mouldering away with sickness and want, he at length began to withdraw them nearer to the source of his supplies.

He abandoned his position, opposite to us, on the night of the 9th of November, leaving some stuffed straw gentlemen occupying their usual posts. Some of them were cavalry, some infantry; and they seemed such respectable representatives of their spectral predecessors, that in the haze of the following morning, we thought they had been joined by some well-fed ones from the rear; and it was late in the day before we discovered the mistake and advanced in pursuit. In passing by the edge of a millpond, after dark, our adjutant and his horse tumbled in; and as the latter had no tail to hold on by, they were both very nearly drowned.

It was late ere we halted for the night, on the side of the road, near to Allenquer, and I got under cover in a small house, which looked as if it had been honoured as the head quarters of the tailor-general of the French army, for the floor was strewed with variegated threads, various complexioned buttons, with particles and remnants of cabbage; and, if it could not boast of the flesh and fowl of Noah's ark, there was an abundance of the creeping things which I could have wished had not been included in the sea stock of that commander.

We marched before daylight next morning, leaving a rousing fire in the chimney, which shortly became too small to hold it; for we had not proceeded far before we perceived that the well-dried thatched roof had joined in the general blaze, a circumstance which caused us no little uneasiness, for our general, the late Major-general Robert Crawfurd, had brought us up in the fear of our master; and, as he was a sort of person who would not see a fire, of that kind, in the same light that we did, I was by no means satisfied that my commission lay snug in my pocket, until we had fairly marched it out of sight, and in which we were aided not a little by a slight fire of another kind, which he was required to watch with the advanced guard.

On our arrival at Vallé, on the 12th of November, we found the enemy behind the Rio Maior, occupying the heights of Santarem, and exchanged some shots with their advanced posts. In the course of the night we experienced one of those tremendous thunder-storms which used to precede the Wellington victories, and which induced us to expect a general action on the following day. I had disposed myself to sleep in a beautiful green hollow, and, before I had time to dream of the effects of their heavy rains, I found myself floating most majestically towards the river, in a fair way of becoming food for the fishes. I ever after gave those inviting-looking spots a wide berth, as I found that they were regular watercourses.

Next morning our division crossed the river, and commenced a false attack on the enemy's left, with a view of making them show their force; and it was to have been turned into a real one, if their position was found to be occupied by a rearguard only; but after keeping up a smart skirmishing fire the greater part of the day, Lord Wellington was satisfied that their whole army was present, and we were consequently withdrawn.

This affair terminated the campaign of 1810. Our division took possession of the village of Vallé and its adjacents, and the rest of the army was placed in cantonments, under whatever cover the neighbouring country afforded.

Our battalion was stationed in some empty farmhouses, near the end of the bridge of Santarem, which was nearly half a mile long; and our sentries and those of the enemy were within pistol shot of each other on the bridge.

I do not mean to insinuate that a country is never so much at peace as when at open war; but I do say, that a soldier can nowhere sleep so soundly, nor is he anywhere so secure from surprise, as when within musket shot of his enemy.

We lay four months in this situation, divided only by a rivulet, without once exchanging shots. Every evening at the hour

When bucks to dinner go,
And cits to sup,

it was our practice to dress for sleep; we saddled our horses, buckled on our armour, and lay down, with the bare floor for a bed and a stone for a pillow, ready for anything, and reckless of everything but the honour of our corps and country; for I will say, (to save the expense of a trumpeter,) that a more devoted set of fellows were never associated.

We stood to our arms every morning at an hour before daybreak, and remained there until a grey horse could be seen a mile off, (which is the military criterion by which daylight is acknowledged, and the hour of surprise past,) when we proceeded to unharness, and to indulge in such luxuries as our toilet and our table afforded.

The Maior, as far as the bridge of Vallé, was navigable for the small craft from Lisbon; so that our table, while we remained there, cut as respectable a figure, as regular supplies of rice, salt fish, and potatoes could make it: not to mention that our pigskin was, at all times, at least three parts full of a common red wine, which used to be dignified by the name of black-strap. We had the utmost difficulty, however, in keeping up appearances in the way of dress. The jacket, in spite of shreds and patches, always maintained something of the original about it; but woe befell the regimental small-clothes, and they could only be replaced by very extraordinary apologies, of which I had two pair at this period, one of a common brown Portuguese cloth, and the other, or Sunday's pair, of black velvet.

We had no women with the regiment; and the ceremony of washing a shirt amounted to my servant's taking it by the collar and giving it a couple of shakes in the water, and then hanging it up to dry. Smoothing irons were not the fashion of the times, and, if a fresh well-dressed *aide-de-camp* did occasion-ally come from England, we used to stare at him with about as much respect as Hotspur did at his "waiting gentlewoman."

The winter here was uncommonly mild. I am not the sort of person to put myself much in the way of ice, except on a warm summer's day; but the only inconvenience that I felt in bathing, in the middle of December, was the quantity of leeches that used to attach themselves to my personal supporters, obliging me to cut a few capers to shake them off, after leaving the water.

Our piquet post, at the bridge, became a regular lounge, for the winter, to all manner of folks.

I used to be much amused at seeing our naval officers come up from Lisbon riding on mules, with huge ships' spy-glasses, like six-pounders, strapped across the backs of their saddles. Their first question invariably was, "Who is that fellow there?"

pointing to the enemy's sentry, close to us, and, on being told that he was a Frenchman, "Then why the devil don't you shoot him?"

Repeated acts of civility passed between the French and us during this tacit suspension of hostilities. The greyhounds of an officer following a hare, on one occasion, ran into their lines, and they very politely returned them.

I was one night on piquet, at the end of the bridge, when a ball came from the French sentry, and struck the burning billet of wood round which we were sitting, and they sent in a flag of truce, next morning, to apologize for the accident, saying that it had been done by a stupid fellow of a sentry, who imagined that people were advancing upon him. We admitted the apology, though we well knew that it had been done by a malicious rather than a stupid fellow, from the elevated situation we occupied.

General Junot, one day reconnoitring, was severely wounded by a sentry, and Lord Wellington, knowing they were at that time destitute of everything in the shape of comfort, sent to request his acceptance of whatever Lisbon afforded that could be of any service to him; but the French general was too much of a politician to admit the want of anything.

CHAPTER 4

Campaign of 1811 Opens

The campaign of 1811 commenced on the 6th of March, by the retreat of the enemy from Santarem.

Lord Wellington seemed to be perfectly acquainted with their intentions, for he sent to apprize our piquets, the evening before, that they were going off, and to desire that they should feel for them occasionally during the night, and give the earliest information of their having started. It was not, however, until daylight that we were quite certain of their departure, and our division was instantly put in motion after them, passing through the town of Santarem, around which their camp fires were still burning.

Santarem is finely situated, and probably had been a handsome town. I had never seen it in prosperity, but it now looked like a city of the plague, represented by empty dogs and empty houses; and, but for the tolling of a convent bell by some unseen hand, its appearance was altogether inhuman.

We halted for the night near Pyrnes. This little town and the few wretched inhabitants who had been induced to remain, under the faithless promises of the French generals, showed fearful signs of a late visit from a barbarous and merciless foe. Young women were lying in their houses brutally violated,—the streets were strewed with broken furniture, intermixed with the putrid carcasses of murdered peasants, mules, and donkeys, and every description of filth, that filled the air with pestilential nausea. The few starved male inhabitants who were stalking amid the wreck of their friends and property, looked like so many skeletons who had been permitted to leave their graves for the purpose of taking vengeance on their oppressors; and the mangled body of every Frenchman who was unfortunate or imprudent enough to stray from his column, showed how religiously they performed their mission.

March 8th.—We overtook their rear-guard this evening, snugly put up for the night in a little village, the name of which I do not recollect; but a couple of six-pounders, supported by a few of our rifles, induced them to extend their walk.

March 9th.—While moving along the road this morning, we found a man, who had deserted from us a short time before, in the uniform of a French dragoon, with his head laid open by one of our bullets. He was still alive, exciting anything but sympathy among his former associates. Towards the afternoon we found the enemy in force, on the plain in front of Pombal, where we exchanged some shots.

March 11th.—They retired yesterday to the heights behind Pombal, leaving advanced posts occupying the town and Moorish castle. This morning our battalion, assisted by some *Caçadores*, attacked and dislodged them with considerable loss. Dispositions were then made for a general assault on their position, but the other divisions of our army did not arrive until too late in the evening. We bivouacked for the night in a ploughed field, under the castle, with our sentries within pistol shot, while it rained in torrents.

As it is possible that some of my readers may never have had the misfortune to experience the comfort of a bivouac, and as the one which I am now in contains but a small quantity of sleep, I shall devote a waking hour for their edification.

When a regiment arrives at its ground for the night, it is formed in columns of companies, at full, half, or quarter distance, according to the space which circumstances will permit it to occupy. The officer commanding each company then receives his orders; and, after communicating whatever may be necessary to the men, he desires them to "pile arms, and make themselves comfortable for the night."

Now, I pray thee, most sanguine reader, suffer not thy fervid imagination to transport thee into Elysian fields at the pleasing exhortation conveyed in the concluding part of the captain's address, but rest thee contentedly in the one where it is made, which in all probability is a ploughed one, and that, too, in a state of preparation to take a model of thy very beautiful person, under the melting influence of a shower of rain.

The soldiers of each company have an hereditary claim to the ground next to their arms, as have their officers to a wider range on the same line, limited to the end of a bugle sound, if not by a neighbouring corps, or one that is not neighbourly, for the nearer a man is to his enemy, the nearer he likes to be to his friends.

Suffice it, that each individual knows his place as well as if he had been born on the estate, and takes immediate possession accordingly. In a ploughed or a stubble field there is scarcely a choice of quarters; but whenever there is a sprinkling of trees, it is always an object to secure a good one, as it affords shelter from the sun by day and the dews by night, besides being a sort of home or sign-post for a group of officers, as denoting the best place of entertainment; for they hang their spare clothing and accoutrements among the branches, barricade themselves on each side with their saddles, canteens, and portmanteaus, and, with a blazing fire in their front, they indulge, according to their various humours, in a complete state of gipsyfication.

There are several degrees of comfort to be reckoned in a bivouac, two of which will suffice.

The first, and worst, is to arrive at the end of a cold wet day, too dark to see your ground, and too near the enemy to be permitted to unpack the knapsacks or to take off accoutrements; where, unencumbered with baggage or eatables of any kind, you have the consolation of knowing that things are now at their worst, and that any change must be for the better. You keep yourself alive for awhile, in collecting materials to feed your fire with; you take a smell at your empty calabash, which recalls to your remembrance the delicious flavour of its last drop of wine; you curse your servant for not having contrived to send you something or other from the baggage, (though you know that it was impossible).

You then damn the enemy for being so near you, though probably, as in the present instance, it was you that came so near them; and, finally, you take a whiff at the end of a cigar, if you have one, and keep grumbling through the smoke, like distant thunder through a cloud, until you tumble into a most warlike sleep.

The next, the most common one, is, when you are not required to look quite so sharp, and when the light baggage and provisions come in at the heel of the regiment. If it is early in the day, the first thing to be done is to make some tea, the most sovereign restorative for jaded spirits. We then proceed to our various duties. The officers of each company form a mess of themselves.

One remains in camp to attend to the duties of the regiment; a second attends to the mess: he goes to the regimental butcher, and bespeaks a portion of the only purchasable commodities, hearts, livers, and kidneys; and also to see whether he cannot do the commissary out of a few extra biscuit, or a canteen of brandy; and the remainder are gentlemen at large for the day. But while they go hunting among the neighbouring regiments for news, and the neighbouring houses for curiosity, they have always an eye to their mess, and omit no opportunity of adding to the general stock.

Dinner hour, for fear of accidents, is always the hour when dinner can be got ready; and the 14th section of the articles of war is always most rigidly attended to, by every good officer parading himself round the camp-kettle at the time fixed, with his haversack in his hand. A haversack on service is a sort of dumb waiter. The mess have a good many things in common, but the contents of the haversack are exclusively the property of its owner; and a well regulated one ought never to be without the following furniture, unless when the perishable part is consumed, in consequence of every other means of supply having failed, *viz*. a couple of biscuit, a sausage, a little tea and sugar, a knife, fork, and spoon, a tin cup, (which answers to the names of teacup, soup-plate, wine-glass, and tumbler), a pair of socks, a piece of soap, a tooth brush, towel, and comb, and half-a-dozen cigars.

After doing justice to the dinner, if we feel in a humour for additional society, we transfer ourselves to some neighbouring mess, taking our cups, and whatever we mean to drink, along with us; for in those times there is nothing to be expected from our friends beyond the pleasure of their conversation: and, finally, we retire to rest. To avoid inconvenience by the tossing off of the bedclothes, each officer has a blanket sewed up at the sides, like a sack, into which he scrambles, and, with a green sod or a smooth stone for a pillow, composes himself to sleep; and, under such a glorious reflecting canopy as the heavens, it would be a subject of mortification to an astronomer to see the celerity with which he tumbles into it.

Habit gives endurance, and fatigue is the best nightcap; no matter that the veteran's countenance is alternately stormed with torrents of rain, heavy dews, and hoar-frosts; no matter that his ears are assailed by a million mouths of chattering locusts, and by some villainous donkey, who every half hour pitches a bray note, which, as a congregation of Presbyterians follow their clerk, is instantly taken up by every mule and donkey in the army, and sent echoing from regiment to regiment, over hill and valley, until it dies away in the distance; no matter that the scorpion is lurking beneath his pillow, the snake winding his slimy way by his side, and the lizard galloping over his face, wiping his eyes with its long cold tail.

All are unheeded, until the warning voice of the brazen instrument sounds to arms. Strange it is, that the ear which is impervious to what would disturb the rest of all the world besides, should alone be alive to one, and that, too, a sound which is likely to soothe the sleep of others, or, at most, to set them dreaming of their loves. But so it is: the first note of the melodious bugle places the soldier on his legs like lightning; when, muttering a few curses at the unseasonableness of the hour, he plants himself on his alarm post, without knowing or caring about the cause.

Such is a bivouac; and our sleep-breaker having just sounded, the reader will find what occurred by reading on.

March 12th.—We stood to our arms before daylight. Finding that the enemy had quitted the position in our front, we proceeded to follow them; and had not gone far before we heard the usual morning's salutation, of a couple of shots, between their rear and our advanced guard. On driving in their outposts, we found their whole army drawn out on the plain, near Redinha, and instantly quarrelled with them on a large scale.

As everybody has read *Waverley* and the *Scottish Chiefs*, and knows that one battle is just like another, inasmuch as they always conclude by one or both sides running away; and as it is nothing to me what this or t'other regiment did, nor do I care three buttons what this or t'other person thinks he did, I shall limit all my descriptions to such events as immediately concerned the important personage most interested in this history.

Be it known, then, that I was one of a crowd of skirmishers who were enabling the French ones to carry the news of their own defeat through a thick wood, at an infantry canter, when I found myself all at once within a few yards of one of their regiments in line, which opened such a fire, that had I not, rifleman-like, taken instant advantage of the cover of a good fir tree, my name would have unquestionably been transmitted to posterity by that night's gazette.

And, however opposed to it may be the usual system of drill, I will maintain from that day's experience, that the cleverest method of teaching a recruit to stand at attention, is to place him behind a tree and fire balls at him; as, had our late worthy disciplinarian, Sir David Dundas, himself, been looking on, I think that even he must have admitted that he never saw any one stand so fiercely upright as I did behind mine, while the balls were rapping into it as fast as if a fellow had been hammering a nail on the opposite side, not to mention the number that were whistling past within the eighth of an inch of every part of my body, both before and behind, particularly in the vicinity of my nose, for which the upper part of the tree could barely afford protection.

This was a last and desperate stand made by their rear-guard, for their own safety, immediately above the town, as their sole chance of escape depended upon their being able to hold the post until the only bridge across the river was clear of the other fugitives. But they could not keep it long enough; for while we were undergoing a temporary sort of purgatory in their front, our comrades went working round their flanks, which quickly sent them flying, with us intermixed, at full cry, down the streets.

Whether in love or war, I have always considered that the pursuer has a decided advantage over the pursued. In the first, he may gain and cannot lose; but, in the latter, when one sees his enemy at full speed before him, he has such a peculiar conscious sort of feeling of being on the right side, that I would not exchange places for any consideration.

When we reached the bridge, the scene became exceedingly interesting, for it was choked up by the fugitives who were, as usual, impeding each other's progress; and we did not find that the application of our swords to those nearest to us tended at all towards lessening their disorder, for it induced about a hundred of them to rush into an adjoining house for shelter. But that was getting regularly out of the frying-pan into the fire, for the house happened to be really in flames, and too hot to hold them, so that the same hundred were quickly seen unkennelling again, half cooked, into the very jaws of their consumers .

John Bull, however, is not a bloodthirsty person, so that those who could not better themselves, had only to submit to a simple transfer of personal property to ensure his protection. We, consequently, made many prisoners at the bridge, and followed their army about a league beyond it, keeping up a flying fight until dark.

Just as Captain Simmons and myself had crossed the river, and were talking over the events of the day, not a yard asunder, there was a Portuguese soldier in the act of passing between us, when a cannon ball plunged into his belly—his head doubled down to his feet, and he stood for a moment in that posture before he rolled over a lifeless lump.

March 13th.—Arrived on the hill above Condacia in time to see that handsome little town in flames. Every species of barbarity continued to mark the enemy's retreating steps. They burnt every town or village through which they passed; and if we entered a church, which by accident had been spared, it was to see the murdered bodies of the peasantry on the altar.

While Lord Wellington, with his staff, was on a hill a little in front of us, waiting the result of a flank movement which he had directed, some of the enemy's sharpshooters stole, unperceived, very near to him and began firing, fortunately without effect. We immediately detached a few of ours to meet them, but the others ran off on their approach.

We lay by our arms until towards evening, when the enemy withdrew behind Condacia, and we closed up to them. There was a continued popping between the advanced posts all night.

March 14th.—Finding, at daylight, that the enemy still continued to hold the strong ground before us, some divisions of the army were sent to turn their flanks, while ours attacked them in front.

We drove them from one stronghold to another, over a large tract of very difficult country, mountainous and rocky, and thickly intersected with stone walls, and were involved in one continued hard skirmish from daylight until dark. This was the most harassing day's fighting that I ever experienced.

Daylight left the two armies looking at each other, near the village of Illama. The smoking roofs of the houses showed that the French had just quitted, and, as usual, set fire to it, when the company to which I belonged was ordered on piquet there for the night. After posting our sentries, my brother officer and myself had the curiosity to look into a house, and were shocked to find in it a mother and her child dead, and the father, with three more, living, but so much reduced by famine, as to be unable to remove themselves from the flames.

We carried them into the open air, and offered the old man our few remaining crumbs of biscuit, but he told us that he was too far gone to benefit by them, and begged that we would give them to his children. We lost no time in examining such of the other houses as were yet safe to enter, and rescued many more individuals from one horrible death, probably to reserve them for another equally so, and more lingering, as we had nothing to give them, and marched at daylight the following morning.

Our post that night was one of terrific grandeur. The hills behind were in a blaze of light with the British campfires, as were those in our front with the French ones. Both hills were abrupt and lofty, not above eight hundred yards asunder, and we were in the burning village in the valley between. The roofs of houses every instant falling in, and the sparks and flames ascending to the clouds.

The streets were strewed with the dying and the dead—some had been murdered and some killed in action, which, together with the half-famished wretches whom we had saved from burning, contributed in making it a scene which was well calculated to shake a stout heart, as was proved in the instance of one of our sentries, a well known "devil-may-care" sort of fellow. I know not what appearances the burning rafters might have reflected on the neighbouring trees at the time, but he had not been long on his post before he came running into the piquet, and swore by all the saints in the calendar, that he saw six dead Frenchmen advancing upon him with hatchets over their shoulders!

We found by the buttons on the coats of some of the fallen foe, that we had this day been opposed to the French Ninety-Fifth regiment, (the same number as we were then,) and I cut off several of them, which I preserved as trophies.

March 15th.—We overtook the enemy a little before dark this afternoon. They were drawn up behind the Ceira, at Foz

D'Aronce, with their rear-guard, under Marshal Ney, imprudently posted on our side of the river, a circumstance of which Lord Wellington took immediate advantage; and, by a furious attack, dislodged them, in such confusion, that they blew up the bridge before their own people had time to get over.

Those who were thereby left behind, not choosing to put themselves to the pain of being shot, took to the river, which received them so hospitably that few of them ever quitted it. Their loss, on this occasion must have been very great, and we understood, at the time, that Ney had been sent to France in consequence of it.

About the middle of the action, I observed some inexperienced light troops rushing up a deep road-way to certain destruction, and ran to warn them out of it; but I only arrived in time to partake the reward of their indiscretion, for I was instantly struck with a musket ball above the left ear, which deposited me, at full length, in the mud.

I know not how long I lay insensible, but, on recovering, my first feeling was for my head, to ascertain if any part of it was still standing, for it appeared to me as if nothing remained above the mouth; but, after repeated applications of all my fingers and thumbs to the doubtful parts, I at length proved to myself, satisfactorily, that it had rather increased than diminished by the concussion.

Jumping on my legs, and hearing, by the whistling of the balls from both sides, that the rascals who had got me into the scrape had been driven back and left me there, I snatched my cap, which had saved my life, and which had been spun off my head to the distance of ten or twelve yards, and joined them, a short distance in the rear, when one of them, a soldier of the Sixtieth, came and told me that an officer of ours had been killed, a short time before, pointing to the spot where I myself had fallen, and that he had tried to take his jacket off, but that the advance of the enemy prevented him.

I told him that I was the one who had been killed, and that I was deucedly obliged to him for his kind intentions, while I felt still more so to the enemy for their timely advance, otherwise I have no doubt but my friend would have taken a fancy to my trousers also, for I found that he had absolutely unbuttoned the jacket.

There is nothing so gratifying to frail mortality as a good dinner when most wanted and expected. It was perfectly dark before the action finished, but, on going to take advantage of the fires which the enemy had evacuated, we found their soup-kettles in full operation, and every man's mess of biscuit lying beside them, in stockings, as was the French mode of carrying them; and it is needless to say how unceremoniously we proceeded to do the honours of the feast. It ever after became a saying among the soldiers, whenever they were on short allowance, "Well, d—n my eyes, we must either fall in with the French or the commissary today, I don't care which."

As our baggage was always in the rear on occasions of this kind, the officers of each company had a Portuguese boy, in charge of a donkey, on whom their little comforts depended. He carried our boat-cloaks and blankets, was provided with a small pig-skin for wine, a canteen for spirits, a small quantity of tea and sugar, a goat tied to the donkey, and two or three dollars in his pocket, for the purchase of bread, butter, or any other luxury which good fortune might throw in his way in the course of the day's march.

We were never very scrupulous in exacting information regarding the source of his supplies; so that he had nothing to dread from our wrath, unless he had the misfortune to make his appearance empty-handed. They were singularly faithful and intelligent in making their way to us every evening, under the most difficult circumstances. This was the only night during Massena's retreat in which ours failed to find us; and, wandering the greater part of the night in the intricate maze of campfires, it appeared that he slept, after all, among some dragoons, within twenty yards of us.

Chapter 5

Passage of the Mondego

March 17th.—Found the enemy's rear-guard behind the Mondego, at Ponte de Marcella, cannonaded them out of it, and then threw a temporary bridge across the river, and followed them until dark.

The late Sir Alexander Campbell, who commanded the division next to ours, by a wanton excess of zeal in expecting an order to follow, would not permit anything belonging to us to pass the bridge, for fear of impeding the march of his troops; and, as he received no order to march, we were thereby prevented from getting anything whatever to eat for the next thirty-six hours. I know not whether the curses of individuals are recorded under such circumstances, but, if they are, the gallant general will have found the united hearty ones of four thousand men registered against him for that particular act.

March 19th.—We, this day, captured the *aide-de-camp* of General Loison, together with his wife, who was dressed in a splendid hussar uniform. He was a Portuguese, and a traitor, and looked very like a man who would be hanged. She was a Spaniard, and very handsome, and looked very like a woman who would get married again.

March 20th.—We had now been three days without anything in the shape of bread; and meat without it, after a time, becomes almost loathsome. Hearing that we were not likely to march quite so early as usual this morning, I started, before daylight, to a village about two miles off, in the face of the Sierra D'Estrella, in the hopes of being able to purchase something, as it lay out of the hostile line of movements.

On my arrival there, I found some nuns who had fled from a neighbouring convent, waiting outside the building of the village oven, for some Indian corn leaven, which they had carried there to be baked; and, when I explained my pressing wants, two of them very kindly transferred me their shares, for which I gave each a kiss and a dollar between. They took the former as an unusual favour; but looked at the latter, as much as to say, "our poverty, and not our will, consents." I ran off with my half-baked dough, and joined my comrades, just as they were getting under arms.

March 21st.—We this day reached the town of Mello, and had so far outmarched our commissary that we found it necessary to wait for him; and in stopping to get a sight of our friends, we lost sight of our foes, a circumstance which I was by no means sorry for, as it enabled my shoulders, once more, to rejoice under the load of a couple of biscuits, and made me no longer ashamed to look a cow or a sheep in the face, now that they were not required to furnish more than their regulated proportions of my daily food.

March 30th.—We had no difficulty in tracing the enemy, by the wrecks of houses and the butchered peasantry; and overtook their rear-guard, this day, busy grinding corn in some windmills, near the village of Frexedas. As their situation offered a fair opportunity for us to reap the fruits of their labours, we immediately attacked and drove them from it, and, after securing what we wanted, withdrew again, across the valley, to the village of Alverca, where we were not without some reasonable expectations that they would have returned the compliment, as we had only a few squadrons of dragoons in addition to our battalion, and we had seen them withdraw a much stronger force from the opposite village; but by keeping a number of our men all night employed in making extensive fires on the hill above, it induced

Three times did the very same thing occur. In our third attempt we got possession of one of their howitzers, for which a desperate struggle was making, when we were at the same moment charged by infantry in front and cavalry on the right, and again compelled to fall back; but fortunately, at this time, we were reinforced by the arrival of the second brigade, and, with their aid, we once more stormed their position and secured the well-earned howitzer, while the third division came at the same time upon their flank, and they were driven from the field in the greatest disorder.

Lord Wellington's dispatch on this occasion did ample justice to Sir Sidney Beckwith and his brave brigade. Never were troops more judiciously or more gallantly led. Never was a leader more devotedly followed.

In the course of the action a man of the name of Knight fell dead at my feet, and though I heard a musket ball strike him, I could neither find blood nor wound.

There was a little spaniel belonging to one of our officers running about the whole time, barking at the balls, and I once saw him smelling at a live shell, which exploded in his face without hurting him.

The strife had scarcely ended among mortals, when it was taken up by the elements with terrific violence. The Scotch mist of the morning had now increased to torrents, enough to cool the fever of our late excitement, and accompanied by thunder and lightning. As a compliment for our exertions in the fight, we were sent into the town, and had the advantage of whatever cover its dilapidated state afforded; while those who had not had the chance of getting broken skins, had now the benefit of sleeping in wet ones.

On the 5th of April we entered the frontiers of Spain, and I slept in a bed for the first time since I left the ship. Passing from the Portuguese to the Spanish frontier is about equal to taking one step from the coal-hole into the parlour, for the cottages on the former are reared with filth, furnished with *ditto*, and peopled accordingly; whereas, those of Spain, even within the same mile, are neatly white-washed, both without and within, and the poorest of them can furnish a good bed, with clean linen, and the pillow-cases neatly adorned with pink and sky-blue ribbons, while their dear little girls look smiling and neat as their pillow-cases.

After the action at Sabugal, the enemy retired to the neighbourhood of Ciudad Rodrigo, without our getting another look at them, and we took up the line of the Agueda and Axava rivers, for the blockade of the fortress of Almeida, in which they had left a garrison indifferently provisioned.

The garrison had no means of providing for their cattle, but by turning them out to graze upon the glacis; and we sent a few of our rifles to practise against them, which very soon reduced them to salt provisions.

Towards the end of April the French army began to assemble on the opposite bank of the Agueda, to attempt the relief of the garrison, while ours began to assemble in position at Fuentes de Onor to dispute it.

Our division still continued to hold the same line of outposts, and had several sharp affairs between the piquets at the bridge of Marialva.

As a general action seemed now to be inevitable, we anxiously longed for the return of Lord Wellington, who had been suddenly called to the corps of the army under Marshal Beresford, near Badajos; as we would rather see his long nose in the fight than a reinforcement of ten thousand men any day. Indeed, there was a charm not only about himself but all connected with him, for which no odds could compensate. The known abilities of Sir George Murray, the gallant bearing of the lamented Pakenham, of Lord Fitzroy Somerset, of the present Duke of Richmond, Sir Colin Campbell, with others, the flower of our young nobility and gentry, who, under the auspices of such a chief, seemed always a group attendant on victory; and I'll venture to say that there was not a heart in that army that did not beat more lightly, when we heard the joyful news of his arrival, the day before the enemy's advance.

He had ordered us not to dispute the passage of the river; so that when the French army advanced, on the morning of the 3rd of May, we retired slowly before them, across the plains of Espeja, and drew into the position where the whole army was now assembled. Our division took post in reserve, in the left centre. Towards evening, the enemy made a furious attack on the village of Fuentes, but were repulsed with loss.

On the 4th both armies looked at each other all day without exchanging shots.

Battle of Fuentes De Onor
May 5th, 1811

The day began to dawn, this fine May morning, with a rattling fire of musketry on the extreme right of our position, which the enemy had attacked, and to which point our division was rapidly moved.

Our battalion was thrown into a wood, a little to the left and front of the division engaged and was instantly warmly opposed to the French skirmishers; in the course of which I was struck with a musket ball on the left breast, which made me stagger a yard or two backward, and, as I felt no pain, I concluded that I was dangerously wounded; but it turned out to be owing to my not being hurt.

While our operations here were confined to a tame skirmish, and our view to the oaks with which we were mingled, we found, by the evidence of our ears, that the division which we had come to support was involved in a more serious onset, for there was the successive rattle of artillery, the wild hurrah of charging squadrons, and the repulsing volley of musketry; until Lord Wellington, finding his right too much extended, directed the Seventh Division to fall back behind the small river Tuuronne, and ours to join the main body of the army.

The execution of our movement presented a magnificent military spectacle, as the plain, between us and the right of the army, was by this time in the possession of the French cavalry, and, while we were retiring through it with the order and precision of a common field-day, they kept dancing around us, and every instant threatening a charge, without daring to execute it.

We took up our new position at a right angle of the then right of the British line, on which our left rested, and with our right on the Touronnes. The enemy followed our movement with a heavy column of infantry; but when they came near enough to exchange shots, they did not seem to like our looks, as we occupied a low ridge of broken rocks, against which even a rat could scarcely have hoped to advance alive; and they again fell back, and opened a tremendous fire of artillery, which was returned by a battery of our guns. In the course of a short time, seeing no further demonstration against this part of the position, our division was withdrawn, and placed in reserve in rear of the centre.

The battle continued to rage with fury in and about Fuentes. Whilst we were lying by our arms under a burning sun, some stray cannon-shot passed over and about us, whose progress we watched for want of other employment. One of them bounded along in the direction of an *amateur,* whom we had for some time been observing securely placed, as he imagined, behind a piece of rock, which stood about five feet above the ground, and over which nothing but his head was shown, sheltered from the sun by an umbrella.

The shot in question touched the ground three or four times between us and him: he saw it coming—lowered his umbrella, and withdrew his head. Its expiring bound carried it into the very spot where he had that instant disappeared. I hope he was not hurt; but the thing looked so ridiculous that it excited a shout of laughter, and we saw no more of him.

A little before dusk, in the evening, our battalion was ordered forward to relieve the troops engaged in the village, part of which still remained in possession of the enemy, and I saw, by the mixed nature of the dead, in every part of the streets, that it had been successively in possession of both sides. The firing ceased with the daylight, and I was sent, with a section of men, in charge of one of the streets for the night. There was a wounded serjeant of highlanders lying on my post.

A ball had passed through the back part of his head, from which the brain was oozing, and his only sign of life was a convulsive hiccough every two or three seconds. I sent for a medical friend to look at him who told me that he could not survive; I then got a mattress from the nearest house, placed the poor fellow on it, and made use of one corner as a pillow for myself, on which, after the fatigues of the day, and though called occasionally to visit my sentries, I slept most soundly. The highlander died in the course of the night.

When we stood to our arms, at daybreak next morning, we found the enemy busy throwing up a six-gun battery, immediately in front of our company's post; we therefore set to work, with our whole hearts and souls, and placed a wall, about twelve feet thick, between us, which, no doubt, still remains there in the same garden, as a monument of what can be effected in a few minutes, by a hundred modern men, when their personal safety is concerned; not but that the proprietor, in the midst of his admiration, would rather see a good bed of garlic on the spot, manured with the bodies of the architects.

When the sun began to shine on the pacific disposition of the enemy, we proceeded to consign the dead to their last earthly mansions, giving every Englishman a grave to himself, and putting as many Frenchmen into one as it could conveniently accommodate. Whilst in the superintendence of this melancholy duty, and ruminating on the words of the poet:—

There's not a form of all that lie
Thus ghastly, wild and bare,
Toss'd, bleeding, in the stormy sky,
Black in the burning air,
But to his knee some infant clung,
But on his heart some fond heart hung!

I was grieved to think that the souls of deceased warriors should be so selfish as to take to flight in their regimentals, for I never saw the body of one with a rag on after a battle.

The day after one of those negative victories is always one of intense interest. The movements on either side are most jealously watched, and each is diligently occupied in strengthening such points as the fight of the preceding day had proved to be the most vulnerable.

Lord Wellington was too deficient in his cavalry force to justify his following up the victory; and the enemy, on their parts, had been too roughly handled, in their last attempt, to think of repeating the experiment; so that, during the next few days, though both armies continued to hold the same ground, there was scarcely a shot exchanged.

They had made a few prisoners, chiefly guards-men and highlanders, whom they marched past the front of our position, in the most ostentatious way, on the forenoon of the 6th; and, the day following, a number of their regiments were paraded in the most imposing manner, for review. They looked uncommonly well, and we were proud to think that we had beaten such fine looking fellows so lately!

Our regiment had been so long and so often quartered in Fuentes that it was like fighting for our firesides. The *padre's* house stood at the top of the town. He was an old friend of ours, and an old fool, for he would not leave his house until it was too late to take anything with him; but, curious enough, although it had been repeatedly in the possession of both sides, and plundered, no doubt, by many expert artists, yet none of them thought of looking so high as the garret, which happened to be the repository of his money and provisions. He came to us the day after the battle, weeping over his supposed loss, like a sensitive Christian, and I accompanied him to the house to see whether there was not some consolation remaining for him; but, when he found his treasure safe, he could scarcely bear its restoration with becoming gravity. I helped him to carry off his bag of dollars, and he returned the compliment with a leg of mutton.

The French army retired on the night of the 7th, leaving Almeida to its fate; but, by an extraordinary piece of luck, the garrison made their escape the night after, in consequence of some mistake or miscarriage of an order, which prevented a British regiment from occupying the post intended for it.

May 8th.—We advanced this morning, and occupied our former post at Espeja, with some hopes of remaining quiet for a few days; but the alarm sounding at daylight on the following morning, we took post on the hill, in front of the village. It turned out to be only a *patrole* of French cavalry, who retired on receiving a few shots from our piquets, and we saw no more of them for a considerable time.

Chapter 6

End of the Campaign of 1811

Lord Wellington, soon after the battle of Fuentes, was again called into Estremadura, to superintend the operations of the corps of the army under Marshal Beresford, who had, in the meantime, fought the battle of Albuera, and laid siege to Badajos. In the beginning of June our division was ordered thither also, to be in readiness to aid his operations. We halted one night at the village of Soito, where there are a great many chestnut trees of very extra-ordinary dimensions. The outside of the trunk keeps growing as the inside decays: I was one of a party of four persons who dined inside of one, and I saw two or three horses put up in several others.

We halted also, one night, on the banks of the Coa, near Sabugal, and visited our late field of battle. We found that the dead had been nearly all torn from their graves, and devoured by wolves, who are in great force in that wild mountainous district, and show very little respect either for man or beast. They seldom, indeed, attack a man; but if one happens to tie his horse to a tree, and leaves him unattended, for a short time, he must not be surprised if he finds, on his return, that he has parted with a good rump steak; that is the piece which they always prefer; and it is, therefore, clear to me, that the father of the wolves must have been born in England!

We experienced, in the course of this very dark night, one of those ridiculous false alarms which will sometimes happen in the best organised body. Some bullocks strayed, by accident, among the piles of arms, the falling clatter of which frightened them so much that they went galloping over the sleeping soldiers. The officers' baggage-horses broke from their moorings and joined in the general charge; and a cry immediately arose, that it was the French cavalry.

The different regiments stood to their arms, and formed squares, looking as sharp as thunder for something to fire at; and it was a considerable time before the cause of the row could be traced. The different followers of the army, in the meantime, went scampering off to the rear, spreading the most frightful reports. One woman of the 52nd succeeded in getting three leagues off before daylight, and swore "that, as God was her judge, she did not leave her regiment until she saw the last man of them cut to pieces!!!"

On our arrival near Elvas, we found that Marshal Beresford had raised the siege of Badajos; and we were, therefore, encamped on the river Caya, near Roquingo. This was a sandy unsheltered district; and the weather was so excessively hot, that we had no enjoyment, but that of living three parts of the day up to the neck in a pool of water.

Up to this period it had been a matter of no small difficulty to ascertain, at any time, the day of the week; that of the month was altogether out of the question, and could only be reckoned by counting back to the date of the last battle; but our division was here joined by a chaplain, whose duty it was to remind us of these things. He might have been a very good man, but he was not prepossessing, either in his appearance or manners.

I remember, the first Sunday after his arrival, the troops were paraded for divine service, and had been some time waiting in square, when he at length rode into the centre of it with his tall, lank, ungainly figure, mounted on a starved, untrimmed, unfurnished horse, and followed by a Portuguese boy, with his canonicals and prayer-books on the back of a mule, with a hay bridle, and having, by way of clothing, about half a pair of straw breeches. This spiritual comforter was the least calculated of any one that I ever saw to excite devotion in the minds of men who had seen nothing in the shape of a divine for a year or two.

In the beginning of August we began to re-trace our steps towards the north. We halted a few days in Portalegré, and a few more at Castello de Vide.

The latter place is surrounded by extensive gardens, belonging to the richer citizens; in each of which there is a small summer house, containing one or two apartments, in which the proprietor, as I can testify, may have the enjoyment of being fed upon by a more healthy and better appetised flea, than is to be met with in town houses in general.

These *quintas* fell to the lot of our battalion; and though their beds, on that account, had not much sleep in them, yet, as those who preferred the voice of the nightingale in a bed of cabbages, to the pinch of a flea in a bed of feathers, had the alternative at their option, I enjoyed my sojourn there very much. Each garden had a bathing tank, with a plentiful supply of water, which at that season was really a luxury; and they abounded in choice fruits. I there formed an attachment to a mulberry tree, which is still fondly cherished in my remembrance.

We reached the scene of our former operations, in the north, towards the end of August.

The French had advanced and blockaded Almeida, during our absence, but they retired again on our approach, and we took up a more advanced position than before, for the blockade of Ciudad Rodrigo.

Our battalion occupied Atalya, a little village at the foot of the Sierra de Gata, and in front of the River Vadilla. On taking possession of my quarter, the people showed me an outhouse, which, they said, I might use as a stable, and I took my horse into it, but seeing the floor strewed with what appeared to be a small brown seed, heaps of which lay in each corner, as if shovelled together in readiness to take to market, I took up a handful, out of curiosity, and, truly, they were a curiosity, for I found that they were all regular fleas, and they were proceeding to eat both me and my horse, without the smallest ceremony. I rushed out of the place, knocking them down by fistfuls, and never yet could comprehend the cause of their congregating together in such a place.

This neighbourhood had been so long the theatre of war, and alternately forced to supply both armies, that the inhabitants, at length, began to dread starvation themselves, and concealed, for their private use, all that remained to them; so that, although they were bountiful in their assurances of good wishes, it was impossible to extract a loaf of their good bread, of which we were so wildly in want that we were obliged to conceal *patroles* on the different roads and footpaths, for many miles around, to search the peasants passing between the different villages, giving them an order on the commissary for whatever we took from them; and we were not too proud to take even a few potatoes out of an old woman's basket.

On one occasion when some of us were out shooting, we discovered about twenty hives of bees, in the face of a glen, concealed among the *gumcestus*, and, stopping up the mouth of one of them, we carried it home on our shoulders, bees and all, and continued to levy contributions on the depot as long as we remained there.

Towards the end of September, the garrison of Ciudad Rodrigo began to get on such "short commons" that Marmont, who had succeeded Masséna, in the command of the French army, found it necessary to assemble the whole of his forces, to enable him to throw provisions into it.

Lord Wellington was still pursuing his defensive system, and did not attempt to oppose him; but Marmont, after having effected his object, thought that he might as well take that opportunity of beating up our quarters, in return for the trouble we had given him: and, accordingly, on the morning of the 25th, he attacked a brigade of the third division, stationed at El Bedon, which, after a brilliant defence and retreat, conducted him opposite to the British position, in front of Fuente Guinaldo, He busied himself the whole of the following day, in bringing up his troops for the attack.

Our division, in the meantime, remained on the banks of

the Vadillo, and had nearly been cut off, through the obstinacy of General Crawfurd, who did not choose to obey an order he received to retire the day before; but we, nevertheless, succeeded in joining the army, by a circuitous route, on the afternoon of the 26th; and, the whole of both armies being now assembled, we considered a battle on the morrow inevitable.

Lord Wellington, however, was not disposed to accommodate them on this occasion; for, about the middle of the night, we received an order to stand to our arms with as little noise as possible, and to commence retiring, the rest of the army having been already withdrawn, unknown to us; an instance of the rapidity and uncertainty of our movements which proved fatal to the liberty of several *amateurs* and followers of the army, who, seeing an army of sixty thousand men lying asleep around their campfires, at ten o'clock at night, naturally concluded that they might safely indulge in a bed in the village behind, until daylight, without the risk of being caught napping; but, long ere that time, they found themselves on the high road to Ciudad Rodrigo, in the rude grasp of an enemy.

Amongst others, was the chaplain of our division, whose outward man, as I have already said, conveyed no very exalted notion of the respectability of his profession, and who was treated with greater indignity than usually fell to the lot of prisoners, for, after keeping him a couple of days, and finding that, however gifted he might have been in spiritual lore, he was as ignorant as Dominie Sampson on military matters; and, conceiving good provisions to be thrown away upon him, they stripped him nearly naked and dismissed him, like the barber in *Gil Blas*, with a kick in the breech, and sent him in to us in a woeful state.

September 27th.—General Crawfurd remained behind us this morning, with a troop of dragoons, to reconnoitre; and, while we were marching carelessly along the road, he and his dragoons galloped right into our column, with a cloud of French ones at his heels. Luckily the ground was in our favour; and dispersing our men among the broken rocks, on both sides of the road, we sent them back somewhat faster than they came on. They were, however, soon replaced by their infantry, with whom we continued in an uninteresting skirmish all day. There was some sharp firing, the whole of the afternoon, to our left; and we retired in the evening, to Soito.

This affair terminated the campaign of 1811. The enemy retired the same night, and we advanced next day to resume the blockade of Rodrigo; and were suffered to remain quietly in cantonments until the commencement of a new year.

In every interval between our active service, we indulged in all manner of childish trick and amusement, with an avidity and delight of which it is impossible to convey an adequate idea. We lived united, as men always are who are daily staring death in the face on the same side, and who, caring little about it, look upon each new day added to their lives as one more to rejoice in.

We invited the villagers, every evening, to a dance at our quarters alternately. A Spanish peasant girl has an address about her which I have never met with in the same class of any other country; as she at once enters into society with the ease and confidence of one who has been accustomed to it all her life. We used to flourish away at the *bolero, fandango*, and waltz, and wound up early in the evening with a supper of roasted chestnuts.

Our village *belles*, as already stated, made themselves perfectly at home in our society, and we, too, should have enjoyed theirs for a season; but when month after month, and year after year, continued to roll along, without producing any change we found that the cherry cheek and sparkling eye of rustic beauty furnished but a very poor apology for the illuminated portion of Nature's fairest works, and ardently longed for an opportunity of once more feasting our eyes on a lady.

In the month of December we heard that the chief magistrate of Rodrigo, with whom we were personally acquainted, had, with his daughter and two other young ladies, taken shelter in Robledillo, a little town in the Sierra de Gata, which, being within range, presented an attraction not to be resisted.

Half-a-dozen of us immediately resolved ourselves into a

committee of ways and means. We had six months' pay due to us; so that the *fandango* might have been danced in either of our pockets without the smallest risk; but we had this consolation for our poverty, that there was nothing to be bought, even if we had the means.

Our only resource, therefore, was to lighten the cares of such of our brother officers as were fortunate enough to have anything to lose; and, at this moment of doubt and difficulty, a small flock of turkeys, belonging to our major, presented themselves, most imprudently, grazing opposite the windows of our council-chamber, two of which were instantly committed to the bottom of a sack, as a foundation to go upon. One of our spies, soon after, apprehended a sheep, the property of another officer, which was committed to the same place; and, getting the commissary to advance us a few extra loaves of bread, some ration beef, and a pig-skin full of wine, we placed a servant on a mule, with the whole concern tackled to him, and proceeded on our journey.

In passing over the mountain, we saw a wild boar bowling along, in the midst of a snowstorm, and voting them fitting companions, we suffered him to pass (particularly as he did not come within shot).

On our arrival at Robledillo, we met with the most cordial reception from the old magistrate; who, entering into the spirit of our visit, provided us with quarters, and filled our room in the evening with everybody worth seeing in the place. We were malicious enough, by way of amusement, to introduce a variety of absurd pastimes, under the pretence of their being English, and which, by virtue thereof, were implicitly adopted.

We, therefore, passed a regular romping evening; and, at a late hour, having conducted the ladies to their homes, some friars, who were of the party, very kindly intended doing us the same favour, and, with that view, had begun to precede us with their lanterns, but, in the frolic of the moment, we set upon them with snowballs, some of which struck upon their broad shoulders, while others fizzed against their fiery faces, and, in their astonishment and alarm, all sanctimony was forgotten;

their oaths flew as thick as our snowballs, while they ran ducking their heads and dousing their lights for better concealment; but we, nevertheless, persevered until we had pelted each to his own home.

We were afterwards afraid that we had carried the joke too far, and entertained some doubts as to the propriety of holding our quarters for another day; but they set our minds at rest on that point, by paying us an early visit in the morning, and seemed to enjoy the joke in a manner that we could not have expected from the gravity of their looks.

We passed two more days much in the same manner, and on the third returned to our cantonments, and found that the division had moved during our absence into some villages nearer to Ciudad Rodrigo, preparatory to the siege of that place,

On inquiry, we found that we had never been suspected for the abduction of the sheep and turkeys, but that the blame, on the contrary, had been attached to the poor soldiers, whose soup had been tasted every day to see if it savoured of such dainties. The proprietor of the turkeys was so particularly indignant, that we thought it prudent not to acknowledge ourselves as the culprits until sometime afterwards, when, as one of our party happened to be killed in action, we, very uncharitably, put the whole of it upon his shoulders.

CHAPTER 7

Death of General Crawford

SIEGE OF CIUDAD RODRIGO
January 8th, 1812

The campaign of 1812 commenced with the siege of Ciudad Rodrigo, which was invested by our division on the 8th of January.

There was a smartish frost, with some snow on the ground; and, when we arrived opposite the fortress, about mid-day, the garrison did not appear to think we were in earnest, for a number of their officers came out, under the shelter of a stone wall, within half musket-shot, and amused themselves in saluting and bowing to us in ridicule; but, ere the day was done some of them had occasion to wear the laugh on the opposite side of the countenance.

We lay by our arms until dark, when a party, consisting of a hundred volunteers from each regiment, under Colonel Colborne, of the Fifty-Second, stormed and carried the fort of St. Francisco, after a short sharp action, in which the whole of its garrison were taken or destroyed. The officer who commanded it was a chattering little fellow, and acknowledged himself to have been one of our saluting friends of the morning. He kept incessantly repeating a few words of English which he had picked up during the assault, and the only ones, I fancy, that were spoken, *viz.* "Dem eyes, b—t eyes!" and in demanding the meaning of them, he required that we should also explain why we stormed a place without first besieging it; for, he said, that another officer would have relieved him of his charge at daylight, had we not relieved him of it sooner.

The enemy had calculated that this outwork would have kept us at bay for a fortnight or three weeks; whereas, its capture the first night, enabled us to break ground at once, within breaching distance of the walls of the town. They kept up a very heavy fire the whole night on the working parties; but as they aimed at random, we did not suffer much; and made such good use of our time that, when daylight enabled them to see what we were doing, we had dug ourselves under tolerable cover.

In addition to ours, the First, Third, and Fourth Divisions were employed in the siege. Each took the duties for twenty-four hours alternately, and returned to their cantonments during the interval.

We were relieved by the first division, under Sir Thomas Graham, on the morning of the 9th, and marched to our quarters.

Jan. 12.—At ten o'clock this morning we resumed the duties of the siege. It still continued to be dry frosty weather j and, as we were obliged to ford the Agueda, up to the middle, every man carried a pair of iced breeches into the trenches with him.

My turn of duty did not arrive until eight in the evening, when I was ordered to take thirty men with shovels to dig holes for ourselves as near as possible to the walls, for the delectable amusement of firing at the embrasures for the remainder of the night. The enemy threw frequent fire-balls among us, to see where we were; but as we always lay snug until their blaze was extinguished, they were not much the wiser, except by finding, from having someone popped off from their guns every instant, that they had got some neighbours whom they would have been glad to get rid of.

We were relieved as usual at ten next morning, and returned to our cantonments.

January 16th.—Entered on our third day's duty, and found the breaching batteries in full operation, and our approaches close to the walls on every side. When we arrived on the ground I was sent to take command of the highland company, which we had at that time in the regiment, and which was with the left wing, under Colonel Cameron. I found them on piquet, between the right of the trenches and the river, half of them posted at a mud cottage, and the other half in a ruined convent, close under the walls. It was a very tolerable post when at it; but it is no joke travelling by daylight up to within a stone's throw of a wall, on which there is a parcel of fellows who have no other amusement but to fire at everybody they see.

We could not show our noses at any point without being fired at; but, as we were merely posted there to protect the right flank of the trenches from any sortie, we did not fire at them, and kept as quiet as could be, considering the deadly blast that was blowing around us. There are few situations in life where something cannot be learnt, and I myself stand indebted to my twenty-four hours' residence there, for a more correct knowledge of martial sounds than in the study of my whole lifetime besides.

They must be an unmusical pair of ears that cannot inform the wearer whether a cannon or a musket played last; but the various notes emanating from their respective mouths admit of nice distinctions. My party was too small and too well sheltered to repay the enemy for the expense of shells and round shot; but the quantity of grape and musketry aimed at our particular heads, made a good concert of first and second whistles, while the more sonorous voice of the round shot, travelling to our friends on the left, acted as a thorough bass; and there was not a shell that passed over us to the trenches, that did not send back a fragment among us as soon as it burst, as if to gratify a curiosity that I was far from expressing.

We went into the cottage soon after dark to partake of something that had been prepared for dinner; and, when in the middle of it, a round shot passed through both walls, immediately over our heads, and garnished the soup with a greater quantity of our parent earth than was quite palatable.

We were relieved, as usual, by the first division, at ten next morning; and, to avoid as much as possible the destructive fire from the walls, they sent forward only three or four men at a time, and we sent ours away in the same proportions.

Everything is by comparison in this world, and it is curious to observe how men's feelings change with circumstances. In cool blood a man would rather go a little out of his way than expose himself to unnecessary danger; but we found, this morning, that by crossing the river where we then were, and running the gauntlet for a mile, exposed to the fire of two pieces of artillery, that we should be saved the distance of two or three miles in returning to our quarters. After coming out of such a furnace as we had been frying in, the other fire was not considered a fire at all, and passed without a moment's hesitation.

STORMING OF CIUDAD RODRIGO

January 19th, 1812.—We moved to the scene of operations about two o'clock this afternoon; and, as it was a day before our regular turn, we concluded that we were called there to lend a hand in finishing the job we had begun so well. Nor were we disappointed; for we found that two practicable breaches had been effected, and that the place was to be stormed in the evening by the third and light divisions, the former by the right breach, and the latter by the left, while some Portuguese troops were to attempt an escalade on the opposite sides of the town.

About eight o'clock in the evening our division was accordingly formed for the assault, behind a convent, near the left breach, in the following order, *viz*.

1st. Four companies of our battalion, under Colonel Cameron, to line the crest of the glacis, and fire upon the ramparts.

2nd. Some companies of Portuguese, carrying bags filled with hay and straw, for throwing into the ditch, to facilitate the passage of the storming party.

3rd. The forlorn hope, consisting of an officer and twenty-five volunteers.

4th. The storming party, consisting of three officers and

one hundred volunteers from each regiment. The officers from ours were Captain Mitchell, Mr. Johnstone, and myself, and the whole under the command of Major Napier of the Fifty-Second.

5th. The main body of the division, under General Crawford, with one brigade, under Major-General Vandeleur, and the other under Colonel Barnard.

At a given signal the different columns advanced to the assault. The night was tolerably clear, and the enemy evidently expected us; for as soon as we turned the corner of the convent wall, the space between us and the breach became one blaze of light with their fire-balls, which, while they lighted us on to glory, lightened not a few of their lives and limbs; for the whole glacis was in consequence swept by a well-directed fire of grape and musketry,—and they are the devil's own brooms; but our gallant fellows walked through it, to the point of attack, with the most determined steadiness, excepting the Portuguese sack-bearers, most of whom lay down behind their bags, to wait the result, while the few that were thrown into the ditch looked so like dead bodies, that, when I leapt into it, I tried to avoid them.

The advantage of being on a storming party is considered as giving the prior claim to be put out of pain, for they receive the first fire, which is generally the best, not to mention that they are also expected to receive the earliest salutation from the beams of timber, hand-grenades, and other missiles, which the garrison are generally prepared to transfer from the top of the wall, to the tops of the heads of their foremost visitors. But I cannot say that I myself experienced any such preference, for every ball has a considerable distance to travel, and I have generally found them equally ready to pick up their man at the end, as at the beginning of their flight; luckily, too, the other preparations cannot always be accommodated to the moment: so that, on the whole, the odds are pretty even, that all concerned come in for an equal share of whatever happens to be going on.

We had some difficulty at first in finding the breach, as we had entered the ditch opposite to a ravelin, which we mistook for a bastion. I tried first one side of it and then the other, and seeing one corner of it a good deal battered, with a ladder placed against it, I concluded that it must be the breach, and, calling to the soldiers near me to follow, I mounted with the most ferocious intent, carrying a sword in one hand and a pistol in the other; but, when I got up, I found nobody to fight with, except two of our own men, who were already laid over dead across the top of the ladder.

I saw, in a moment, that I had got into the wrong box, and was about to descend again, when I heard a shout from the opposite side, that the breach was there; and, moving in that direction, I dropped myself from the ravelin, and landed in the ditch, opposite to the foot of the breach, where I found the head of the storming party just beginning to fight their way into it. The combat was of short duration; and, in less than half an hour from the commencement of the attack, the place was in our possession.

After carrying the breach, we met with no further opposition, and moved round the ramparts to see that they were perfectly clear of the enemy, previous to entering the town. I was fortunate enough to take the left hand circuit, by accident, and thereby escaped the fate which befell a great portion of those who went to the right, and who were blown up, along with some of the Third Division, by the accidental explosion of a magazine.

I was highly amused, in moving round the ramparts, to find some of the Portuguese troops just commencing their escalade, on the opposite side, near the bridge, in ignorance of the place having already fallen. Gallantly headed by their officers, they had got some ladders placed against the wall, while about two thousand voices from the rear were cheering, with all their might, for mutual encouragement; and, like most other troops, under similar circumstances, it appeared to me that their feet and their tongues went at a more equal pace after we gave them the hint.

On going a little further, we came opposite to the ravelin,

which had been my chief annoyance during my past day's piquet. It was still crowded by the enemy who had now thrown down their arms, and endeavoured to excite our pity by virtue of their being "*Pauvres Italianos*"; but our men had somehow imbibed a horrible antipathy to the Italians, and every appeal they made in that name was invariably answered with,—"You're Italians, are you? then, d—n you, here's a shot for you"; and the action instantly followed the word.

A town taken by storm presents a frightful scene of outrage. The soldiers no sooner obtain possession of it, than they think themselves at liberty to do what they please. It is enough for them that there had been an enemy on the ramparts; and, without considering that the poor inhabitants may nevertheless be friends and allies, they, in the first moment of excitement, all share one common fate; and nothing but the most extraordinary exertions on the part of the officers can bring them back to a sense of their duty.

We continued our course round the ramparts until we met the head of the column which had gone by the right, and then descended into the town. At the entrance of the first street, a French officer came out of a door and claimed my protection, giving me his sword. He told me that there was another officer in the same house who was afraid to venture out, and entreated that I would go in for him. I accordingly followed him up to the landing-place of a dark stair, and, while he was calling to his friend, by name, to come down, "as there was an English officer present who would protect him," a violent screaming broke through a door at my elbow.

I pushed it open, and found the landlady struggling on the floor with an English soldier, whom I immediately transferred to the bottom of the stair head foremost. The French officer had followed me in at the door, and was so astonished at all he saw, that he held up his hands, turned up the whites of his eyes, and resolved himself into a state of the most eloquent silence. When he did recover the use of his tongue, it was to recommend his landlady to my notice, as the most amiable of women. She, on her part, professed the most unbounded gratitude and entreated that I would henceforth make her house my home; but, when I called upon her, a few days after, her husband happening to be present, she denied having ever seen me before, and stuck to it most religiously.

As the other officer could not be found, I descended into the street again with my prisoner; and, finding the current of soldiers setting towards the centre of the town, I followed the stream, which conducted me into the great square, on one side of which the late garrison were drawn up as prisoners, and the rest of it was filled with British and Portuguese intermixed, without any order or regularity.

I had been there but a very short time, when they all commenced firing, without any ostensible cause; some fired in at the doors and windows, some at the roofs of houses, and others at the clouds; and, at last, some heads began to be blown from their shoulders in the general hurricane, when the voice of Sir Thomas Picton, with the power of twenty trumpets, began to proclaim damnation to everybody, while Colonel Barnard, Colonel Cameron, and some other active officers, were carrying it into effect with a strong hand; for, seizing the broken barrels of muskets, which were lying about in great abundance, they belaboured every fellow, most unmercifully, about the head who attempted either to load or fire, and finally succeeded in reducing them to order. In the midst of the scuffle, however, three of the houses in the square were set on fire; and the confusion was such that nothing could be done to save them; but by the extraordinary exertions of Colonel Barnard, during the whole of the night, the flames were prevented from communicating to the adjoining buildings.

We succeeded in getting a great portion of our battalion together by one o'clock in the morning, and withdrew with them to the ramparts, where we lay by our arms until daylight.

There is nothing in this life half so enviable as the feelings of a soldier after a victory. Previous to a battle, there is a certain sort of something that pervades the mind, which is not easily defined; it is neither akin to joy nor fear, and, probably, anxiety may be nearer to it than any other word in the dictionary; but, when the battle is over, and crowned with victory, he finds himself elevated for awhile into the regions of absolute bliss!

It had ever been the summit of my ambition to attain a post at the head of a storming party:—my wish had now been accomplished, and gloriously ended; and I do think, after all was over, and our men laid asleep on the ramparts, that I strutted about as important a personage, in my own opinion, as ever trod the face of the earth; and had the ghost of the renowned Jack-the-Giant-killer itself passed that way at the time, I'll venture to say, that I would have given it a kick in the breech without the smallest ceremony. But, as the sun began to rise, I began to fall from heroics; and, when he showed his face, I took a look at my own, and found that I was too unclean a spirit to worship, for I was covered with mud and dirt, with the greater part of my dress torn to rags.

The Fifth Division, which had not been employed in the siege, marched in, and took charge of the town, on the morning of the 20th, and we prepared to return to our cantonments. Lord Wellington happened to be riding in at the gate at the time that we marched out, and had the curiosity to ask the officer of the leading company what regiment it was, for there was scarcely a vestige of uniform among the men. Some of them were dressed in Frenchmen's coats, some in white breeches and huge jackboots, some with cocked hats and queues; most of their swords were fixed on their rifles, and stuck full of hams, tongues, and loaves of bread, and not a few were carrying bird-cages! There never was a better masked corps!

General Crawford fell on the glacis, at the head of our division, and was buried at the foot of the breach which they so gallantly carried. His funeral was attended by Lord Wellington, and all the officers of the division, by whom he was, ultimately, much liked. He had introduced a system of discipline into the Light Division which made them unrivalled. A very rigid exaction of the duties pointed out in his code of regulations made him very unpopular at its commencement; and it was not until a short time before he was lost to us forever, that we were capable of appreciating his merits, and fully sensible of the incalculable advantages we derived from the perfection of his system.

Among other things carried from Ciudad Rodrigo, one of our men had the misfortune to carry his death in his hands, under the mistaken shape of amusement. He thought it was a cannonball, and took it up for the purpose of playing at the game of nine-holes; but it happened to be a live shell. In rolling it along it went over a bed of burning ashes, and ignited without his observing it. Just as he had got it between his legs, and was in the act of discharging it a second time, it exploded, and blew him nearly to pieces.

Several men of our division who had deserted while we were blockading Ciudad Rodrigo, were taken when it fell, and sentenced to be shot. Lord Wellington extended mercy to everyone who could procure anything like a good character from his officers; but six of them, who could not, were paraded and shot, in front of the division, near the village of Ituera. Shooting appears to me to be a cruel kind of execution, for twenty balls may pierce a man's body without touching a vital part. On the occasion alluded to, two of the men remained standing after the first fire, and the provost-marshal was obliged to put an end to their sufferings, by placing the muzzle of a musket at each of their heads.

Chapter 8

March again for the North

We remained about six weeks in cantonments, after the fall of Ciudad Rodrigo; and, about the end of February, were again put in motion towards Estremadura.

March 7th.—Arrived near Castello de Vide, and quartered in the neighbouring villages. Another deserter, who had also been taken at the storming of Ciudad Rodrigo, was here shot, under the sentence of court-martial. When he was paraded for that purpose, he protested against their right to shoot him, until he first received the arrears of pay which was due at the time of his desertion.

March 14th.—Two of us rode out this afternoon to kill time until dinner hour (six); but, when we returned to our quarters, there was not a vestige of the regiment remaining, and our appetites were considerably whetted, by having an additional distance of fourteen miles to ride, in the dark, over roads on which we could not trust our horses out of a walk. We joined them, at about eleven at night, in the town of Portalegré.

March 16th.—Quartered in the town of Elvas.

I received a billet on a neat little house, occupied by an old lady and her daughter, who were very desirous of evading such an encumbrance. For, after resisting my entrance, until successive applications of my foot had reduced the door to a condition which would no longer second their efforts, the old lady resolved to try me on another tack; for, opening the door, and making a sign for me to make no noise, she said, in a whisper, that her daughter was lying dangerously ill of a fever, in the only bed in the house, and that she was therefore excessively sorry that she could not accommodate me. As this information did not at all accord with my notions of consistency, after their having suffered the preceding half-hour's bombardment, I requested to be shown to the chamber of the invalid, saying that I was a *medico*, and might be of service to her. When she found remonstrance unavailing, she at length showed me into a room upstairs, where there was a very genteel-looking young girl, the very picture of Portuguese health, lying with her eyes shut, in full dress, on the top of the bedclothes, where she had hurriedly thrown herself.

Seeing at once how matters stood, I walked up to the bedside and hit her a slap on the thigh with my hand, asking her at the same time how she felt herself! Never did Prince Hohenloe himself perform a miracle more cleverly, for she bounced almost as high as the ceiling, and flounced about the room, as well and as actively as ever she did, with a countenance in which shame, anger, and a great portion of natural humour were so amusingly blended, that I was tempted to provoke her still further by a salute.

Having thus satisfied the mother that I had been the means of restoring her daughter to her usual state of health, she thought it prudent to put the best face upon it, and therefore invited me to partake of their family dinner; in the course of which I succeeded so well in eating my way into their affections, that we parted next morning with mutual regret. They told me that I was the best officer they had ever seen, and begged that I would always make their house my home; but I was never fated to see them again. We marched in the morning for Badajos.

Siege of Badajos

On the 17th of March, 1812, the Third, Fourth, and Light Divisions, encamped around Badajos, embracing the whole of the inland side of the town on the left bank of the Guadiana, and commenced breaking ground before it immediately after dark the same night.

The elements, on this occasion, adopted the cause of the besieged; for we had scarcely taken up the ground when a heavy rain commenced, and continued, almost without inter-mission, for a fortnight: in consequence thereof, the pontoon bridge, connecting us with our supplies from Elvas, was carried away by the rapid increase of the river, and the duties of the trenches were otherwise rendered extremely harassing.

We had a smaller force employed than at Rodrigo; and the scale of operations was so much greater, that it required every man to be actually in the trenches six hours every day, and the same length of time every night, which with the time required to march to and from them, through fields more than ankle-deep in stiff mud, left us never more than eight hours out of the twenty-four in camp, and we never were dry the whole time.

One day's trench-work is as like another as the days themselves; and like nothing better than serving an apprenticeship to the double calling of grave-digger and game-keeper, for we found ample employment for both the spade and the rifle.

The only varieties during the siege were,—

First,—The storming of Picuvina, a formidable outwork, occupying the centre of our operations. It was carried one evening in the most gallant style, by Major-General Sir James Kempt, at the head of the covering parties.

Secondly,—A sortie made by the garrison, which they got the worst of, although they succeeded in stealing some of our pickaxes and shovels.

Thirdly,—A *circumbendibus* described by a few daring French dragoons, who succeeded in getting into the rear of our engineers' camp, at that time unguarded, and lightened some of the officers of their epaulettes.

Lastly,—Two field-pieces taken by the enemy to the opposite side of the river, enfilading one of our parallels, and materially disturbing the harmony within, as a cannon shot is no very welcome guest among gentlemen who happened to be lodged in a straight ditch, without the power of cutting it.

Our batteries were supplied with ammunition, by the Portuguese militia, from Elvas, a string of whom used to arrive every day, reaching nearly from the one place to the other, (twelve miles), each man carrying a twenty-four pound shot, and cursing all the way and back again.

The Portuguese artillery, under British officers, was uncommonly good. I used to be much amused in looking at a twelve gun breaching-battery of theirs.

They knew the position of all the enemy's guns that could bear upon them, and had one man posted to watch them, to give notice of what was coming, whether a shot or a shell, who, accordingly, kept calling out, "*Bomba, balla, balla, bomba!*" and they ducked their heads until the missile passed; but sometimes would see a general discharge from all arms, when he would throw himself down, screaming out "*Jesus, todos, todos!*" meaning "everything."

An officer of ours, was sent one morning before daylight, with ten men, to dig holes for themselves opposite to one of the enemy's guns, which had been doing a great deal of mischief the day before; and he had soon the satisfaction of knowing the effect of his practice, by seeing them stopping up the embrasure with sand bags. After waiting a little, he saw them beginning to remove the sand bags; but, renewing his fire upon it, they were instantly replaced without the guns being fired.

Presently he saw the huge cocked hat of a French officer make its appearance on the rampart, near to the embrasure; but knowing by experience that the head was somewhere in the neighbourhood, he watched until the flash of a musket, through the long grass, showed the position of the owner, and, calling one of his best shots, he desired him to take deliberate aim at the spot, and lent his shoulder as a rest, to give it more elevation. Bang went the shot; and it was the finishing flash for the Frenchman, for they saw no more of him, although his cocked hat maintained its post until dark.

In proportion as the grand crisis approached, the anxiety of the soldiers increased; not on account of any doubt or dread as to the result, but for fear that the place should be surrendered without standing an assault; for, singular as it may appear, although there was a certainty of about one man out of every three being knocked down, there were, perhaps, not three men in the three divisions, who would not rather have braved all the chances than receive it tamely from the hands of the enemy. So great was the rage for passports into eternity, in our battalion, on that occasion, that even the officers' servants insisted on taking their places in the ranks; and I was obliged to leave my baggage in charge of a man who had been wounded some days before.

On the 6th of April, three practicable breaches had been effected, and arrangements were made for assaulting the town that night. The Third Division, by escalade, at the castle; a brigade of the Fifth Division, by escalade, at the opposite side of the town; while the Fourth and Light Divisions were to storm the breaches. The whole were ordered to be formed for the attack at eight o'clock.

Storming of Badajos
April 6th, 1812

Our division formed for the attack of the left breach in the same order as at Ciudad Rodrigo: the command of it had now devolved upon our commandant, Colonel Barnard. I was then the acting adjutant of four companies, under Colonel Cameron, who were to line the crest of the glacis, and to fire at the ramparts and the top of the left breach.

The enemy seemed aware of our intentions. The fire of artillery and musketry, which, for three weeks before, had been incessant, both from the town and trenches, had now entirely ceased, as if by mutual consent, and a death-like silence, of nearly an hour, preceded the awful scene of carnage.

The signal to advance was made about nine o'clock, and our four companies led the way. Colonel Cameron and myself had reconnoitred the ground so accurately by daylight, that we succeeded in bringing the head of our column to the very spot agreed on, opposite to the left breach, and then formed line to the left, without a word being spoken, each man lying down as he got into line, with the muzzle of his rifle over the edge of the ditch, between the palisades, all ready to open.

It was tolerably clear above, and we distinctly saw their heads lining the ramparts; but there was a sort of haze on the ground, which, with the colour of our dress, prevented them from seeing us, although only a few yards asunder. One of their sentries, however, challenged us twice, "*qui vive*" and receiving no reply, he fired off his musket, which was followed by their drums beating to arms; but we still remained perfectly quiet, and all was silence again for the space of five or ten minutes, when the head of the forlorn hope at length came up, and we took advantage of the first fire, while the enemy's heads were yet visible.

The scene that ensued furnished as respectable a representation of hell itself as fire, and sword, and human sacrifices could make it; for, in one instant, every engine of destruction was in full operation.

It is in vain to attempt a description of it. We were entirely excluded from the right breach by an inundation which the heavy rains had enabled the enemy to form; and the two others were rendered totally impracticable by their interior defences.

The five succeeding hours were therefore passed in the most gallant but hopeless attempts on the part of individual officers, forming up fifty or a hundred men at a time at the foot of the breach, and endeavouring to carry it by desperate bravery; and fatal as it proved to each gallant band, in succession, yet, fast as one dissolved, another was formed. We were informed, about twelve at night, that the Third Division had established themselves in the castle; but, as its situation and construction did not permit them to extend their operations beyond it at the moment, it did not in the least affect our opponents at the breach, whose defence continued as obstinate as ever.

I was near Colonel Barnard after midnight, when he received repeated messages from Lord Wellington to withdraw from the breach, and to form the division for a renewal of the attack at daylight; but as fresh attempts continued to be made, and the troops were still pressing forward into the ditch, it went against his gallant soul to order a retreat while yet a chance remained; but, after heading repeated attempts himself, he saw that it was hopeless, and the order was reluctantly given about two o'clock in the morning. We fell back about three hundred yards, and re-formed all that remained to us.

Our regiment, alone, had to lament the loss of twenty-two officers killed and wounded, ten of whom were killed, or afterwards died of their wounds. We had scarcely got our men together when we were informed of the success of the Fifth Division in their escalade, and that the enemy were, in consequence, abandoning the breaches, and we were immediately ordered forward to take possession of them.

On our arrival, we found them entirely evacuated, and had not occasion to fire another shot; but we found the utmost difficulty, and even danger, in getting in, in the dark, even without opposition. As soon as we succeeded in establishing our battalion inside, we sent piquets into the different streets and lanes leading from the breach, and kept the remainder in hand until day should throw some light on our situation.

When I was in the act of posting one of the piquets, a man of ours brought me a prisoner, telling me that he was the governor; but the other immediately said that he had only called himself so, the better to ensure his protection; and then added, that he was the colonel of one of the French regiments, and that all his surviving officers were assembled at his quarters, in a street close by, and would surrender themselves to any officer who would go with him for that purpose. I accordingly took two or three men with me, and, accompanying him there, found fifteen or sixteen of them assembled, all seemingly very much surprised at the unexpected termination of the siege.

They could not comprehend under what circumstances the town had been lost, and repeatedly asked me how I got in; but I did not choose to explain further than simply telling them that

I entered at the breach, coupling the information with a look which was calculated to convey somewhat more than I knew myself; for, in truth, when I began to reflect that a few minutes before had seen me retiring from the breach, under a fanciful overload of degradation, I thought that I had now as good a right as any man to be astonished at finding myself lording it over the officers of a French battalion; nor was I much wiser than they were, as to the manner of its accomplishment.

They were all very much dejected, except their major, who was a big, jolly-looking Dutchman, with medals enough on his left breast to have furnished the window of a tolerable toyshop. His accomplishments were after the manner of Captain Dugald Dalgetty; and, while he cracked his joke, he was not inattentive to the cracking of the corks from the many wine bottles which his colonel placed on the table successively, along with some cold meat, for general refreshment prior to marching into captivity, and which I, though a free man, was not too proud to join them in.

When I had allowed their chief a reasonable time to secure what valuables he wished, about his person, he told me that he had two horses in the stable, which, as he would no longer be permitted to keep, he recommended me to take; and as a horse is the only thing on such occasions that an officer can permit himself to consider a legal prize, I caused one of them to be saddled; and his handsome black mare thereby became my charger during the remainder of the war.

In proceeding with my prisoners towards the breach, I took, by mistake, a different road to that I came: and as numbers of Frenchmen were lurking about for a safe opportunity of surrendering themselves, about a hundred additional ones added themselves to my column, as we moved along, jabbering their native dialect so loudly, as nearly to occasion a dire catastrophe, as it prevented me from hearing someone challenge in my front; but, fortunately, it was repeated, and I instantly answered; for Colonel Barnard and Sir Colin Campbell had a piquet of our men, drawn across the street, on the point of sending a volley into us, thinking that we were a rallied body of the enemy.

The whole of the garrison were marched off as prisoners, to Elvas, about ten o'clock in the morning, and our men were then permitted to fall out, to enjoy themselves for the remainder of the day, as a reward for having kept together so long as they were wanted. The greater part of the three divisions were, by this time, loose in the town; and the usual frightful scene of plunder commenced, which the officers thought it prudent to avoid for the moment, by retiring to the camp.

We went into the town on the morning of the 8th, to endeavour to collect our men, but only succeeded in part, as the same extraordinary scene of plunder and rioting still continued. Wherever there was anything to eat or drink (the only saleable commodities), the soldiers had turned the shopkeepers out of doors, and placed themselves regularly behind the counter, selling off the contents of the shop. By and bye, another and a stronger party would kick those out in their turn, and there was no end to the succession of self-elected shopkeepers, until Lord Wellington found that, to restore order, severe measures must be resorted to.

On the third day, he caused a Portuguese brigade to be marched in, and kept standing to their arms, in the great square, where the provost-marshal erected a gallows, and proceeded to suspend some of the delinquents, which very quickly cleared the town of the remainder, and enabled us to give a more satisfactory account of our battalion than we had hitherto been able to do.

It is wonderful how such scenes as these will deaden men's finer feelings, and with what apathy it enables them to look upon the sufferings of their fellow-creatures! The third day after the fall of the town, I rode, with Colonel Cameron, to take a bathe in the Guadiana, and, in passing the verge of the camp of the 5th Division, we saw two soldiers standing at the door of a small shed, or outhouse, shouting, waving their caps, and making signs that they wanted to speak to us.

We rode up to see what they wanted, and found that the

poor fellows had each lost a leg. They told us that a surgeon had dressed their wounds on the night of the assault, but that they had ever since been without food or assistance of any kind, although they, each day, had opportunities of soliciting the aid of many of their comrades, from whom they could obtain nothing but promises. In short, surrounded by thousands of their countrymen within call, and not more than three hundred yards from their own regiment, they were unable to interest any one in their behalf, and were literally starving.

It is unnecessary to say that we instantly galloped back to the camp and had them removed to the hospital.

On the morning of the 7th, when some of our officers were performing the last duties to their fallen comrades, one of them had collected the bodies of four of our young officers, who had been slain. He was in the act of digging a grave for them, when an officer of the guards arrived on the spot, from a distant division of the army, and demanded tidings of his brother, who was at that moment lying a naked lifeless corpse under his very eyes. The officer had the presence of mind to see that the corpse was not recognised, and, wishing to spare the other's feelings, told him that his brother was dangerously wounded, but that he would hear more of him by going out to the camp; and thither the other immediately bent his steps, with a seeming *presentiment* of the sad intelligence that awaited him.

April 9th.—As I had not seen my domestic since the storming of the town, I concluded that he had been killed; but he turned up this morning, with a tremendous gash on his head, and mounted on the top of a horse nearly twenty feet high, carrying under his arm one of those glass cases which usually stand on the counters of jewellers' shops, filled with all manner of trinkets. He looked exactly like the ghost of a horse pedler.

April 10th.—The devil take the man who stole my donkey last night.

April 11th.—Marched again for the neighbour-hood of Ciudad Rodrigo, with the long-accustomed sounds of cannon and musketry ringing in my fanciful ears as merrily as if the instruments themselves were still playing.

    Sir Sidney Beckwith, one of the fathers of the rifles, was, at this time, obliged to proceed to England for the recovery of health, and did not again return to the Peninsula. In his departure, that army lost one of the ablest of its outpost generals. Few officers knew so well how to make the most of a small force. His courage, coupled with his thorough knowledge of the soldier's character, was of that cool, intrepid kind, that would, at any time, convert a routed rabble into an orderly effective force. A better officer, probably, never led a brigade into the field!

CHAPTER 9

Affairs on the 18th and 19th of July

April 13th, 1812. Quartered at Portalegré.

Dear Portalegré! I cannot quit thee, for the fourth and last time, without a parting tribute to the remembrance of thy wild romantic scenery, and to the kindness and hospitality of thy worthy citizens! May thy gates continue shut to thine enemies as heretofore, and, as heretofore, may they ever prove those of happiness to thy friends! Dear nuns of Santa Clara! I thank thee for the enjoyment of many an hour of nothingness; and thine, Santa Barbara, for many of a more intellectual cast! May the voice of thy chapel-organ continue unrivalled but by the voices of thy lovely choristers! and may the piano in thy refectory be replaced by better, in which the harmony of strings may supersede the clattering of ivories! May the sweets which thou hast lavished on us be showered upon thee ten-thousand fold! And may those accursed iron bars divide thee as effectually from death as they did from us!!!

April 15th.—Quartered at Castello Branco.

This town had been so often visited by the French and us alternately, that the inhabitants at length confounded their friends with their foes; and by treating both sides as enemies, they succeeded in making them so.

When I went this evening to present my billet on a respectable-looking house, the door was opened by the lady of it, wearing a most gingerly aspect. She told me, with an equivocal sort of look, that she had two spare beds in the house, and that either of them were at my service; and, by way of illustration, showed me into a sort of servant's room, off the kitchen, half full of apples, onions, potatoes, and various kinds of lumber, with a dirty-looking bed in one corner; and, on my requesting to see the other, she conducted me up to the garret, into the very counterpart of the one below, though the room was somewhat differently garnished. I told her that they were certainly two capital beds; but as I was a modest person and disliked all extremes, that I should be quite satisfied with any one on the floor which I had not yet seen.

This, however, she told me was impossible, as every one of them were required by her own family. While we were descending the stair, disputing the point, I caught the handle of the first door I came to, twisted it open, and seeing it a neat little room, with nothing but a table and two or three chairs, I told her that it would suit me perfectly; and, desiring her to have a good mattress, with clean linen, laid in one corner of it by nine o'clock (adding a few hints, to satisfy her that I was quite in earnest), I went to dine with my messmates.

When I returned to the house, about ten o'clock, I was told that I should find a light in the room, and my bed ready. I accordingly ascended, and found everything as represented; and, in addition thereto, I found another bed lying alongside of mine, containing a huge fat friar, with bald pate, fast asleep, and blowing the most tremendous nasal trumpet that I ever heard!

As my friend had evidently been placed there for my annoyance, I did not think it necessary to use much ceremony in getting rid of him; and catching him by the two ears, I raised him up on his legs, while he groaned in a seeming agonizing doubt, whether the pain was inflicted by a man or a nightmare; and before he had time to get himself broad awake, I had chucked him and his clothing, bed and bedding, out at the door, which I locked, and enjoyed a sound sleep the remainder of the night.

They offered me no further molestation; but in taking my

departure at daylight next morning, I observed my landlady reconnoitring me from an upstairs' window, and thought it prudent not to go too near it.

While we had been employed at Badajos, Marmont had advanced in the north, and blockaded Ciudad Rodrigo and Almeida, sending advanced parties into the frontier towns of Portugal, to the confusion and consternation of the Portuguese militia, who had been stationed for their protection; and who, quite satisfied with the report of their coming, did not think it necessary to wait the report of their cannon. Marshal Beresford, in his paternal address to "*Los Valerosos*," in commemoration of their conduct on this occasion, directed that the colours of each regiment should be lodged in the town-halls of their respective districts, until they each provided themselves with a pair out of the ranks of the enemy; but I never heard that any of them were redeemed in the manner prescribed.

The French retired upon Salamanca on our approach; and we resumed our former quarters without opposition.

Hitherto we had been fighting the description of battle in which John Bull glories so much—gaining a brilliant and useless victory against great odds. But we were now about to contend for fame on equal terms; and having tried both, I will say, without partiality, that I would rather fight one man than two any day; for I have never been quite satisfied that the additional *quantum* of glory altogether compensated for the proportionate loss of substance; a victory of that kind being a doubtful and most unsatisfactory one to the performers, with each occupying the same ground after, that they did before; and the whole merit resting with the side which did not happen to begin it.

We remained about two months in cantonments, to recover the effects of the late sieges; and as by that time all the perforated skins and repairable cracked limbs had been mended, the army was assembled in front of Ciudad Rodrigo, to commence what may be termed the second campaign of 1812.

The enemy retired from Salamanca on our approach, leaving garrisons in three formidable little forts, which they had erected on the most commanding points of the city, and which were immediately invested by a British division.

Salamanca, as a city, appeared to me to be more ancient than respectable; for excepting an old cathedral and a new square, I saw nothing in it worth looking at, always saving and excepting their pretty little girls, who (the deuce take them) cost me two nights' good sleep. For, by way of doing a little dandy in passing through such a celebrated city, I disencumbered the under part of my saddle of the blanket, and the upper part of the boat-cloak with which it was usually adorned; and the penalty which I paid for my gentility was, sleeping the next two nights in position two miles in front of the town, while these useful appendages were lying on the baggage two miles in rear of it.

The heights of St. Christoval, which we occupied as a position to cover the siege, were strong, but quite unsheltered, and unfurnished with either wood or water. We were indebted for our supplies of the latter to the citizens of Salamanca; while stubbles and dry grass were our only fuel.

Marmont came down upon us the first night with a thundering cannonade, and placed his army *en masse* on the plain before us, almost within gunshot, I was told that while Lord Wellington was riding along the line, under a fire of artillery, and accompanied by a numerous staff, that a brace of greyhounds, in pursuit of a hare, passed close to him. He was at the moment in earnest conversation with General Castanos; but the instant he observed the chase, he gave the view hallo, and went after them at full speed, to the utter astonishment of his foreign accompaniments. Nor did he stop until he saw the hare killed; when he returned, and resumed the commander-in-chief, as if nothing had occurred.

The enemy next morning commenced a sharp attack on our advanced post, in the village of Moresco; and as it continued to be fed by both sides, there was every appearance of its bringing on a general action; but they desisted towards the afternoon, and the village remained divided between us.

Marmont, after looking at us for several days, did not think it prudent to risk an attack on our present post; and as the telegraph rockets from the town told him that his garrison was reduced to extremity, he crossed the Tormes, on the night of the 26th June, in the hopes of being able to relieve them from that side of the river.

Our division followed his movement, and took post for the night at Aldea Lingua. They sent forward a strong reconnoitring party at daylight next morning, but they were opposed by General Bock's brigade of heavy German dragoons, who would not permit them to see more than was necessary; and as the forts fell into our hands the same night, Marmont had no longer an object in remaining there, and fell back behind the Douro, occupying the line of Toro and Torodesillas.

By the accidental discharge of a musket, one day last year, the ramrod entered the belly, passed through the body, and the end of it stuck in the backbone of one of the soldiers of our division, from whence it was actually hammered out with a stone. The poor fellow recovered and joined his regiment, as well as ever he had been, and was last night unfortunately drowned while bathing in the Tormes.

When the enemy retired, our division advanced and occupied Rueda, a handsome little town on the left bank of the Douro.

It abounded in excellent wines; and our usual evening dances began there to be graced by a superior class of females to what they had hitherto been accustomed. I remember that in passing the house of the sexton one evening, I saw his daughter baking a loaf of bread; and falling desperately in love with both her and the loaf, I carried the one to the ball and the other to my quarters.

A woman was a woman in those days; and every officer made it a point of duty to marshal as many as he could to the general assembly, no matter whether they were countesses or *sextonesses*; and although we, in consequence, frequently incurred the most indelible disgrace among the better orders of our indiscriminate collection, some of whom would retire in disgust; yet, as a sufficient number generally remained for our evening's amusement, and we were only birds of passage, it was a matter of the most perfect indifference to us what they thought. We followed the same course wherever we went.

The French army having, in the meantime, been largely reinforced, and as they commanded the passage of the Douro, we were in hourly expectation of an offensive movement from them. As a precautionary measure, one-half of our division bivouacked every night in front of the town. On the evening of the 16th of July, it was our turn to be in quarters, and we were in the full enjoyment of our usual evening's amusement, when the bugles sounded to arms.

As we had previously experienced two false alarms in the same quarters, we thought it more than probable that this might prove one also; and therefore prevailed upon the ladies to enjoy themselves, until our return, upon the good things which we had provided for their refreshment, and out of which I hope they drew enough of consolation for our absence, as we have not seen them since.

After forming on our alarm post, we were moved off, in the dark, we knew not whither; but every man following the one before him, with the most implicit confidence, until, after marching all night, we found ourselves, on the following morning, at daylight, near the village of Castrejon, where we bivouacked for the day.

I was sent on piquet on the evening of the 17th, to watch a portion of the plain before us; and, soon after sunrise on the following morning, a cannonade commenced behind a hill to my right; and, though the combatants were not visible, it was evident that they were not dealing in blank cartridge, as mine happened to be the pitching post of all the enemy's round shot.

While I was attentively watching its progress, there arose, all at once, behind the rising ground to my left, a yell of the most terrific import; and feeling convinced that it would give instantaneous birth to as hideous a body, it made me look, with an eye of lightning, at the ground around me; and, seeing a broad deep ditch within a hundred yards, I lost not a moment in placing it between my piquet and the extraordinary sound. I had scarcely effected the movement, when Lord Wellington, with his staff, and a cloud of French and English dragoons and horse artillery intermixed, came over the hill at full cry, all hammering at each others' heads in one confused mass, over the very ground I had that instant quitted.

It appeared that his Lordship had gone there to reconnoitre, covered by two guns and two squadrons of cavalry, who, by some accident, were surprised, and charged by a superior body of the enemy, and sent tumbling in upon us in the manner described. A piquet of the Forty-Third had formed on our right, and we were obliged to remain passive spectators of such an extraordinary scene going on within a few yards of us, as we could not fire without an equal chance of shooting some of our own side.

Lord Wellington and his staff, with the two guns, took shelter for the moment behind us, while the cavalry went sweeping along our front, where I suppose they picked up a reinforcement, for they returned, almost instantly, in the same confused mass; but the French were now the flyers; and I must do them the justice to say, that they got off in a manner highly creditable to themselves. I saw one, in particular, defending himself against two of ours; and he would have made his escape from both, but an officer of our dragoons came down the hill, and took him in flank, at full speed, sending man and horse rolling headlong on the plain.

I was highly interested, all this time, in observing the distinguished characters which this unlooked-for turn-up had assembled around us. Marshal Beresford and the greater part of the staff remained with their swords drawn, and the Duke himself did not look more than half-pleased, while he silently despatched some of them with orders. General Alten, and his huge German orderly dragoon, with their swords drawn, cursed the whole time to a very large amount; but, as it was in German, I had not the full benefit of it.

He had an opposition swearer in Captain Jenkinson of the

artillery, who commanded the two guns, and whose oaths were chiefly aimed at himself for his folly, as far as I could understand, in putting so much confidence in his covering party, that he had not thought it necessary to unfix the catch which horse-artillerymen, I believe, had to prevent their swords quitting the scabbards when they are not wanted, and which, on this occasion, prevented their jumping forth when they were so unexpectedly called for.

The straggling enemy had scarcely cleared away from our front, when Lord Combermere came, from the right, with a reinforcement of cavalry; and our piquet was, at the same moment, ordered to join the battalion.

The movements which followed presented the most beautiful military spectacle imaginable. The enemy were endeavouring to turn our left; and, in making a counteracting movement, the two armies were marching in parallel lines, close to each other, on a perfect plain, each ready to take advantage of any opening of the other, and exchanging round shot as they moved along. Our division brought up the rear of the infantry, marching with the order and precision of a field day, in open column of companies, and in perfect readiness to receive the enemy in any shape; who, on their part, had a huge cavalry force close at hand, and equally ready to pounce upon us.

Our movement was supported by a formidable body of our own dragoons; and, as we drew near the bank of the small river Guerrena, our horse-artillery continued to file in the same line, to attract the attention of the enemy, while we gradually distanced them a little, and crossed the river into a position on the high grounds beyond it. The enemy passed the river, on our left, and endeavoured to force that part of the position; but the troops who were stationed there drove them back with great loss, and at dark the firing ceased.

During the early part of the 19th there appeared to be no movements on either side; but, in the afternoon, having fallen asleep in my tent, I was awoke by the whistling of a cannon shot; and was just beginning to abuse my servant for not having called me sooner, when we were ordered to stand to our arms; and, as the enemy were making a movement to our right, we made a corresponding one. The cannonade did not cease until dark, when we lay down by our arms, the two armies very near to each other, and fully expecting a general action on the morrow.

July 20th.—We stood to our arms an hour before daylight, and Lord Wellington held out every inducement for his opponent to attack him; but Marmont evaded it, and continued his movement on our right, which obliged us to continue ours, towards Salamanca; and we were a great part of this day in parallel lines with them, the same as on the 18th.

July 21st.—We crossed the Tormes just before dark this evening, about two miles above Salamanca, the enemy having passed it higher up. Before reaching our ground, we experienced one of the most tremendous thunderstorms that I ever witnessed. A sheet of lightning struck the head of our column, where I happened to be riding, and deprived me of the use of my optics for at least ten minutes. A great many of our dragoon horses broke from their piqueting during the storm, and galloped past us into the French lines. We lay by our arms on the banks of the river, and it continued to rain in torrents the whole of the night.

Battle of Salamanca

July 22nd.—A sharp fire of musketry commenced at daylight in the morning; but, as it did not immediately concern us, and was nothing unusual, we took no notice of it, but busied ourselves in getting our arms and our bodies disengaged from the rust and the wet, engendered by the storm of the past night.

About ten o'clock our division was ordered to stand to their arms, and then moved into position with our left resting on the Tormes, and our right extended along a ridge of rising ground, thinly interspersed with trees, beyond which the other divisions were formed in continuation, with the exception of the third, which still remained on the opposite bank of the river.

The enemy were to be seen in motion on the opposite ridges, and a straggling fire of musketry, with an occasional gun, acted as a sort of prelude to the approaching conflict. We heard, about this time, that Marmont had just sent to his *ci-devant* landlord, in Salamanca, to desire that he would have the usual dinner ready for himself and staff at six o'clock; and so satisfied was "mine host" of the infallibility of the French marshal, that he absolutely set about making the necessary preparations.

There assuredly never was an army so anxious as ours was to be brought into action on this occasion. They were a magnificent body of well-tried soldiers, highly equipped, and in the highest health and spirits, with the most devoted confidence in their leader, and an invincible confidence in themselves. The retreat of the four preceding days had annoyed us beyond measure, for we believed that we were nearly equal to the enemy in point of numbers; and the idea of our retiring before an equal number of any troops in the world was not to be endured with common patience.

We were kept the whole of the forenoon in the most torturing state of suspense through contradictory reports. One passing officer telling us that he had just heard the order given to attack, and the next asserting, with equal confidence, that he had just heard the order to retreat; and it was not until about two o'clock in the afternoon that affairs began to wear a more decided aspect, and when our own eyes and ears at length conveyed the wished-for tidings that a battle was inevitable; for we saw the enemy beginning to close upon our right, and the cannonade had become general along the whole line.

Lord Wellington, about the same time, ordered the movement which decided the fate of the day—that of bringing the Third Division, from beyond the river on our left, rapidly to our extreme right, turning the enemy in their attempt to turn us, and commencing the offensive with the whole of his right wing.

The effect was instantaneous and decisive; for although some obstinate and desperate fighting took place in the centre, with various success, yet the victory was never for a moment in doubt; and the enemy were soon in full retreat, leaving seven thousand prisoners, two eagles, and eleven pieces of artillery in our hands. Had we been favoured with two hours more daylight, their loss would have been incalculable, for they committed a blunder at starting, which they never got time to retrieve; and their retreat was, therefore, commenced in such disorder, and with a river in their rear, that nothing but darkness could have saved them.

Chapter 10

Enter Madrid

The Third Division, under Sir Edward Pakenham, the artillery, and some regiments of dragoons, particularly distinguished themselves. But our division, very much to our annoyance, came in for a very slender portion of this day's glory. We were exposed to a cannonade the whole of the afternoon; but, as we were not per-mitted to advance until very late, we had only an opportunity of throwing a few straggling shot at the fugitives, before we lost sight of them in the dark; and then bivouacked for the night near the village of Huerta (I think it was called).

We started after them at daylight next morning; and, crossing at a ford of the Tormes, we found their rear-guard, consisting of three regiments of infantry, with some cavalry and artillery, posted on a formidable height above the village of Serna. General Bock, with his brigade of heavy German dragoons, immediately went at them: and, putting their cavalry to flight, he broke through their infantry, and took or destroyed the whole of them.

This was one of the most gallant charges recorded in history. I saw many of these fine fellows lying dead along with their horses, on which they were still astride, with the sword firmly grasped in the hand, as they had fought the instant before; and several of them still wearing a look of fierce defiance, which death itself had been unable to quench.

We halted for the night at a village near Penaranda. I took possession of the church; and finding the floor strewed with the paraphernalia of priesthood, I selected some silk gowns, and other gorgeous trappings, with which I made a bed for myself in the porch, and where, "if all had been gold that glittered," I should have looked a jewel indeed; but it is lamentable to think, that, among the multifarious blessings we enjoy in this life, we should never be able to get a dish of glory and a dish of beef-steak on the same day; in consequence of which, the heart, which ought properly to be soaring in the clouds, or, at all events, in a castle half way up, is more generally to be found grovelling about a hen-roost, in the vain hope that, if it cannot get hold of the hen herself, it may at least hit upon an egg; and such, I remember, was the state of my feelings on this occasion, in consequence of my having dined the three preceding days on the half of my inclinations.

We halted the next night in the handsome little town of Olmeda, which had just been evacuated by the enemy. The French general, Ferez, died there, in consequence of the wounds which he received at the battle of Salamanca, and his remains had the night before been consigned to the earth with the highest honours, and a canopy of laurel placed over his grave: but the French had no sooner left the town, than the inhabitants exhumed the body, cut off the head, and spurned it with the greatest indignity.

They were in hopes that this line of conduct would have proved a passport to our affections, and conducted us to the spot, as to a trophy that they were proud of; but we expressed the most unfeigned horror and indignation at their proceeding; and, getting some soldiers to assist, his remains were carefully and respectfully replaced in the grave. His was a noble head; and, even in death, it looked the brave, the gallant soldier. Our conduct had such an effect on the Spaniards, that they brought back the canopy of their own accord, and promised solemnly that the grave should henceforth rest undisturbed.

July 26th.—We arrived on the banks of the Douro, within a league of Valladolid, where, after halting two days, Lord Wellington detaching a division of infantry and some cavalry to watch the movements of the defeated army, proceeded with the remainder towards Madrid.

August 1st.—On approaching near to our bivouac this afternoon, I saw a good large farmhouse, about a mile off the road; and, getting permission from my commandant, I made a cast thereto, in search of something for dinner. There were two women belonging to the German Legion smoking their pipes in the kitchen, when I arrived; and, having the highest respect for their marauding qualifications, I began to fear that nothing was to be had, as they were sitting there so quietly. I succeeded, nevertheless, in purchasing two pair of chickens; but, neglecting the precaution of unscrewing their necks, I merely grasped a handful of their legs, and mounting my horse, proceeded towards the camp.

I had scarcely, however, gone a couple of hundred yards, when they began opening their throats and flapping their wings, which startled my horse and sent him off at full speed. I lost the rein on one side, and, in attempting to pull him up with the other, I brought his foot into a rut, and down he came, sending me head-foremost into a wet ditch! When I got on my legs and shook myself a little, I saw each particular hen galloping across the field, screeching with all its might, while the horse was off in a different direction. Casting a rueful look at the chickens, I naturally followed him, as the most valuable of the collection. Fortunately, a heavy boat-cloak caused the saddle to roll under his belly; and finding that he could not make way in consequence, he quietly waited for me about a quarter of a mile off.

When I had remounted, I looked back to the scene of my disaster, and saw my two German friends busily employed in catching the chickens. They were, no doubt, in hopes that I had broken my neck, that they might have the sacking of me also; for, as I was returning, I observed them concealing the fowls under their clothes, while the one took up a suspicious sort of position behind the other.

After reconnoitring them a short time, I rode up and demanded the fowls, when the one looking at the other in well-feigned astonishment, asked in Dutch, what I could possibly mean? She then gave me to understand that they could not comprehend English; but I immediately said, "Come, come! none of your gammon! you have got my fowls, here's half a dollar for your trouble in catching them, so hand them out."

"Oh!" said one of them in English, "it is de fowl you want," and they then produced them. After paying the stipulated sum, I wished them all the compliments of the season, and thought myself fortunate in getting off so well; for they were each six feet high, and strong as horses, and I felt convinced that they had often thrashed a better man than me in the course of their military career.

August 7th.—Halted near the ancient town of Segovia, which bears a strong resemblance to the old town of Edinburgh, built on a lofty ridge, which terminates in an abrupt summit, on which stands the fortified tower, celebrated in the *Adventures of Gil Blas*. It is a fine old town, boasts of a superb Roman aqueduct, and is famous for ladies' shoes.

Our bivouac this evening was on the banks of El Rio Frio, near to a new hunting-palace of the King of Spain. It was a large quadrangular building, each side full of empty rooms, with nothing but their youth to recommend them.

On the 9th, we crossed the Guadarama Mountains, and halted for the night in the park of the Escurial.

I had, from childhood upwards, considered this palace as the eighth wonder of the world, and was therefore proportionately disappointed at finding it a huge, gloomy, unmeaning pile of building, looking somewhat less interesting than the wild craggy mountain opposite, and not containing a single room large enough to flog a cat in. The only apartment that I saw worth looking at, was the one in which their dead kings live!

Entered Madrid
August 13th, 1812

As we approached the capital, imagination was busy in speculating on the probable nature of our reception. The peasantry, with whom we had hitherto been chiefly associated, had imbibed a rooted hatred to the French, caused by the wanton cruelties experienced at their hands, both in their persons and their property; otherwise they were a cheerful, hospitable, and orderly people, and, had they been permitted to live in peace and quietness, it was a matter of the most perfect indifference to them whether Joseph, Ferdinand, or the ghost of Don Quixote was their king.

But, as the citizens of Madrid had been living four years in comparative peace, under the dominion of a French Government, and in the enjoyment of all the gaieties of that luxurious court, to which, if I add that we entertained, at that time, some slight jealousy regarding the pretensions of the French officers to the favours of the fair, I believe the prevailing opinion was that we should be considered as the intruders; and it was therefore a matter of the most unexpected exultation, when we entered it on the afternoon of the 13th of August, to find ourselves hailed as liberators, with the most joyous acclamations, by surrounding multitudes, who continued their rejoicings for three successive days.

By day, the riches of each house were employed in decorations to its exterior; and by night, they were brilliantly illuminated, during which time all business was suspended, and the whole population of the city crowded the streets, emulating each other in heaping honours and caresses upon us.

King Joseph had retired on our approach, leaving a garrison in the fortified palace of El Retiro; but they surrendered some days afterwards, and we remained there three months, basking in the sunshine of beauty, harmony, and peace. I shall ever look back to that period as the most pleasing event of my military life.

The only bar to our perfect felicity was the want of money, as, independent of long arrears, already due, the military chest continued so very poor that it could not afford to give us more than a fortnight's pay during these three months; and as nobody could, would, or should give cash for bills, we were obliged to sell silver spoons, watches, and everything of value that we stood possessed of, to purchase the common necessaries of life.

My Irish *criado*, who used to take uncommon liberties with my property, having been two or three days in the rear, with the baggage, at the time of the battle of Salamanca, took upon himself to exchange my baggage-horse for another; and his apology for so doing was, that the one he had got was twice as big as the one he gave! The additional size, however, so far from being an advantage, proved quite the reverse; for I found that he could eat as much as he could carry, and, as he was obliged to carry all that he had to eat, I was forced to put him on half allowance, to make room for my baggage; in consequence of which, every bone in his body soon became so pointed that I could easily have hung my hat on any part of his hind quarters.

I therefore took advantage of our present repose to let him have the benefit of a full allowance, which enabled me to effect an exchange between him and a mule, getting five dollars to the bargain, which made me one of the happiest, and, I believe, also one of the richest men in the army. I expended the first dollar next day, in getting admission to a bullfight, in their national amphitheatre, where the first thing that met my astonished eyes was a mad bull giving the finishing *prode* to my unfortunate big horse.

Lord Wellington, with some divisions of the army, proceeded, about the beginning of September, to undertake the siege of Burgos, leaving those at Madrid under the orders of Sir Rowland Hill. Towards the end of October, our delightful sojourn there drew perceptibly to a close, for it was known that King Joseph, with the forces under Soult and Jourdan, now united, were moving upon Aranjuez, and that all, excepting our own division, were already in motion, to dispute the passage of the Tagus, and to cover the capital. About four o'clock on the morning of the 23rd of October, we received orders to be on our alarm posts at six, and as soon as we had formed, we were marched to the city of Alcala.

October 27th.—We were all this day marching to Arganda,

and all night marching back again. If any one thing is more particularly damned than another it is a march of this kind.

October 30th—An order arrived, from Lord Wellington, for our corps of the army to fall back upon Salamanca; we therefore returned to Madrid, and, after halting outside the gates until we were joined by Skerret's division, from Cadiz, we bade a last sorrowful *adieu* to our friends in the city, and commenced our retreat.

October 31st.—Halted for the night in the park of the Escurial. It is amusing, on a division's first taking up its ground, to see the numbers of hares that are every instant starting up among the men, and the scrambling and shouting of the soldiers for the prize. This day, when the usual shout was given, every man ran, with his cap in his hand, to endeavour to capture poor puss, as he imagined, but which turned out to be two wild boars, who contrived to make room for themselves so long as there was nothing but men's caps to contend with; but they very soon had as many bayonets as bristles in their backs. We recrossed the Guadarama Mountains next morning.

November 2nd.—Halted this night in front of a small town, the name of which I do not recollect. It was beginning to get dark by the time I had posted our guards and piquets, when I rode into it to endeavour to find my messmates, who I knew had got a dinner waiting for me somewhere.

I entered a large square, or market-place, and found it crowded with soldiers of all nations, most of them three-parts drunk, and in the midst of whom a mad bull was performing the most extraordinary feats, quite unnoticed, excepting by those who had the misfortune to attract his attention. The first intimation that I had of him, was his charging past me, and making a thrust at our quarter-master, carrying off a portion of his regimental trousers.

He next got a fair toss at a Portuguese soldier, and sent him spinning three or four turns up in the air. I was highly amused in observing the fellow's astonishment, when he alighted, to see that he had not the remotest idea to what accident he was indebted for such an evolution, although he seemed fully prepared to quarrel with anyone who chose to acknowledge any participation in the deed; but the cause of it was, all the while, finding fresh customers, and making the grand tour of the square with such velocity, that I began to fear I should be on his list also, if I did not take shelter in the nearest house, a measure no sooner thought of than executed.

I therefore opened a door and drove my horse in before me; but there instantly arose such an uproar within, that I began to wish myself once more on the outside on any terms; for it happened to be occupied by English, Portuguese, and German bullock drivers, who had been seated round a table, scrambling for a dinner, when my horse upset the table, lights, and everything on it. The only thing that I could make out amid their confused curses was, that they had come to the determination of putting the cause of the row to death; but, as I begged to differ with them on that point, I took the liberty of knocking one or two of them down, and finally succeeded in extricating my horse, with whom I retraced my way to the camp, weary, angry, and hungry.

On my arrival there, I found an orderly waiting to show me the way to dinner, which once more restored me to good humour with myself and all the world; while the adventure afforded my companions a hearty laugh at my expense.

November 6th.—In the course of this day's march, while our battalion formed the rear-guard, at a considerable distance in the rear of the column, we found a Portuguese soldier, who had been left by his regiment, lying in the middle of the road, apparently dead; but on examining him more closely, we had reason to think that he was merely in a state of stupor, occasioned by fatigue and the heat of the weather—an opinion which caused us no little uneasiness.

For although we did not think it quite fair to bury a living man, yet we had no means whatever of carrying him off; and to leave him where he was, would, in all probability, have cost us a number of better lives than his had ever been, for the French (who were then in sight) had hitherto been following us at a very respectable distance; but had they found that we were retiring in such a hurry as to leave our half-dead people on the road, they would not have been Frenchmen if they did not give us an extra push, to help us along.

Under all the circumstances of the case, therefore, and although our doctor was of opinion that with time and attention he might recover, yet not having either the one or the other to spare, the remainder of us who had voted ourselves into a sort of coroner's inquest, thought it most prudent to find him dead; and carrying him a little off the road to the edge of a ravine, we scraped a hole in the sand with our swords, and placed him in it. We covered him but very lightly, and left his head and arms at perfect liberty; so that, although he might be said to have had both feet in the grave, he might still have scrambled out of it if he could.

Chapter 11

End of the Campaign of 1812

November 7th.—Halted this night at Alba de Tormes, and next day marched into quarters in Salamanca, where we rejoined Lord Wellington with the army from Burgos.

On the 14th the British army concentrated on the field of their former glory, in consequence of a part of the French army having effected the passage of the river above Alba de Tormes. On the 15th the whole of the enemy's force having passed the river, a cannonade commenced early in the day; and it was the general belief that ere night a second battle of Salamanca would be recorded. But as all the French armies in Spain were now united in our front, and outnumbered us so far, Lord Wellington, seeing no decided advantage to be gained by risking a battle, at length ordered a retreat, which we commenced about three in the afternoon. Our division halted for the night at the entrance of a forest about four miles from Salamanca.

The heavy rains which usually precede the Spanish winter had set in the day before; and as the roads in that part of the country cease to be roads for the remainder of the season, we were now walking nearly knee deep in a stiff mud into which no man could thrust his foot with the certainty of having a shoe at the end of it when he pulled it out again; and that we might not be miserable by halves, we had this evening to regale our chops with the last morsel of biscuit that they were destined to grind during the retreat.

We cut some boughs of trees to keep us out of the mud, and

lay down to sleep on them, wet to the skin; but the cannonade of the afternoon had been succeeded, after dark, by a continued firing of musketry, which led us to believe that our piquets were attacked; and in momentary expectation of an order to stand to our arms, we kept ourselves awake the whole night, and were not a little provoked to find, next morning, that it had been occasioned by numerous stragglers from the different regiments, shooting at the pigs belonging to the peasantry, which were grazing in the wood.

November 16th.—Retiring from daylight until dark through the same description of roads. The French dragoons kept close behind, but did not attempt to molest us. It still continued to rain hard, and we again passed the night in a wood. I was very industriously employed during the early part of it, in feeling in the dark for acorns, as a substitute for bread.

November 17th.—At daylight this morning the enemy's cavalry advanced in force; but they were kept in check by the skirmishers of the 14th Light Dragoons, until the road became open, when we continued our retreat. Our brigade-major was at the time obliged to go to the rear, sick, and I was appointed to act for him.

We were much surprised, in the course of the forenoon, to hear a sharp firing commence behind us, on the very road by which we were retiring; and it was not until we reached the spot that we learnt that the troops who were retreating, by a road parallel to ours, had left it too soon, and enabled some French dragoons, under cover of the forest, to advance unperceived to the flank of our line of march, who, seeing an interval between two divisions of infantry, which was filled with light baggage, and some passing officers, dashed at it, and made some prisoners in the scramble of the moment, amongst whom was Lieutenant-General Sir Edward Paget.

Our division formed on the heights above Samunoz to cover the passage of the rivulet, which was so swollen with the heavy rains as only to be passable at particular fords. While waiting there for the passage of the rest of the army, the enemy, under cover of the forest, were, at the same time, assembling in force close around us; and the moment that we began to descend the hill, towards the rivulet, we were assailed by a heavy fire of cannon and musketry, while their powerful cavalry were in readiness to take advantage of any confusion which might have occurred. We effected the passage, however, in excellent order, and formed on the opposite bank of the stream, where we continued under a cannonade, and engaged in a sharp skirmish until dark.

Our loss on this occasion was considerable; but it would have been much greater, had not the enemy's shells buried themselves so deep in the soft ground, that their explosion did little injury. It appeared singular to us, who were not medical men, that an officer and several of our division, who were badly wounded on this occasion in the leg, and who were sent to the rear on gun carriages, should have died of a mortification in the limb which was not wounded.

When the firing ceased, we received the usual order "to make ourselves comfortable for the night"; but I never remember an instance in which we had so much difficulty in obeying it; for the ground we occupied was a perfect flat, which was flooded more than ankle deep with water, excepting here and there, where the higher ground around the roots of trees presented circles of a few feet of visible earth, upon which we grouped ourselves. Some few fires were kindled, at which we roasted some bits of raw beef on the points of our swords, and ate them by way of a dinner. There was plenty of water to apologize for the want of better fluids, but bread sent no apology at all.

Some divisions of the army had commenced retiring as soon as it was dark, and the whole had been ordered to move, so that the roads might be clear for us before daylight. I was sent twice in the course of the night to see what progress they had made; but such was the state of the roads, that even within an hour of daylight, two divisions, besides our own, were still unmoved, which would consequently delay us so long, that we looked forward to a severe harassing day's fighting; a kind of fighting, too, that is the least palatable of any, where much might be lost, and nothing was to be gained.

With such prospects before us, it made my very heart rejoice to see my brigadier's servant commence boiling some chocolate and frying a beef-steak. I watched its progress with a keenness which intense hunger alone could inspire, and was on the very point of having my desires consummated when the general, getting uneasy at not having received any communication relative to the movements of the morning, and without considering how feelingly my stomach yearned for a better acquaintance with the contents of his frying-pan, desired me to ride to General Alten for orders. I found the general at a neighbouring tree; but he cut off all hopes of my timely return, by desiring me to remain with him until he received the report of an officer whom he had sent to ascertain the progress of the other divisions.

While I was toasting myself at his fire, so sharply set that I could have eaten one of my boots, I observed his German orderly dragoon, at an adjoining fire, stirring up the contents of a camp kettle, which once more revived my departing hopes, and I presently had the satisfaction of seeing him dipping in some basins, presenting one to the general, one to the *aide-de-camp*, and a third to myself. The mess which it contained I found, after swallowing the whole at a draught, was neither more nor less than the produce of a piece of beef boiled in plain water! and, though it would have been enough to have physicked a dromedary at any other time, yet, as I could then have made a good hole in the dromedary himself, it sufficiently satisfied my cravings to make me equal to anything for the remainder of the day.

We were soon after ordered to stand to our arms, and, as day lit up, a thick haze hung on the opposite hills, which prevented our seeing the enemy; and as they did not attempt to feel for us, we, contrary to our expectations, commenced our retreat unmolested; nor could we quite believe our good fortune when, towards the afternoon, we had passed several places where they could have assailed us in flank with great advantage, and caused us a severe loss, almost in spite of fate; but it afterwards appeared that they were quite knocked up with their exertions in overtaking us the day before, and were unable to follow further. We halted on a swampy height, behind St. Espiritu, and experienced another night of starvation and rain.

I now felt considerably more for my horse than myself, as he had been three days and nights without a morsel of any kind to eat. Our baggage animals, too, we knew were equally ill off; and as they always preceded us a day's march, it was highly amusing, whenever we found a dead horse or a mule lying on the roadside, to see the anxiety with which every officer went up to reconnoitre him, each fearing that he should have the misfortune to recognise it as his own.

On the 19th of November we arrived at the convent of Caridad, near Ciudad Rodrigo, and once more experienced the comforts of our baggage and provisions. My boots had not been off since the 13th, and I found it necessary to cut them to pieces, to get my swollen feet out of them.

This retreat terminated the campaign of 1812. After a few days' delay, and some requisite changes about the neighbourhood, while all the world were getting shook into their places, our battalion finally took possession of the village of Alameida for the winter, where, after forming a regimental mess, we detached an officer to Lamego, and secured to ourselves a bountiful supply of the best juice of the grape which the neighbouring banks of the Douro afforded.

The quarter we now occupied was naturally pretty much upon a par with those of the last two winters, but it had the usual advantages attending the march of intellect. The officers of the division united in fitting up an empty chapel, in the village of Galegos, as an amateur theatre, for which, by the bye, we were all regularly cursed from the altar by the Bishop of Rodrigo. Lord Wellington kept a pack of foxhounds, and the Hon. Captain Stewart, of ours, a pack of harriers, so that these, in addition to our old *Bolero* meetings, enabled us to pass a very tolerable winter.

The neighbouring plains abounded with hares: it was one of the most beautiful coursing countries, perhaps, in the world; and there was also some shooting to be had at the numerous vultures preying on the dead carcasses which strewed the roadside on the line of our last retreat.

Up to this period Lord Wellington had been adored by everyone, as well for his brilliant achievements, as for his noble and manly bearing in all things; but, in consequence of some disgraceful irregularities which took place during the retreat, he immediately after issued an order, conveying a sweeping censure on the whole army. His general conduct was too upright for even the finger of malice itself to point at; but as his censure, on this occasion, was not strictly confined to the guilty, it afforded a handle to disappointed persons, and excited a feeling against him, on the part of individuals, which has probably never been obliterated.

It began by telling us that we had suffered no privations; and, though this was hard to be digested on an empty stomach, yet, taking it in its more liberal meaning, that our privations were not of an extent to justify any irregularities, which I readily admit; still, as many regiments were not guilty of any irregularities, it is not to be wondered at if such should have felt, at first, a little sulky to find, in the general reproof, that, no loophole whatever had been left for them to creep through; for I believe I am justified in saying, that neither our own, nor the two gallant corps associated with us, had a single man absent that we could not satisfactorily account for.

But it touched us still more tenderly in not excepting us from his general charge of inexpertness in camp arrangements; for it was our belief, and in which we were in some measure borne out by circumstances, that had he placed us, at the same moment, in the same field, with an equal number of the best troops in France, he would not only have seen our fires as quickly lit, but every Frenchman roasting on them into the bargain, if they waited long enough to be dressed; for there perhaps never was, nor ever again will be, such a war brigade as that which was composed of the Forty-Third, Fifty-Second, and the Rifles.

That not only censure, but condign punishment, was merited in many instances, is certain; and had his Lordship dismissed some officers from the service, and caused some of the disorderly soldiers to be shot, it would not only have been an act of justice, but probably a necessary example. Had he hanged every commissary, too, who failed to issue the regular rations to the troops dependent on them, unless they proved that they themselves were starved, it would only have been a just sacrifice to the offended stomachs of many thousands of gallant fellows.

In our brigade I can safely say, that the order in question excited "more of sorrow than of anger." We thought that, had it been particular, it would have been just; but, as it was general, that it was inconsiderate; and we therefore regretted that he who had been, and still was, the god of our idolatry, should thereby have laid himself open to the attacks of the ill-natured.

Alameida is a Spanish village, situated within a stone's throw of the boundary line of the sister kingdom; and as the headquarters of the army, as well as the nearest towns, from whence we drew our supplies, lay in Portugal, our connexions, while we remained there, were chiefly with the latter kingdom; and having passed the three last winters on their frontier, we, in the month of May, 1813, prepared to bid it a final *adieu*, with very little regret.

The people were kind and hospitable, and not destitute of intelligence; but, somehow, they appeared to be the creatures of a former age, and showed an indolence and want of enterprise which marked them born for slaves; and although the two *Caçadore* regiments attached to our division were at all times in the highest order, and conducted themselves gallantly in the field, yet I am of opinion that, as a nation, they owe their character for bravery almost entirely to the activity and gallantry of the British officers who organized and led them.

The veriest cowards in existence must have shown the same front under such discipline. I did not see enough of their gentry to enable me to form an opinion about them; but the middling and lower orders are extremely filthy, both in their persons and in their houses, and they have all an intolerable itch for gambling. The soldiers, though fainting with fatigue on the line of march, invariably group themselves in card-parties whenever they are allowed a few minutes' halt; and a non-commissioned officer with half-a-dozen men, on any duty of fatigue, are very generally to be seen as follows,—*viz.* one man as a sentry, to watch the approach of the superintending officer, one man at work, and the non-commissioned officer, with the other four, at cards.

The cottages in Alameida, and, indeed, in all the Spanish villages, generally contain two mud-floored apartments; the outer one, though more cleanly than the Irish, is nevertheless fashioned after the same manner, and is common alike to the pigs and the people; while the inner looks more like the gun-room of a ship of war, having a sitting apartment in the centre, with small sleeping cabins branching from it, each illuminated by a port-hole about a foot square.

We did not see daylight "through a glass darkly," as on London's Ludgate Hill, for there the air circulated freely, and mild it came, and pure, and fragrant, as if it had stolen over a bed of roses. If a man did not like that, he had only to shut his port, and remain in darkness, inhaling his own preferred sweetness! The outside of my sleeping cabin was interwoven with ivy and honeysuckle, and among the branches a nightingale had established itself, and sung sweetly, night after night, during the whole of the winter. I could not part from such a pleasing companion, and from a bed in which I had enjoyed so many tranquil slumbers, without a sigh, though I was ungrateful enough to accompany it with a fervent wish that I might never see them again; for I looked upon the period that I had spent there as so much time lost.

CHAPTER 12

March to Salamanca

May, 1813.—In the early part of this month our division was reviewed by Lord Wellington, preparatory to the commencement of another campaign; and I certainly never saw a body of troops in a more highly efficient state. It did one's very heart good to look at our battalion that day, seeing each company standing a hundred strong, and the intelligence of several campaigns stamped on each daring, bronzed countenance, which looked you boldly in the face, in the fullness of vigour and confidence, as if it cared neither for man nor devil.

On the 21st of May, our division broke up from winter quarters, and assembled in front of Ciudad Rodrigo, with all excepting the left wing of the army, which, under Sir Thomas Graham, had already passed the Douro, and was ascending its right bank.

An army that has seen some campaigns in the field, affords a great deal of amusement in its assembling after winter quarters. There is not only the greeting of long parted friends and acquaintances in the same walks of life, but, among the different divisions which the nature of the service generally threw a good deal together, there was not so much as a mule or a donkey that was not known to each individual, and its absence noticed; nor a scamp of a boy, or a common Portuguese *trull*, who was not as particularly inquired after, as if the fate of the campaign depended on their presence.

On the 22nd, we advanced towards Salamanca, and the next day halted at Samunoz, on our late field of action. With what different feelings did we now view the same spot! In our last visit, winter was on the face of the land, as well as on our minds; we were worn out with fatigue, mortification, and starvation: now, all was summer and sunshine. The dismal swamps had now become verdant meadows; we had plenty in the camp, vigour in our limbs, and hope in our bosoms.

We were this day joined by the household brigade of cavalry from England; and as there was a report in the morning that the enemy were in the neighbourhood, some of the Life Guards concluded that everything in front of their camp must be a part of them, and they, accordingly, apprehended some of the light dragoon horses, which happened to be grazing near. One of their officers came to dine with me that day, and he was in the act of reporting their capture, when my orderly book was brought at the moment, containing an offer of reward for the detection of the thieves!

On the 27th, we encamped on the banks of the Tormes, at a ford about a league below Salamanca. A body of the enemy, who had occupied the city, suffered severely before they got away, in a brush with some part of Sir Rowland Hill's corps; chiefly, I believe, from some of his artillery.

On the 28th, we crossed the river, and marched near to Aldea Nueva, where we remained stationary for some days, under Sir Rowland Hill; Lord Wellington having proceeded from Salamanca to join the left wing of the army, beyond the Douro.

On the 2nd of June, we were again put in motion; and, after a very long march, encamped near the Douro, opposite the town of Toro.

Lord Wellington had arrived there the day before, without being opposed by the enemy; but there had been an affair of cavalry, a short distance beyond the town, in which the hussar brigade particularly distinguished themselves, and took about three hundred prisoners.

On the morning of the 3rd, we crossed the river; and marching through the town of Toro, encamped about half a league beyond it. The enemy had put the castle in a state of repair, and constructed a number of other works to defend the passage of the river; but the masterly eye of our chief, having seen his way round the town, spared them the trouble of occupying the works; yet, loath to think that so much labour should be altogether lost, he garrisoned their castle with the three hundred taken by the hussar brigade, for which it made a very good jail.

On the 4th, we were again in motion, and had a long, warm, fatiguing march; as also on the 5th and 6th. On the 7th, we encamped outside of Palencia, a large rickety-looking old town, with the front of every house supported by pillars, like so many worn out old bachelors on crutches.

The French did not interfere with our accommodation in the slightest, but made it a point to leave every place an hour or two before we came to it; so that we quietly continued our daily course, following nearly the line of the Canal de Castile, through a country luxuriant in corn fields and vineyards, until the lath, when we arrived within two or three leagues of Burgos (on its left), and where we found a body of the enemy in position, whom we immediately proceeded to attack; but they evaporated on our approach, and fell back upon Burgos.

We encamped for the night on the banks of a river, a short distance to the rear. Next morning, at daylight, an explosion shook the ground like an earthquake, which made every man jump upon his legs; and it was not until some hours after, when Lord Wellington returned from reconnoitring, that we learnt that the castle of Burgos had been just blown up, and the town evacuated by the enemy.

We continued our march on the 13th, through a very rich country.

On the 14th, we had a long harassing day's march, through a rugged mountainous country, which afforded only an occasional glimpse of fertility, in some pretty little valleys with which it was intersected.

We started at daylight on the 15th, through a dreary region of solid rock, bearing an abundant crop of loose stones, without a particle of soil or vegetation visible to the naked eye in any direction. After leaving nearly twenty miles of this horrible wilderness behind us, our weary minds clogged with an imaginary view of nearly as much more of it in our front, we found ourselves all at once looking down upon the valley of the Ebro, near the village of Arenas, one of the richest, loveliest, and most romantic spots that I ever beheld.

The influence of such a scene on the mind can scarcely be believed. Five minutes before we were all as lively as stones; in a moment we were all fruits and flowers; and many a pair of legs, that one would have thought had not a kick left in them, were, in five minutes after, seen dancing across the bridge, to the tune of "The Downfall of Paris," which struck up from the bands of the different regiments.

I lay down that night in a cottage garden, with my head on a melon, and my eye on a cherry tree, and resigned myself to a repose which did not require a long courtship.

We resumed our march at daybreak on the 16th. The road, in the first instance, wound through orchards and luxurious gardens, and then closed in to the edge of the river, through a difficult and formidable pass, where the rocks on each side, arising to a prodigious height, hung over each other in fearful grandeur, and in many places nearly met together over our heads.

After following the course of the river for nearly two miles, the rocks on each side gradually expanded into another valley, lovely as the one we had left, and where we found the fifth division of our army lying encamped. They were still asleep; and the rising sun, and a beautiful morning, gave additional sublimity to the scene; for there was nothing but the tops of the white tents peeping above the fruit trees, and an occasional sentinel pacing his post, that gave any indication of what a nest of hornets the blast of a bugle could bring out of that apparently peaceful solitude.

Our road now wound up the mountain to our right; and almost satiated with the continued grandeur around us, we arrived in the afternoon at the town of Medina, and encamped a short distance beyond it.

We were welcomed into every town or village through which we passed by the peasant girls, who were in the habit of meeting us with garlands of flowers, and dancing before us in a peculiar style of their own; and it not unfrequently happened, that while they were so employed with one regiment, the preceding one was diligently engaged in pulling down some of their houses for firewood—a measure which we were sometimes obliged to have recourse to where no other fuel could be had, and for which they were ultimately paid by the British Government; but it was a measure that was more likely to have set the poor souls dancing mad than for joy, had they foreseen the consequences of our visit.

June 17th.—We had not seen anything of the enemy since we left the neighbourhood of Burgos; but after reaching our ground this evening, we were aware that some of their *videttes* were feeling for us.

On the morning of the 18th, we were ordered to march to San Milan, a small town about two leagues off; and where, on our arrival on the hill above, we found a division of French infantry, as strong as ourselves, in the act of crossing our path. The surprise, I believe, was mutual, though I doubt whether the pleasure was equally so; for we were red hot for an opportunity of retaliating for the Salamanca retreat; and as the old saying goes, *There is no opportunity like the present.* Their leading brigade had nearly passed before we came up, but not a moment was lost after we did.

Our battalion dispersing among the brushwood, went down the hill upon them; and, with a destructive fire, broke through their line of march, supported by the rest of the brigade. Those that had passed made no attempt at a stand, but continued their flight, keeping up as good a fire as their circumstances would permit; while we kept hanging on their flank and rear, through a good rifle country, which enabled us to make considerable havoc among them.

Their general's *aide-de-camp*, among others, was mortally wounded: and a lady, on a white horse, who probably was his wife, remained beside him until we came very near. She appeared to be in great distress; but though we called to her to remain, and not to be alarmed, yet she galloped off as soon as a decided step became necessary. The object of her solicitude did not survive many minutes after we reached him. We followed the retreating foe until late in the afternoon.

On this occasion our brigade came in for all the blows, and the other for all the baggage, which was marching between the two French brigades; the latter of which, seeing the scrape into which the first had fallen, very prudently left it to its fate, and dispersed on the opposite mountains, where some of them fell into the hands of a Spanish force that was detached in pursuit; but I believe the greater part succeeded in joining their army the day after the battle of Vittoria.

We heard a heavy cannonade all day to our left, occasioned, as we understood, by the Fifth Division falling in with another detachment of the enemy, which the unexpected and rapid movements of Lord Wellington was hastening to their general point of assembly.

On the early part of the 19th, we were fagging up the face of a mountain, under a sultry hot sun, until we came to a place where a beautiful clear stream was dashing down the face of it, when the division was halted, to enable the men to refresh themselves. Every man carries a cup, and every man ran and swallowed a cup full of it—it was salt water from the springs of Salinas; and it was truly ludicrous to see their faces after taking such a voluntary dose.

I observed an Irishman, who, not satisfied with the first trial, and believing that his cup had been infested by some salt breaking loose in his haversack, washed it carefully and then drank a second, when, finding no change, he exclaimed,—"By J—s, boys, we must be near the sea, for the water's getting salt!"

We soon after passed through the village of Salinas, situated at the source of the stream, where there is a considerable salt manufactory. The inhabitants were so delighted to see us, that they placed buckets full of it at the doors of the different houses, and entreated our men to help themselves as they passed along. It rained hard in the afternoon, and it was late before we got to our ground. We heard a good deal of firing in the neighbourhood in the course of the day, but our division was not engaged.

We retained the same bivouac all day on the 20th; it was behind a range of mountains within a short distance of the left of the enemy's position, as we afterwards discovered; and though we heard an occasional gun, from the other side of the mountain, in the course of the day, fired at Lord Wellington's reconnoitring party, the peace of our valley remained undisturbed.

Chapter 13

Defeat of the Enemy

Battle of Vittoria
June 21st, 1813

Our division got under arms this morning before daylight, and passed the base of the mountain by its left, through the camp of the fourth division, who were still asleep in their tents, to the banks of the River Zadora, at the village of Tres Puentes. The opposite side of the river was occupied by the enemy's advanced posts, and we saw their army on the hills beyond, while the spires of Vittoria were visible in the distance. We felt as if there was likely to be a battle; but as that was an event we were never sure of, until we found ourselves actually in it, we lay for some time just out of musket shot, uncertain what was likely to turn up, and waiting for orders.

At length a sharp fire of musketry was heard to our right, and, on looking in that direction, we saw the head of Sir Rowland Hill's corps, together with some Spanish troops, attempting to force the mountain which marked the enemy's left. The three battalions of our regiment were, at the same moment, ordered forward to feel the enemy, who lined the opposite banks of the river, and with whom we were quickly engaged in a warm skirmish. The affair with Sir Rowland Hill became gradually warmer, but ours had apparently no other object than to amuse those who were opposite to us for the moment; so that, for about two hours longer, it seemed as if there would be nothing but an affair of outposts.

About twelve o'clock, however, we were moved rapidly to our left, followed by the rest of the division, till we came to an abrupt turn of the river, where we found a bridge unoccupied by the enemy, which we immediately crossed, and took possession of what appeared to me to be an old field-work on the other side. We had not been many seconds there before we observed the bayonets of the Third and Seventh Divisions glittering above the standing corn, and advancing upon another bridge, which stood about a quarter of a mile further to our left, and where, on their arrival, they were warmly opposed by the enemy's light troops, who lined the bank of the river, (which we ourselves were not on), in great force, for the defence of the bridge.

As soon as this was observed by our division, Colonel Barnard advanced with our battalion, and took them in flank with such a furious fire as quickly dislodged them, and thereby opened a passage for these two divisions free of expense, which must otherwise have cost them dearly. What with the rapidity of our movement, the colour of our dress, and our close contact with the enemy, before they would abandon their post, we had the misfortune to be identified with them for some time, by a battery of our own guns, who, not observing the movement, continued to serve it out indiscriminately, and all the while admiring their practice upon us; nor was it until the red coats of the Third Division joined us, that they discovered their mistake.

The battle now commenced in earnest; and this was perhaps the most interesting moment of the whole day. Sir Thomas Graham's artillery, with the First and Fifth Divisions, began to be heard far to our left, beyond Vittoria. The bridge which we had just cleared, stood so near to a part of the enemy's position, that the Seventh Division was instantly engaged in close action with them at that point.

On the mountain to our extreme right the action continued to be general and obstinate, though we observed that the enemy were giving ground slowly to Sir Rowland Hill. The passage of the river by our division had turned the enemy's outpost at the bridge on our right, where we had been engaged in the morning, and they were now retreating, followed by the Fourth Division. The plain between them and Sir Rowland Hill was occupied by the British cavalry, who were now seen filing out of a wood, squadron after squadron, galloping into form as they gradually cleared it. The hills behind were covered with spectators, and the Third and the Light Divisions, covered by our battalion, advanced rapidly upon a formidable hill, in front of the enemy's centre, which they had neglected to occupy in sufficient force.

In the course of our progress, our men kept picking off the French *videttes*, who were imprudent enough to hover too near us; and many a horse, bounding along the plain, dragging his late rider by the stirrup-irons, contributed in making it a scene of extraordinary and exhilarating interest.

Old Picton rode at the head of the Third Division, dressed in a blue coat and round hat, and swore as roundly all the way as if he had been wearing two cocked ones. Our battalion soon cleared the hill in question of the enemy's light troops; but we were pulled up on the opposite side of it by one of their lines, which occupied a wall at the entrance of a village immediately under us.

During the few minutes that we stopped there, while a brigade of the Third Division was deploying into line, two of our companies lost two officers and thirty men, chiefly from the fire of the artillery bearing on the spot from the French position. One of their shells burst immediately under my nose, part of it struck my boot and stirrup-iron, and the rest of it kicked up such a dust about me that my charger refused to obey orders; and while I was spurring and he capering, I heard a voice behind me, which I knew to be Lord Wellington's, calling out, in a tone of reproof, "Look to keeping your men together, sir!" and though, God knows, I had not the remotest idea that he was within a mile of me at the time, yet so sensible was I that circumstances warranted his supposing that I was a young officer, cutting a caper, by way of bravado, before him, that worlds would not have tempted me to look round at the moment.

The French fled from the wall as soon as they received a volley from a part of the third division, and we instantly dashed down the hill, and charged them through the village, capturing three of their guns; the first, I believe, that were taken that day. They received a reinforcement, and drove us back before our supports could come to our assistance; but, in the scramble of the moment, our men were knowing enough to cut the traces, and carry off the horses, so that when we retook the village, immediately after, the guns still remained in our possession.

The battle now became general along the whole line, and the cannonade was tremendous. At one period we held one side of a wall, near the village, while the French were on the other; so that any person who chose to put his head over from either side, was sure of getting a sword or a bayonet put up his nostrils. This situation was, of course, too good to be of long endurance. The victory, I believe, was never for a moment doubtful. The enemy were so completely out-generalled, and the superiority of our troops was such, that to carry their positions required little more than the time necessary to march to them.

After forcing their centre, the Fourth Division and our own got on the flank and rather in rear of the enemy's left wing, who were retreating before Sir Rowland Hill, and who, to effect their escape, were now obliged to fly in one confused mass. Had a single regiment of our dragoons been at hand, or even a squadron, to have forced them into shape for a few minutes, we must have taken from ten to twenty thousand prisoners.

After marching alongside of them for nearly two miles, and as a disorderly body will always move faster than an orderly one, we had the mortification to see them gradually heading us, until they finally made their escape. I have no doubt but that our mounted gentlemen were doing their duty as they ought in another part of the field; yet it was impossible to deny ourselves the satisfaction of cursing them all, because a portion had not been there at such a critical moment.

Our elevated situation, at this time, afforded a good view of the field of battle to our left, and I could not help being struck with an unusual appearance of unsteadiness and want of confidence among the French troops. I saw a dense mass of many thousands occupying a good defensible post, who gave way in the greatest confusion, before a single line of the Third Division, almost without feeling them. If there was nothing in any other part of the position to justify the movement, and I do not think there was, they ought to have been flogged, every man, from the general downwards.

The ground was particularly favourable to the retreating foe, as every half-mile afforded a fresh and formidable position; so that, from the commencement of the action to the city of Vittoria, a distance of six or eight miles, we were involved in one continued hard skirmish. On passing Vittoria, however, the scene became quite new, and infinitely more amusing, as the French had made no provision for a retreat; and Sir Thomas Graham having seized upon the great road to France, the only one left open was that leading by Pampeluna; and it was not open long, for their fugitive army, and their myriads of followers with baggage, guns, carriages, &c., being all precipitated upon it at the same moment, it got choked up about a mile beyond the town, in the most glorious state of confusion; and the drivers, finding that one pair of legs was worth two pair of wheels, abandoned it all to the victors.

Many of their followers who had light carriages endeavoured to make their escape through the fields; but it only served to prolong their misery.

I shall never forget the first that we overtook: it was in the midst of a stubble-field—for some time between us and the French skirmishers—the driver doing all he could to urge the horses along: but our balls began to whistle so plentifully about his ears, that he at last dismounted in despair, and, getting on his knees, under the carriage, began praying. His place on the box was quickly occupied by as many of our fellows as could stick on it, while others were scrambling in at the doors on each side, and not a few on the roof, handling the baskets there so roughly, as to occasion loud complaints from the fowls within. I rode up to the carriage, to see that the people inside were not improperly treated; but the only one there was an old gouty gentleman, who, from the nature of his cargo, must either have robbed his own house, or that of a very good fellow, for the carriage was literally laden with wines and provisions.

Never did victors make a more legal or useful capture; for it was now six in the evening, and it had evidently been the old gentleman's fault if he had not already dined, whereas it was our misfortune, rather than our fault, that we had not tasted anything since three o'clock in the morning; so that when one of our men knocked the neck off a bottle, and handed it to me, to take a drink, I nodded to the old fellow's health, and drank it off without the smallest scruple of conscience. It was excellent claret; and if he still lives to tell the story, I fear he will not give us the credit of having belonged to such a civil department as his seemed to be.

We did not cease the pursuit until dark, and then halted in a field of wheat, about two miles beyond Vittoria. The victory was complete. They carried off only one howitzer out of their numerous artillery, which, with baggage, stores, provisions, money, and everything that constitutes the *matériel* of an army, fell into our hands.

It is much to be lamented, on those occasions, that the people who contribute most to the victory should profit the least by it: not that I am an advocate for plunder—on the contrary, I would much rather that all our fighting was for pure love; but as everything of value falls into the hands of the followers, and scoundrels who skulk from the ranks for the double purpose of plundering and saving their dastardly carcasses, what I regret is, that the man who deserts his post should thereby have an opportunity of enriching himself with impunity, while the true man gets nothing; but the evil I believe is irremediable.

Sir James Kempt, who commanded our brigade, in passing one of the captured wagons in the evening, saw a soldier loading himself with money, and was about to have him conveyed to the camp as a prisoner, when the fellow begged hard to be released, and to be allowed to retain what he had got, telling the general that all the boxes in the wagon were filled with gold. Sir James, with his usual liberality, immediately adopted the idea of securing it, as a reward to his brigade, for their gallantry; and, getting a fatigue party, he caused the boxes to be removed to his tent, and ordered an officer and some men from each regiment to parade there next morning, to receive their proportions of it; but, when they opened the boxes, they found them filled with hammers, nails, and horse-shoes!

Among the evil chances of that glorious day, I had to regret the temporary loss of Colonel Cameron—a bad wound in the thigh having obliged him to go to England. Of him I can truly say, that, as a friend, his heart was in the right place, and, as a soldier, his right place was at the head of a regiment in the face of an enemy. I never saw an officer feel more at home in such a situation, nor do I know anyone who could fill it better,

A singular accident threw me in the way of a dying French officer, who gave me a group of family portraits to transmit to his friends; but, as it was not until the following year that I had an opportunity of making the necessary inquiries after them, they had then left their residence, and were nowhere to be heard of.

As not only the body, but the mind, had been in constant occupation since three o'clock in the morning, circumstances no sooner permitted (about ten at night) than I threw myself on the ground, and fell into a profound sleep, from which I did not awake until broad daylight, when I found a French soldier squatted near me, intensely watching for the opening of my shutters. He had contrived to conceal himself there during the night; and, when he saw that I was awake, he immediately jumped on his legs, and very obsequiously presented me with a map of France, telling me that as there was now a probability of our visiting his native country, he would make himself very useful, and would be glad if I would accept of his services, I thought it unfair, however, to deprive him of the present opportunity of seeing a little more of the world himself, and therefore sent him to join the rest of the prisoners, which would ensure him a trip to England free of expense.

About mid-day on the 22nd, our three battalions, with some cavalry and artillery, were ordered in pursuit of the enemy.

I do not know how it is, but I have always had a mortal objection to be killed the day after a victory. In the actions preceding a battle, or in the battle itself, it never gave me much uneasiness, as being all in the way of business; but, after surviving the great day, I always felt as if I had a right to live to tell the story; and I therefore did not find the ensuing three days' fighting half so pleasant as they otherwise would have been.

Darkness overtook us this night without our overtaking the enemy; and we halted in a grove of pines, exposed to a very heavy rain. In imprudently shifting my things from one tree to another, after dark, some rascal contrived to steal the valise containing my dressing things, than which I do not know a greater loss, when there is no possibility of replacing any part of them.

We overtook their rear-guard early on the following day, and, hanging on their line of march until dark, we did them all the mischief that we could. They burnt every village through which they passed, under the pretence of impeding our movements; but as it did not make the slightest difference in that respect, we could only view it as a wanton piece of cruelty.

On the 24th, we were again engaged in pressing their rear the greater part of the day; and ultimately, in giving them the last kick under the walls of Pampeluna, we had the glory of capturing their last gun, which literally sent them into France without a single piece of ordnance.

Our battalion occupied, that night, a large, well furnished, but uninhabited *château*, a short distance from Pampeluna.

We got under arms early on the morning of the 25th; and passing, by a mountain-path, to the left of Pampeluna, within range of the guns, though they did not fire at us, circled the town, until we reached the village of Villalba, where we halted for the night. Since I joined that army, I had never, up to that period, been master of anything in the shape of a bed; and though

I did not despise a bundle of straw, when it could conveniently be had, yet my boat-cloak and blanket were more generally to be seen spread out for my reception on the bare earth.

But in proceeding to turn into them as usual this evening, I was not a little astonished to find, in their stead, a comfortable mattress, with a suitable supply of linen, blankets, and pillows; in short, the very identical bedding on which I had slept the night before, in the *château*, three leagues off, and which my rascal of an Irishman had bundled all together on the back of my mule, without giving me the slightest hint of his intentions.

On my taking him to task about it, and telling him that he would certainly be hanged, all that he said in reply was, "By J—s, they had more than a hundred beds in that house, and not a single soul to sleep in them." I was very much annoyed at the time, that there was no possibility of returning them to their rightful owner, as, independent of its being nothing short of a regular robbery, I really looked upon them as a very unnecessary encumbrance; but being forced, in some measure, to indulge in their comforts, I was not long in changing my mind: and was, ultimately, not very sorry that the possibility of restoration never did occur.

CHAPTER 14

Soult's Advance

June 26th, 1813.—Our division fell in this morning, at daylight, and, marching out of Villalba, circled round the southern side of Pampeluna, until we reached the great road leading to Tafalla, where we found ourselves united with the Third and Fourth Divisions, and a large body of cavalry. The whole, under the immediate command of Lord Wellington, proceeded southward, with a view to intercept General Clausel, who, with a strong division of the French army, had been at Logrona, on the day of the battle of Vittoria, and was now endeavouring to pass into the Pyrenees by our right. We marched until sunset, and halted for the night in a wood.

On the morning of the 27th we were again in motion, and passing through a country abounding in fruits, and all manner of delightful prospects; and through the handsome town of Tafalla, where we were enthusiastically cheered by the beauteous occupants of the numerous balconies overhanging the streets. We halted for the night in an olive-grove a short distance from Olite.

At daylight next morning we passed through the town of Olite, and continued our route until we began to enter among the mountains about mid-day, when we halted two hours, to enable the men to cook, and again resumed our march. Darkness overtook us, while struggling through a narrow rugged road, which wound its way along the bank of the Arragon; and we did not reach our destination, at Casada, until near midnight, where, amid torrents of rain, and in the darkness of the night, we could find nothing but ploughed fields on which to repose our weary limbs, nor could we find a particle of fuel to illuminate the cheerless scene.

> Breathed there a man of soul so dead,
> Who would not to himself have said,
> This is —— a confounded comfortless dwelling.

Dear Sir Walter, pray excuse the Casadians from your curse entailed on home haters, for if any one of them ever succeeded in getting beyond the mountain, by the road which I traversed, he ought to be anathematized if ever he seek his home again.

We passed the whole of the next day in the same place. It was discovered that Clausel had been walking blindly into the lion's den, when the *alcalde* of a neighbouring village had warned him of his danger, and he was thereby enabled to avoid us, by turning off towards Zaragossa. We heard that Lord Wellington had caused the informer to be hanged. I hope he did, but I don't believe it.

On the 30th, we began to retrace our steps to Pampeluna, in the course of which we halted two nights at Sanguessa, a populous mountain town, full of old rattle-trap houses, a good many of which we pulled down for firewood, by way of making room for improvements.

I was taking advantage of this extra day's halt to communicate to my friends the important events of the past fortnight, when I found myself all at once wrapped into a bundle, with my tent-pole and tent rolling upon the earth, mixed up with my portable table and writing utensils, while the devil himself seemed to be dancing a hornpipe over my body!

Although this is a sort of thing that one will sometimes submit to, when it comes by way of illusion, at its proper time and place, such as a midnight visit from a nightmare; yet, as I seemed now to be visited by a horse as well as a mare, and that, too, in the middle of the day, and in the midst of a crowded camp, it was rather too much of a joke, and I therefore sung out most lustily. I was not long in getting extricated, and found that the whole scene had been arranged by two rascally donkeys, who, in a frolicsome humour, had been chasing each other about the neighbourhood, until they finally tumbled into my tent, with a force which drew every peg, and rolled the whole of it over on the top of me! It might have been good sport for them, but it was none to me!

On the 3rd of July, we resumed our quarters in Villalba, where we halted during the whole of the next day; and were well supplied with fish, fresh butter, and eggs, brought by the peasantry of Biscay, who are the most manly set of women that I ever saw. They are very square across the shoulders; and, what between the quantity of fish, and the quantity of yellow petticoats, they carry a load which an ordinary mule might boast of.

A division of Spaniards having relieved us in the blockade of Pampeluna, our division, on the 5th of July, advanced into the Pyrenees.

On the 7th, we took up our quarters in the little town of St. Esteban, situated in a lovely valley, watered by the Bidassoa. The different valleys in the Pyrenees are very rich and fertile; the towns are clean and regular, and the natives very handsome. They are particularly smart about the limbs; and in no other part of the world have I seen anything, natural or artificial, to rival the complexions of the ladies, *i.e.* to the admirers of pure red and white.

We were allowed to remain several days on this enchanting spot, and enjoyed ourselves exceedingly. They had an extraordinary style of dancing, peculiar to themselves: at a particular part of the tune, they all began thumping the floor with their feet, as hard and as fast as they were able, not in the shape of a figure or flourish of any kind, but even down pounding.

I could not myself see anything either graceful or difficult in the operation; but they seemed to think that there was only one lady among them who could do it in perfection. She was the wife of a French colonel, and had been left in the care of her friends, (and his enemies): she certainly could pound the ground both harder and faster than any one there, eliciting the greatest applause after every performance; and yet I do not think that she could have caught a French husband by her superiority in that particular step.

After our few days' halt, we advanced along the banks of the Bidassoa, through a succession of beautiful little fertile valleys, thickly studded with clean respectable-looking farmhouses and little villages, and bounded by stupendous, picturesque, and well-wooded mountains, until we came to the hill next to the village of Bera,(*Vera*) which we found occupied by a small force of the enemy, who, after receiving a few shots from our people, retired through the village into their position behind it.

Our line of demarcation was then clearly seen. The mountain which the French army occupied was the last ridge of the Pyrenees; and their sentries stood on the face of it, within pistol shot of the village of Bera, which now became the advanced post of our division. The Bidassoa takes a sudden turn to the left at Bera, and formed a natural boundary between the two armies from thence to the sea; but all to our right was open, and merely marked a continuation of the valley of Bera, which was a sort of neutral ground, in which the French foragers and our own frequently met and helped themselves, in the greatest good humour, while any forage remained, without exchanging either words or blows. The left wing of the army, under Sir Thomas Graham, now commenced the siege of St. Sebastian; and as Lord Wellington had at the time to cover both that and the blockade of Pampeluna, our army occupied an extended position of many miles.

Marshal Soult having succeeded to the command of the French army, and finding, towards the end of July, that St. Sebastian was about to be stormed, and that the garrison of Pampeluna were beginning to get on short allowance, he determined on making a bold push for the relief of both places; and assembling the whole of his army, he forced the pass of Maya, and advanced rapidly upon Pampeluna.

Lord Wellington was never to be caught napping. His army

occupied too extended a position to offer effectual resistance at any of their advanced posts; but by the time that Marshal Soult had worked his way up to the last ridge of the Pyrenees, and within sight of "the haven of his wishes," he found his Lordship waiting for him, with four divisions of the army, who treated him to one of the most signal and sanguinary defeats that he ever experienced.

Our division, during the important movements on our right, was employed in keeping up the communication between the troops under the immediate command of Lord Wellington, and those under Sir Thomas Graham at St. Sebastian. We retired, the first day, to the mountains behind Le Secca; and just as we were about to lie down for the night, we were again ordered under arms, and continued our retreat in utter darkness, through a mountain path, where, in many places, a false step might have rolled a fellow as far as the other world.

The consequence was, that although we were kept on our legs during the whole of the night, we found, when daylight broke, that the tail of the column had not got a quarter of a mile from their starting-post.

On a good broad road it is all very well; but, on a narrow bad road, a night march is like a nightmare, harassing a man to no purpose.

On the 26th, we occupied a ridge of mountain near enough to hear the battle, though not in a situation to see it; and remained the whole of the day in the greatest torture, for want of news. About midnight we heard the joyful tidings of the enemy's defeat with the loss of four thousand prisoners. Our division proceeded in pursuit, at daylight on the following morning.

We moved rapidly by the same road on which we had retired; and, after a forced march, found ourselves, when near sunset, on the flank of their retiring column, on the Bidassoa, near the bridge of Janca, and immediately proceeded to business.

The sight of a Frenchman always acted like a cordial on the spirits of a rifleman; and the fatigues of the day were forgotten as our three battalions extended among the brushwood, and went down to "knock the dust out of their hairy knapsacks,"[1] as our men were in the habit of expressing themselves; but, in place of knocking the dust out of them, I believe that most of their knapsacks were knocked in the dust; for the greater part of those who were not floored along with their knapsacks, shook them off by way of enabling the owner to make a smarter scramble across that portion of the road on which our leaden shower was pouring: and, foes as they were, it was impossible not to feel a degree of pity for their situation; pressed by an enemy in their rear, an inaccessible mountain on their right, and a river on their left, lined by an invisible foe, from whom there was no escape but the desperate one of running the gauntlet.

However, *as every — has his day*, and this was ours, we must stand excused for making the most of it. Each company, as they passed, gave us a volley; but as they had nothing to guide their aim, except the smoke from our rifles, we had very few men hit.

Amongst other papers found on the road that night, one of our officers discovered the letter-book of the French military secretary, with his correspondence included to the day before. It was immediately sent to Lord Wellington.

We advanced next morning, and occupied our former post at Bera. The enemy still continued to hold the mountain of Echalar, which, as it rose out of the right end of our ridge, was, properly speaking, a part of our property; and we concluded, that a sense of justice would have induced them to leave it of their own accord in the course of the day; but when, towards the afternoon, they showed no symptoms of quitting, our division, leaving their kettles on the fire, proceeded to eject them. As we approached the mountain, the peak of it caught a passing cloud, which gradually descended in a thick fog, and excluded the enemy from our view.

Our three battalions, however, having been let loose, under Colonel Barnard, we soon made ourselves *Children of the Mist*; and, guided to our opponents by the whistling of their balls,

---

1. The French knapsack is made of unshorn goatskin.

made them descend from their "high estate"; and, handing them across the valley into their own position, we then retired to ours, where we found our tables already spread, and a comfortable dinner awaiting us.

This was one of the most gentlemanlike days' fighting that I ever experienced, although we had to lament the vacant seats of one or two of our messmates.

August 22nd.—I narrowly escaped being taken prisoner this morning, very foolishly. A division of Spaniards occupied the ground to our left, beyond the Bidassoa; and, having mounted my horse to take a look at their post, I passed through a small village and then got on a rugged path winding along the edge of the river, where I expected to find their outposts. The river, at that place, was not above knee deep, and about ten or twelve yards across; and though I saw a number of soldiers gathering chestnuts from a row of trees which lined the opposite bank, I concluded that they were Spaniards, and kept moving onwards; but, observing at last that I was an object of greater curiosity than I ought to be to people who had been in the daily habit of seeing the uniform, it induced me to take a more particular look at my neighbours; when, to my consternation, I saw the French eagle ornamenting the front of every cap.

I instantly wheeled my horse to the right about; and, seeing that I had a full quarter of a mile to traverse at a walk, before I could get clear of them, I began to whistle with as much unconcern as I could muster, while my eyes were searching, like lightning, for the means of escape, in the event of their trying to cut me off. I had soon the satisfaction of observing that none of them had firelocks, which reduced my capture to the chances of a race; for, though the hill on my right was inaccessible to a horseman, it was not so to a dismounted Scotsman; and I therefore determined, in case of necessity, to abandon my horse, and show them what I could do on my own bottom at a pinch. Fortunately they did not attempt it; and I could scarcely credit my good luck when I found myself once more in my own tent.

Chapter 15

Returns after an Action

The 25th of August, being our regimental anniversary, was observed by the officers of our three battalions with all due conviviality. Two trenches, calculated to accommodate seventy gentlemen's legs, were dug in the green sward; the earth between them stood for a table, and behind was our seat; and though the table could not boast of all the delicacies of a civic entertainment, yet

The worms they crept in, and. the worms they crept out:

As the earth almost quaked with the weight of the feast, and the enemy certainly did, from the noise of it. For so many fellows, holding such precarious tenures of their lives, could not meet together in commemoration of such an event, without indulging in an occasional cheer,—not a whispering cheer, but one that echoed far and wide into the French lines; and as it was a sound that had often pierced them before, and never yet boded them any good, we heard afterwards that they were kept standing at their arms the greater part of the night in consequence.

At the time of Soult's last irruption into the Pyrenees, Sir Thomas Graham had made an unsuccessful attempt to carry St. Sebastian by storm; and having ever since been prosecuting the siege with unremitting vigour, the works were now reduced to such a state as to justify a second attempt, and our division sent forth their three hundred volunteers to join the storming party.[1]

---

1. Lieutenants Percival and Hamilton commanded those from our battalion, and were both desperately wounded.

The morning on which we expected the assault to take place, we had turned out before daylight, as usual; and as a thick fog hung on the French position, which prevented our seeing them, we turned in again at the usual time, but had scarcely done so, when the mist rode off on a passing breeze, showing us the opposite hills bristling with their bayonets, and their columns descending rapidly towards us. The bugles instantly sounded to arms, and we formed on our alarm posts.

We thought at first that the attack was intended for us, but they presently began to pass the river, a little below the village of Bera, and to advance against the Spaniards on our left. They were covered by some mountain guns, from which their first shell fell short, and made such a breach in their own leading column, that we could not resist giving three cheers to their marksman. Leaving a strong covering party to keep our division in check at the bridge of Bera, their main body followed the Spaniards, who, offering little opposition, continued retiring towards St. Sebastian.

We remained quiet the early part of the day, under a harmless fire from their mountain guns; but, towards the afternoon, our battalion, with part of the Forty-Third, and supported by a brigade of Spaniards, were ordered to pass by the bridge of Le Secca, and to move in a parallel direction with the French, along the same ridge of hills.

The different flanking posts of the enemy permitted the Forty-Third and us to pass them quietly, thinking, I suppose, that it was their interest to keep the peace; but not so with the Spaniards, whom they kept in a regular fever, under a smart fire, the whole way. We took up a position at dark, on a pinnacle of the same mountain, within three or four hundred yards of them. There had been a heavy firing all day to our left, and we heard, in the course of the night, of the fall of St. Sebastian, as well as of the defeat of the force which we had seen following the Spaniards in that direction.

As we always took the liberty of abusing our friends, the commissaries, whether with or without reason, whenever we happened to be on short allowance, it is but fair to say, that when our supporting Spanish brigadier came to compare notes with us here, we found that we had three days' rations in the haversack against his none. He very politely proposed to relieve us from half of ours, and to give a receipt for it, but we told him that the trouble in carrying it was a pleasure!

At daylight next morning we found that the enemy had altogether disappeared from our front. The heavy rains during the past night had rendered the Bidassoa no longer fordable; and the bridge of Bera being the only retreat left open, it was fortunate for them that they took advantage of it before we had time to occupy the post with a sufficient force to defend the passage, otherwise they would have been compelled, in all probability, to have laid down their arms.

As it was, they suffered very severely from two companies of our Second Battalion, who were on piquet there. The two captains commanding them were, however, killed in the affair.

We returned in the course of the day and resumed our post at Bera, the enemy continuing to hold theirs beyond it.

The ensuing month passed by, without producing the slightest novelty, and we began to get heartily tired of our situation. Our souls, in fact, were strung for war, and peace afforded no enjoyment, unless the place did; and there was none to be found in a valley of the Pyrenees, which the ravages of contending armies had reduced to a desert. The labours of the French on the opposite mountain had, in the first instance, been confined to fortification; but, as the season advanced, they seemed to think that the branch of a tree, or a sheet of canvass, was too slender a barrier between them and a frosty night, and their fortified camp was gradually becoming a fortified town, of regular brick and mortar.

Though we were living under the influence of the same sky, we did not think it necessary to give ourselves the same trouble, but reasoned on their proceedings like philosophers, and calculated, from the aspect of the times, that there was a probability of a speedy transfer of property, and that it might still be reserved for us to give their town a name: nor were we disappointed. Late on the night of the 7th of October, Colonel Barnard arrived from head-quarters, with the intelligence that the next was to be the day of trial. Accordingly, on the morning of the 8th, the Fourth Division came up to support us, and we immediately marched down to the foot of the enemy's position, shook off our knapsacks before their faces, and went at them.

The action commenced by five companies of our third battalion advancing, under Colonel Ross, to dislodge the enemy from a hill which they occupied in front of their intrenchments; and there never was a movement more beautifully executed, for they walked quietly and steadily up, and swept them regularly off without firing a single shot until the enemy had turned their backs, when they then served them out with a most destructive discharge. The movement excited the admiration of all who witnessed it, and added another laurel to the already crowded wreath which adorned the name of that distinguished officer.

At the first look of the enemy's position, it appeared as if our brigade had got the most difficult task to perform; but, as the capture of this hill showed us a way round the flank of their intrenchments, we carried one after the other, until we finally gained the summit, with very little loss. Our Second brigade, however, were obliged to take *the bull by the horns*, on their side, and suffered more severely; but they rushed at everything with a determination that defied resistance, carrying redoubt after redoubt at the point of the bayonet, until they finally joined us on the summit of the mountain, with three hundred prisoners in their possession.

We now found ourselves firmly established within the French territory, with a prospect before us that was truly refreshing, considering that we had not seen the sea for three years, and that our views, for months, had been confined to fogs and the peaks of mountains. On our left, the Bay of Biscay lay extended as far as the horizon, while several of our ships of war were seen sporting upon her bosom. Beneath us lay the pretty little town of St. Jean de Luz, which looked as if it had just been framed out of the Lilliputian scenery of a toyshop. The town of Bayonne, too, was visible in the distance; and the view to the right embraced a beautiful well-wooded country, thickly studded with towns and villages, as far as the eye could reach.

Sir Thomas Graham, with the left wing of the army, had, the same morning, passed the Bidassoa, and established them also within the French boundary. A brigade of Spaniards, on our right, had made a simultaneous attack on La Rhune, the highest mountain on this part of the Pyrenees, and which, since our last advance, was properly now a part of our position. The enemy, however, refused to quit it; and the firing between them did not cease until long after dark.

The affair in which we were engaged terminated, properly speaking, when we had expelled the enemy from the mountain; but some of our straggling skirmishers continued to follow the retiring foe into the valley beyond, with a view, no doubt, of seeing what a French house contained.

Lord Wellington, preparatory to this movement, had issued an order requiring that private property, of every kind, should be strictly respected; but we had been so long at war with France, that our men had been accustomed to look upon them as their natural enemies, and could not, at first, divest themselves of the idea that they had not a right to partake of the good things abounding about the cottage doors.

Our commandant, however, was determined to see the order rigidly enforced; and it was therefore highly amusing to watch the return of the depredators. The first who made his appearance was a bugler, carrying a goose, which, after he had been well beaten about the head with it, was transferred to the provost-marshal. The next was a soldier, with a calf; the soldier was immediately sent to the quarter-guard, and the calf to the provost-marshal. He was followed by another soldier, mounted on a horse, who were also both consigned to the same keeping; but, on the soldier stating that he had only got the horse in charge from a volunteer, who was at that time attached to the regiment, he was set at liberty.

Presently the volunteer himself came up, and, not observing the colonel lying on the grass, called out among the soldiers, "Who is the —— rascal that sent my horse to the provost-marshal?"

"It was I!" said the colonel, to the utter confusion of the querist. Our chief was a good deal nettled at these irregularities; and, some time after, on going to his tent, which was pitched between the roofless walls of a house, conceive his astonishment at finding the calf and the goose hanging in his own larder! He looked serious for a moment, but on receiving an explanation, and after the row he had made about them, the thing was too ridiculous, and he burst out laughing. It is due to all concerned to state that they had, at last, been honestly come by, for I, as one of his messmates, had purchased the goose from the proper quarter, and another had done the same by the calf.

Not anticipating this day's fight, I had given my pay-serjeant twenty-five guineas, the day before, to distribute among the company: and I did not discover, until too late, that he had neglected to do it, as he disappeared in the course of the action, and was never afterwards heard of. If he was killed, or taken prisoner, he must have been a prize to somebody, though he left me a blank.

Among other incidents of the day, one of our men had a son and heir presented to him by his Portuguese wife, soon after the action. She had been taken in labour while ascending the mountain; but it did not seem to interfere with her proceedings in the least, for she, and her child, and her donkey, came all three screeching into the camp, immediately after, telling the news, as if it had been something very extraordinary, and none of them a bit the worse.

On the morning of the 9th, we turned out, as usual, an hour before daylight. The sound of musketry, to our right, in our own hemisphere, announced that the French and Spaniards had resumed their unfinished argument of last night, relative to the occupation of La Rhune; while at the same time, *from our throne of clouds*, we had an opportunity of contemplating, with some astonishment, the proceedings of the nether world.

A French ship of war, considering St. Jean de Luz no longer a free port, had endeavoured under cover of the night, to steal alongshore to Bayonne; and, when daylight broke, they had an opportunity of seeing that they were not only within sight of their port, but within sight of a British gun-brig, and, if they entertained any doubts as to which of the two was nearest, their minds were quickly relieved on that point, by finding that they were not within reach of their port, and strictly within reach of the guns of the brig, while two British frigates were bearing down with a press of canvass.

The Frenchman returned a few broadsides: he was double the size of the one opposed to him; but, conceiving his case to be hopeless, he at length set fire to the ship, and took to his boats. We watched the progress of the flames until she finally blew up, and disappeared in a column of smoke. The boats of our gun-brig were afterwards seen employed in picking up the odds and ends.

Our friends, the Spaniards, I have no doubt, would have been very glad to have got rid of their opponents in the same kind of way, either by their going without the mountain, or by their taking it with them. But the mountain stood and the French stood, until we began to wish the mountain, the French, and the Spaniards at the devil; for, although we knew that the affair between them was a matter of no consequence whichever way it went, yet it was impossible for us to feel quite at ease, while a fight was going on so near. It was therefore a great relief when, in the afternoon, a few companies of our second brigade were sent to their assistance, as the French then retired without firing another shot.

Between the French and us there was no humbug; it was either peace or war. The war, on both sides, was conducted on the grand scale, and, by a tacit sort of understanding, we never teased each other unnecessarily.

The French, after leaving La Rhune, established their advanced post on La Petite Rhune, a mountain that stood as high as most of its neighbours; but, as its name betokens, it was but a child to its gigantic namesake, of which it seemed as if it had, at a former period, formed a part; but having been shaken off, like a useless *galloche*, it stood gaping, open-mouthed, at the place it had left, (and which had now become our advanced post,) while the enemy proceeded to furnish its jaws with a set of teeth, or, in other words, to face it with breastworks, &c. a measure which they invariably had recourse to in every new position.

Encamped on the face of La Rhune, we remained a whole month idle spectators of their preparations, and dearly longing for the day that should afford us an opportunity of penetrating into the more hospitable-looking low country beyond them; for the weather had become excessively cold, and our camp stood exposed to the utmost fury of the almost nightly tempest.

Oft have I, in the middle of the night, awoke from a sound sleep, and found my tent on the point of disappearing in the air, like a balloon, and, leaving my warm blankets, been obliged to snatch the mallet, and rush out in the midst of a hail-storm, to peg it down. I think that I now see myself looking like one of those gay creatures of the elements who dwelt (as Shakespeare has it) among the rainbows!

By way of contributing to the warmth of my tent, I dug a hole inside, which I arranged as a fireplace, carrying the smoke underneath the walls, and building a turf chimney outside. I was not long in proving the experiment, and, finding that it went exceedingly well, I was not a little vain of the invention. However, it came on to rain very hard while I was dining at a neighbouring tent, and on my return to my own, I found the fire not only extinguished, but a fountain playing from the same place, up to the roof, watering my bed and baggage, and all sides of it, most refreshingly. This showed me, at the expense of my night's repose, that the rain oozed through the thin spongy surface of the earth, and, in particular places, rushed down in torrents between the earth and the rock which it covered; and any incision in the former was sure to produce a fountain.

It was very singular that, notwithstanding our exposure to all the severities of the worst of weather, we had not a single sick man in the battalion while we remained there.

Chapter 16

An Enemy's Gratitude

Battle of Nivelle
November 10th, 1813

The fall of Pampeluna having at length left our further movements unshackled by an enemy in the rear, preparations were made for an attack on their position, which, though rather too extended, was formidable by nature, and rendered doubly so by art.

La Petite Rhune was allotted to our division, as their first point of attack; and accordingly, the 10th being the day fixed, we moved to our ground at midnight on the 9th. The abrupt ridges in the neighbourhood enabled us to lodge ourselves, unperceived, within half musket shot of their piquets; and we had left every description of animal behind us in camp, in order that neither the barking of dogs nor the neighing of steeds should give indication of our intentions.

Our signal of attack was to be a gun from Sir John Hope, who had now succeeded Sir Thomas Graham in the command of the left wing of the army.

We stood to our arms at dawn of day, which was soon followed by the signal gun; and each commanding officer, according to previous instructions, led gallantly off to his point of attack. The French must have been, no doubt, astonished to see such an armed force spring out of the ground almost under their noses; but they were, nevertheless, prepared behind their intrenchments, and caused us some loss in passing the short space between us; but the whole place was carried within the time required to walk over it; and, in less than half-an-hour from the commencement of the attack, it was in our possession, with all their tents left standing.

La Petite Rhune was more of an outpost than a part of their position, the latter being a chain of stupendous mountains in its rear; so that while our battalion followed their skirmishers into the valley between, the remainder of our division were forming for the attack on the main position, and waiting for the co-operation of the other divisions, the thunder of whose artillery, echoing along the valleys, proclaimed that they were engaged, far and wide, on both sides of us.

About mid-day our division advanced to the grand attack, on the most formidable-looking part of the whole of the enemy's position, and, much to our surprise, we carried it with more ease and less loss than the outpost in the morning; a circumstance which we could only account for by supposing that it had been defended by the same troops, and that they did not choose to sustain two hard beatings on the same day. The attack succeeded at every point; and in the evening we had the satisfaction of seeing the left wing of the army marching into St. Jean de Luz.

Towards the end of the action, Colonel Barnard was struck with a musket ball, which carried him clean off his horse. The enemy, seeing that they had shot an officer of rank, very maliciously kept up a heavy fire on the spot, while we were carrying him under the brow of the hill. The ball having passed through the lungs, he was spitting blood, and, at the moment, had every appearance of being in a dying state; but, to our joy and surprise he, that day month, rode up to the battalion when it was in action, near Bayonne, and, I need not add, that he was received with three hearty cheers.

A curious fact occurred in our regiment at this period. Prior to the action of the Nivelle, an owl had perched itself on the tent of one of our officers (Lieutenant Doyle). This officer was killed in the battle, and the owl was afterwards seen on Captain Duncan's tent. His brother officers quizzed him on the subject, by telling him that he was the next on the list, a joke which Captain Duncan did not much relish; and it was prophetic, as he soon afterwards fell at Tarbes.

The movements of the two or three days following placed the enemy within their intrenchments at Bayonne, and the head-quarters of our battalion in the Château D'Arcangues, with the outposts of the division at the village of Bassasarry and its adjacents.

I now felt myself both in a humour and a place to enjoy an interval of peace and quietness. The country was abundant in every comfort; the *château* was large, well-furnished, and unoccupied, except by a bed-ridden grandmother, and young Arcangues, a gay rattling young fellow, who furnished us with plenty of good wine, (by our paying for the same,) and made one of our mess.

On the 20th of November a strong reconnoitring party of the enemy examined our chain of posts. They remained a considerable time within half musket shot of one of our piquets; but we did not fire, and they seemed at last as if they had all gone away. The place where they had stood bounded our view in that direction, as it was a small sand hill with a mud cottage at the end of it. After watching the spot intensely for nearly an hour, and none showing themselves, my curiosity would keep no longer, and, desiring three men to follow, I rode forward to ascertain the fact.

When I cleared the end of the cottage, I found myself within three yards of at least a dozen of them, who were seated in a group behind a small hedge, with their arms laid against the wall of the cottage, and a sentry with sloped arms, and his back towards me, listening to their conversation.

My first impulse was to gallop in amongst them, and order them to surrender; but my three men were still twenty or thirty yards behind, and, as my only chance of success was by surprise, I thought the risk of the delay too great, and, reining back my horse, I made a signal to my men to retire, which, from the soil being a deep sand, we were enabled to do without the slightest noise; but all the while I had my ears pricked up, expecting every instant to find a ball whistling through my body; however, as none of them afterwards showed themselves past the end of the cottage, I concluded that they had remained ignorant of my visit.

We had an affair of some kind once a week, while we remained there; and as they were generally trifling, and we always found a good dinner and a good bed in the *château* on our return, we considered them rather a relief than otherwise.

The only instance of a want of professional generosity that I ever had occasion to remark in a French officer, occurred on one of these occasions. We were about to push in their outposts, for some particular purpose, and I was sent with an order for Lieutenant Gardiner of ours, who was on piquet, to attack the posts in his front, as soon as he should see a corresponding movement on his flank, which would take place almost immediately. The enemy's sentries were so near, as to be quite at Lieutenant Gardiner's mercy, who immediately said to me, "Well, I won't kill these unfortunate rascals at all events, but shall tell them to go in and join their piquet."

I applauded his motives, and rode off; but I had only gone a short distance when I heard a volley of musketry behind me; and, seeing that it had come from the French piquet, I turned back to see what had happened, and found that the officer commanding it had no sooner got his sentries so generously 'restored to him, than he instantly formed his piquet and fired a volley at Lieutenant Gardiner, who was walking a little apart from his men, waiting for the expected signal. The balls all fell near, without touching him, and, for the honour of the French army, I was glad to hear afterwards that the officer alluded to was a militiaman.

BATTLES NEAR BAYONNE
December 9th, 10th, 11th, 12th, and 13th, 1813

The centre and left wing of our army advanced on the morning of the 9th of December, and drove the enemy within their intrenchments, threatening an attack on their lines. Lord Wellington had the double object, in this movement, of reconnoitring their works, and effecting the passage of the Nive with his right wing. The rivers Nive and Adour unite in the town of Bayonne; so that while we were threatening to storm the works on one side, Sir Rowland Hill passed the Nive, without opposition, on the other, and took up his ground, with his right on the Adour and his left on the Nive, on a contracted space, within a very short distance of the walls of the town. On our side we were engaged in a continual skirmish until dark, when we retired to our quarters, under the supposition that we had got our usual week's allowance, and that we should remain quiet again for a time.

We turned out at daylight on the 10th; but, as there was a thick drizzling rain which prevented us from seeing anything, we soon turned in again. My servant soon after came to tell me that Sir Lowry Cole, and some of his staff, had just ascended to the top of the *château*, a piece of information which did not quite please me, for I fancied that the general had just discovered our quarter to be better than his own, and had come for the purpose of taking possession of it. However, in less than five minutes, we received an order for our battalion to move up instantly to the support of the piquets; and, on my descending to the door to mount my horse, I found Sir Lowry standing there, who asked if we had received any orders; and, on my telling him that we had been ordered up to support the piquets, he immediately desired a staff officer to order up one of his brigades to the rear of the *château*.

This was one of the numerous instances in which we had occasion to admire the prudence and forethought of the great Wellington. He had foreseen the attack that would take place, and had his different divisions disposed to meet it. We no sooner moved up, than we found ourselves a party engaged along with the piquets; and under a heavy skirmishing fire, retiring gradually from hedge to hedge, according as the superior force of the enemy compelled us to give ground, until we finally retired within our home, the *château*, which was the first part of our position that was meant to be defended in earnest.

We had previously thrown up a mud rampart around it, and loopholed the different outhouses, so that we had nothing now to do, but to line the walls and show determined fight. The Forty-Third occupied the churchyard to our left, which was also partially fortified; and the Third *Caçadores*, and our Third Battalion, occupied the space between, behind the hedgerows, while the Fourth Division was in readiness to support us from the rear.

The enemy came up to the opposite ridge, in formidable numbers, and began blazing at our windows and loopholes, and showing some disposition to attempt it by storm; but they thought better of it. and withdrew their columns a short distance to the rear, leaving the nearest hedge lined with their skirmishers. An officer of ours, Mr. Hopewood, and one of our serjeants, had been killed in the field opposite, and were lying within twenty yards of the enemy's skirmishers. We were very anxious to get possession of their bodies, but had not force enough to effect it. Several French soldiers came through the hedge, at different times, with the intention, as we thought, of plundering, but our men shot everyone who attempted to go near them, until towards evening, when a French officer approached, waving a white handkerchief and pointing to some of his men who were following him with shovels. Seeing that his intention was to bury them, we instantly ceased firing, nor did we renew it again that night.

The Forty-Third, from their post at the church, kept up an incessant shower of musketry the whole of the day, at what was conceived, at the time, to be a very long range; but from the quantity of balls which were afterwards found sticking in every tree where the enemy stood, it was evident that their berth must have been rather uncomfortable.

One of our officers, in the course of the day, had been passing through a deep roadway, between two banks, with hedgerows, when, to his astonishment, a dragoon and his horse tumbled heels over head into the road, as if they had been fired out of a cloud. Neither of them were the least hurt; but it must have been no joke that tempted him to take such a flight.

Soult expected, by bringing his whole force to bear on our centre and left wing, that he would have succeeded in forcing it, or, at all events, of obliging Lord Wellington to withdraw Sir Rowland Hill from beyond the Nive; but he effected neither, and darkness left the two armies on the ground which they had fought on.

General Alten and Sir James Kempt took up their quarters with us in the *château*: our sentries and those of the enemy stood within pistol shot of each other in the ravine below.

Young Arcangues, I presume, must have been rather disappointed at the result of the day; for, even giving him credit for every kindly feeling towards us, his wishes must still have been in favour of his countrymen; but when he found that his *château* was to be a bone of contention, it then became his interest that we should keep possession of it; and he held out every inducement for us to do so; which, by the bye, was quite unnecessary, seeing that our own comfort so much depended on it.

However, though his supplies of claret had failed some days before, he now discovered some fresh cases in the cellar, which he immediately placed at our disposal; and, that our dire resolve to defend the fortress should not be melted by weak woman's wailings, he fixed an armchair on a mule, mounted his grandmother on it, and sent her off to the rear, while the balls were whizzing about the neighbourhood in a manner to which even she, poor old lady, was not altogether insensible, though she had become a mounted heroine at a period when she had given up all idea of ever sitting on anything more lively than a coffin.

During the whole of the 11th each army retained the same ground; and though there was an occasional exchange of shots at different points, yet nothing material occurred.

The enemy began throwing up a six gun battery opposite our *château*; and we employed ourselves in strengthening the works, as a precautionary measure, though we had not much to dread from it, as they were so strictly within range of our rifles, that he must have been a lucky artilleryman who stood there to fire a second shot.

In the course of the night a brigade of Belgians, who were with the French army, having heard that their country had declared for their legitimate king, passed over to our side, and surrendered.

On the 12th there was heavy firing and hard fighting all day, to our left, but we remained perfectly quiet. Towards the afternoon, Sir James Kempt formed our brigade, for the purpose of expelling the enemy from the hill next the *château*, to which he thought them rather too near; but, just as we reached our different points for commencing the attack, we were recalled, and nothing further occurred.

I went, about one o'clock in the morning, to visit our different piquets; and seeing an unusual number of fires in the enemy's lines, I concluded that they had lit them to mask some movement; and taking a *patrole* with me, I stole cautiously forward, and found that they had left the ground altogether. I immediately returned, and reported the circumstance to General Alten, who sent off a despatch to apprize Lord Wellington.

As soon as day began to dawn, on the morning of the 13th, a tremendous fire of artillery and musketry was heard to our right. Soult had withdrawn everything from our front in the course of the night, and had now attacked Sir Rowland Hill with his whole force. Lord Wellington, in expectation of this attack, had, last night, reinforced Sir Rowland Hill with the Sixth Division; which enabled him to occupy his contracted position so strongly, that Soult, unable to bring more than his own front to bear upon him, sustained a signal and sanguinary defeat.

Lord Wellington galloped into the yard of our *château*, soon after the attack had commenced, and demanded, with his usual quickness, what was to be seen. Sir James Kempt, who was spying at the action from an upper window, told him; and, after desiring Sir James to order Sir Lowry Cole to follow him with the Fourth Division, he galloped off to the scene of action. In the afternoon, when all was over, he called in again, on his return to head-quarters, and told us, "that it was the most glorious affair that he had ever seen; and that the enemy had absolutely left upwards of five thousand men, killed and wounded, on the ground."

This was the last action in which we were concerned near Bayonne. The enemy seemed quite satisfied with what they had got, and offered us no further molestation, but withdrew within their works.

CHAPTER 17

Passage of the Garonne

Towards the end of the month, some divisions of the French army having left Bayonne, and ascended the right bank of the Adour , it produced a corresponding movement on our side, by which our division then occupied Ustaritz, and some neighbouring villages; a change of quarters we had no reason to rejoice in.

At Arcangues, notwithstanding the influence of our messmate, the "*Seigneur du Village,*" our table had, latterly, exhibited gradual symptoms of decay. But here, our voracious predecessors had not only swallowed the calf, but the cow, and literally left us nothing; so that, from an occasional turkey, or a pork pie, we were now, all at once, reduced to our daily ration of a withered pound of beef.

A great many necessaries of life could certainly be procured from St. Jean de Luz; but the prices there were absolutely suicidal. The suttlers' shops were too small to hold both their goods and their consciences, so that every pin's worth they sold cost us a dollar; and as every dollar cost us seven shillings, they were, of course, not so plenty as bad dinners. I have often regretted that the enemy never got an opportunity of having the run of their shops for a few minutes, that they might have been, in some measure, punished for their sins, even in this world.

The house that held our table, too, was but a wretched apology for the one we had left. A bitter wind continued to blow; and as the granary of a room which we occupied, on the first floor, had no fireplace, we immediately proceeded to provide it with one, and continued filling it up with such a load of bricks and mortar, that the first floor was on the point of becoming the ground one; and having only a choice of evils on such an emergency, we, as usual, adopted that which appeared to us to be the least, cutting down the only two fruit trees in the garden to prop it up with. We were rather on doubtful terms with the landlord before, but this put us all square—no terms at all.

Our animals, too, were in a woeful plight, for want of forage. We were obliged to send our baggage ones, every week, for their rations of corn, three days' march, through oceans of mud, which might have been navigated with boats. The whole cavalcade always moved under the charge of an officer; and many were the anxious looks that we took with our spy-glasses, from a hill overlooking the road, on the days of their expected return, each endeavouring to descry his own. Mine came back to me twice; but *the pitcher that goes often to the well* was verified in his third trip, for—he perished in a muddy grave.

His death, however, was not so unexpected as it might have been; for although I cannot literally say that he had been dying by inches, seeing that he had walked all the way from the frontiers of Portugal, yet he had nevertheless been doing it on the grand scale—by miles. I only fell in with him the day before the commencement of the campaign, and, after reconnoitring him with my usual judgment, and seeing that he was in possession of the regulated quantity of eyes, legs, and mouth, and concluding that they were all calculated to perform their different functions, I took him, as a man does his wife, for better and for worse; and it was not until the end of the first day's march that I found he had a broken jaw-bone, and could not eat, and I had therefore been obliged to support him all along on spoon diet. He was a capital horse only for that!

It has already been written, in another man's book, that *we always require just a little more than we have got to make us perfectly happy*; and, as we had given this neighbourhood a fair trial, and that little was not to be found in it, we were very glad when, towards the end of February, we were permitted to look for it a little further on. We broke up from quarters on the 21st, and leaving Sir John Hope, with the left wing of the army, in the investment of Bayonne, Lord Wellington followed Soult with the remainder.

The new clothing for the different regiments of the army had, in the meantime, been gradually arriving at St. Jean de Luz; and as the commissariat transport was required for other purposes, not to mention that a man's new coat always looks better on his own back than it does on a mule's, the different regiments marched there for it in succession. It did not come to our turn until we had taken a stride to the front, as far as La Bastide: our retrograde movement, therefore, obliged us to bid *adieu* to our division for some time.

On our arrival at St. Jean de Luz, we found our new clothing, and some new friends in the family of our old friend, Arcangues, which was one of the most respectable in the district, and who showed us a great deal of kindness. As it happened to be the commencement of Lent, the young ladies were, at first, doubtful as to the propriety of joining in any of the gaieties; but, after a short consultation, they arranged it with their consciences, and joined in the waltz right merrily. *Mademoiselle* was really an exceedingly nice girl, and the most lively companion in arms (in a waltz) that I ever met.

Our clothing detained us there two days: on the third, we proceeded to rejoin the division.

The pride of ancestry is very tenaciously upheld among the Basques, who are the mountaineers of that district. I had a fancy that most of them grew wild, like their trees, without either fathers or mothers, and was therefore much amused one day to hear a fellow with a Tam O'Shanter's bonnet, and a pair of bare legs, tracing his descent from the first man, and maintaining that he spoke the same language too. He might have added, if further proof were wanting, that he also wore the same kind of shoes and stockings.

On the 27th February, 1814, we marched all day to the tune

of a cannonade: it was the battle of Orthes; and on our arrival, in the evening, at the little town of St. Palais, we were very much annoyed to find the Seventy-Ninth regiment stationed there, who handed us a general order, desiring that the last arrived regiment should relieve the preceding one in charge of the place. This was the more vexatious, knowing that there was no other regiment behind to relieve us.

It was a nice little town, and we were treated by the inhabitants like friends and allies, experiencing much kindness and hospitality from them; but a rifleman in the rear, is *like a fish out of the water:* he feels that he is not in his place. Seeing no other mode of obtaining a release, we at length began detaining the different detachments who were proceeding to join their regiments, with a view of forming a battalion of them; but by the time that we had collected a sufficient number for that purpose, we received an order from head-quarters to join the army; when, after a few days' forced marches, we had at length the happiness of overtaking our division a short distance beyond the town of Aire. The battle of Orthes was the only affair of consequence that had taken place during our absence.

We remained stationary, near Aire, until the middle of March, when the army was again put in motion.

On the morning of the 19th, while we were marching along the road, near the town of Tarbes, we saw what appeared to be a small piquet of the enemy, on the top of a hill to our left, looking down upon us, when a company of our second battalion was immediately sent to dislodge them. The enemy, however, increased in number in proportion to those sent against them, until not only the whole of the Second, but our own, and the Third battalion were eventually brought into action; and still we had more than double our number opposed to us; but we, nevertheless, drove them from the field with great slaughter, after a desperate struggle of a few minutes, in which we had eleven officers killed and wounded.

As this fight was purely a rifle one, and took place within sight of the whole army, I hope the reader will excuse my blushes while I give the following quotation from the author of *Twelve Years' Military Adventure*, who was a spectator, and who, in allusion to this affair, says:

> Our rifles were immediately sent to dislodge the French from the hills on our left, and our battalion was ordered to support them. Nothing could exceed the manner in which the Ninety-Fifth set about the business. . . . Certainly I never saw such skirmishers as the Ninety-Fifth, now the rifle brigade. They could do the work much better and with infinitely less loss than any other of our best light troops. They possessed an individual boldness, a mutual understanding, and a quickness of eye, in taking advantage of the ground, which, taken all together, I never saw equalled. They were, in fact, as much superior to the French *voltigeurs*, as the latter were to our skirmishers in general. As our regiment was often employed in supporting them, I think I am fairly qualified to speak of their merits.

> We followed the enemy until dark, when, after having taken up our ground and lit our fires, they rather maliciously opened a cannonade upon us; but, as few of their shots took effect, we did not put ourselves to the inconvenience of moving, and they soon desisted.

> We continued in pursuit daily, until we finally arrived on the banks of the Garonne, opposite Toulouse. The day after our arrival an attempt was made, by the engineers, to throw a bridge across the river, above the town; and we had assembled one morning, to be in readiness to pass over, but they were obliged to abandon it for the want of the necessary number of pontoons, and we returned again to quarters.

> We were stationed, for several days, in the suburb of St. Ciprien, where we found ourselves exceedingly comfortable. It consisted chiefly of the citizens' country houses, and an abundance of the public tea and fruit accommodations, with which every large city is surrounded, for the temptation of Sunday parties;

and as the inhabitants had all fled hurriedly into town, leaving their cellars, generally speaking, well stocked with a tolerable kind of wine, we made ourselves at home.

It was finally determined that the passage of the river should be tried below the town, and, preparatory thereto, we took ground to our left, and got lodged in the *château* of a rich old West-India man. He was a tall ramrod of a fellow, upwards of six feet high, withered to a cinder, and had a pair of green eyes, which looked as if they belonged to somebody else, who was looking through his eye-holes; but, despite his imperfections, he had got a young wife, and she was nursing a young child. The "Green Man," (as we christened him) was not, however, so bad as he looked; and we found our billet such a good one, that when we were called away to fight, after a few days' residence with him, I question, if left to our choice, whether we would not have rather remained where we were!

A bridge having at length been established, about a league below the town, two British divisions passed over; but the enemy, by floating timber and other things down the stream, succeeded in carrying one or two of the pontoons from their moorings, which prevented any more from crossing either that day or the succeeding one. It was expected that the French would have taken advantage of this circumstance, to attack the two divisions on the other side; but they thought it more prudent to wait the attack in their own stronghold; and in doing so I believe they acted wisely, for these two divisions had both flanks secured by the river, their position was not too extended for their numbers, and they had a clear space in their front, which was flanked by artillery from the commanding ground on our side of the river; so that, altogether, they would have been found ugly customers, to anybody who chose to meddle with them.

The bridge was re-established on the night of the 9th, and, at daylight next morning, we bade *adieu* to the "Green Man," inviting him to come and see us in Toulouse in the evening. He laughed at the idea, telling us that we should be lucky fellows if ever we got in; and, at all events, he said, that he would bet a *déjeuner à la forchette* for a dozen, that we did not enter it in three days from that time. I took the bet, and won, but the old rogue never came to pay me.

We crossed the river, and advanced sufficiently near the enemy's position to be just out of the reach of their fire, where we waited until dispositions were made for the attack, which took place as follows:—

Sir Rowland Hill, who remained on the left bank of the Garonne, made a show of attacking the bridge and suburb of the town on that side.

On our side of the river the Spanish army, which had never hitherto taken an active part in any of our general actions, now claimed the post of honour, and advanced to storm the strongest part of the heights. Our division was ordered to support them in the low grounds, and, at the same time, to threaten a point of the canal; and Picton, who was on our right, was ordered to make a false attack on the canal. These were all that were visible to us. The remaining divisions of the army were in continuation to the left.

The Spaniards, anxious to monopolize all the glory, I rather think, moved on to the attack a little too soon, and before the British divisions on their left were in readiness to co-operate; however, be that as it may, they were soon in a blaze of fire, and began walking through it, at first, with a great show of gallantry and determination; but their courage was not altogether screwed up to the sticking point, and the nearer they came to the critical pass, the less prepared they seemed to meet it, until they all finally faced to the right-about, and came back upon us as fast as their heels could carry them, pursued by the enemy.

We instantly advanced to their relief, and concluded that they would have rallied behind us; but they had no idea of doing anything of the kind; for, when with Cuesta and some of the other Spanish generals, they had been accustomed, under such circumstances, to run a hundred miles at a time; so that, passing through the intervals of our division, they went clear off to the rear, and we never saw them more. The moment the French found us interpose between them and the Spaniards they retired within their works.

The only remark that Lord Wellington was said to have made on their conduct, after waiting to see whether they would stand after they got out of the reach of the enemy's shot, was,

"Well, d—n me, if ever I saw ten thousand men run a race before!" However, notwithstanding their disaster, many of their officers certainly evinced great bravery; and on their account it is to be regretted that the attack was made so soon, for they would otherwise have carried their point with little loss, either of life or credit, as the British divisions on the left soon after stormed and carried all the other works, and obliged those who had been opposed to the Spaniards to evacuate theirs without firing another shot.

When the enemy were driven from the heights, they retired within the town, and the canal then became their line of defence, which they maintained the whole of the next day; but in the course of the following night they left the town altogether, and we took possession of it on the morning of the 12th.

The inhabitants of Toulouse hoisted the white flag, and declared for the Bourbons the moment the French army left it; and, in the course of the same day, Colonel Cooke arrived from Paris, with the extraordinary news of Napoleon's abdication. Soult has been accused of having been in possession of that fact prior to the battle of Toulouse; but, to disprove such an assertion, it can only be necessary to think a moment, whether he would not have made it public the day after the battle, while he yet held possession of the town, as it would not only have enabled him to keep it, but, to those who knew no better, it might have given him a shadow of claim to the victory, if he chose to avail himself of it; and I have known a victory claimed by a French marshal on more slender grounds. In place of knowing it then, he did not even believe it now; and we were absolutely obliged to follow him a day's march beyond Toulouse before he agreed to an armistice.

The news of the peace, at this period, certainly sounded as

strangely in our ears as it did in those of the French marshal, for it was a change that we had never contemplated. We had been born in war, reared in war, and war was our trade; and what soldiers had to do in peace, was a problem yet to be solved among us.

After remaining a few days at Toulouse, we were sent into quarters, in the town of Castle-Sarrazin, along with our old companions in arms, the Fifty-Second, to wait the necessary arrangements for our final removal from France.

Castle-Sarrazin is a respectable little town, on the right bank of the Garonne; and its inhabitants received us so kindly, that every officer found in his quarter a family home. We there, too, found both the time and the opportunity of exercising one of the agreeable professions to which we had long been strangers, that of making love to the pretty little girls with which the place abounded; and when, after a three months' residence among them, the fatal order arrived for our march to Bordeaux, for embarkation, the bucketsful of salt tears that were shed by men who had almost forgotten the way to weep, was quite ridiculous. I have never yet, however, clearly made out whether people are most in love when they are laughing or when they are crying. Our greatest love writers certainly give the preference to the latter.

Scott thinks that *love is loveliest when it's bathed in tears*; and Moore tells his mistress to *give smiles to those who love her less, but to keep her tears for him*; but what pleasure he can take in seeing her in affliction, I cannot make out; nor, for the soul of me, can I see why a face full of smiles should not be every bit as valuable as one of tears, seeing that it is so much more pleasant to look at.

I have rather wandered, in search of an apology for my own countenance not having gone into mourning on that melancholy occasion; for, to tell the truth, (and if I had a visage sensible to such an impression, I should blush while I tell it,) I was as much in love as anybody, up nearly to the last moment, when I fell out of it, as it were, by a miracle; but, probably, a history of love's last look may be considered as my justification.

The day before our departure, in returning from a ride, I overtook my love and her sister, strolling by the river's side, and instantly dismounting, I joined in their walk. My horse was following, at the length of his bridle-reins, and, while I was engaged in conversation with the sister, the other dropped behind, and, when I looked round, I found her mounted astride on my horse! and with such a pair of legs, too! It was rather too good; and "Richard was himself again."

Although released, under the foregoing circumstances from individual attachment, that of a general nature continued strong as ever; and, without an exception on either side, I do believe that we parted with mutual regret, and with the most unbounded love and good feeling towards each other. We exchanged substantial proofs of it while together; we continued to do so after we had parted; nor were we forgotten when we were no more!

It having appeared, in some of the newspapers, a year afterwards, that every one of our officers had been killed at Waterloo, and that the regiment had been brought out of the action by a volunteer, and the report having come to the knowledge of our Castle-Sarrazin friends, they drew up a letter, which they sent to our commanding officer, signed by every person of respectability in the place, lamenting our fate, expressing a hope that the report might have been exaggerated, and entreating to be informed as to the particular fate of each individual officer, whom they mentioned by name. They were kind good-hearted souls, and may God bless them!

Chapter 18

Join the Regiment at Brussels

I have endeavoured, in this book of mine, to measure out the peace and the war in due proportions, according to the spirit of the times it speaks of; and as there appears to me to be as much peace in the last chapter as occurred in Europe between 1814 and 1815, I shall, with the reader's permission, lodge my regiment at once on Dover heights, and myself in Scotland, taking a shot at the last of the woodcocks, which happened to be our relative positions, when Buonaparte's escape from Elba once more summoned the army to the field.

The first intimation I had of it was by a letter, informing me of the embarkation of the battalion for the Netherlands, and desiring me to join them there, without delay; and, finding that a brig was to sail the following day from Leith to Rotterdam, I took a passage on board of her. She was an odd one to look at, but the captain assured me that she was a good one to go; and, besides, that he had provided everything that was elegant for our entertainment. The latter piece of information I did not think of questioning until too late to profit by it? for I had the mortification to discover, the first day, that his whole stock consisted in a quarter of lamb, in addition to the ship's own, with a few cabbages, and five gallons of whisky.

After having been ten days at sea, I was awoke, one morning before daylight, with the ship's grinding over a sand bank, on the coast of Holland; fortunately it did not blow hard, and a pilot soon after came alongside, who, after exacting a reward suitable to the occasion, at length consented to come on board, and extricated us from our perilous situation, carrying the vessel into the entrance of one of the small branches of the river leading up to Rotterdam, where we came to anchor. The captain was very desirous of appealing to a magistrate for a reduction in the exorbitant demands of the pilot; and I accompanied him on shore for that purpose.

An Englishman made up to us at the landing-place, and said that his name was C——; that he had made his fortune by smuggling, and, though he was not permitted to spend it in his native country, that he had the greatest pleasure in being of service to his countrymen. As this was exactly the sort of person we were in search of, the captain explained his grievance; and the other said, that he would conduct him to a gentleman who would soon put that to rights. We, accordingly, walked to the adjoining village, in one of the houses of which he introduced us, formally, to a tall Dutchman, with a pipe in his mouth, and a pen behind his ear, who, after hearing the story, proceeded to commit it, in large characters, to a quire of foolscap.

The cautious nature of the Scotchman did not altogether like the appearance of the man of business, and demanding, through the interpreter, whether there would be anything to pay for his proceedings? he was told that it would cost five guineas. "Five devils," said Saunders. "What is it for?"

"For a protest," said the other.

"D—n the protest," said the captain: "I came to save five guineas, not to pay five more." I could stand the scene no longer, and rushed out of the house, under the pretence of seeing the village: and on my return to the ship, half-an-hour afterwards, I found the captain fast asleep. I knew not whether he had swallowed the remainder of the five gallons of whisky, in addition to his five-guinea grievance, but I could not shake him out of it, although the mate and I tried, alternately, for upwards of two hours; and indeed I never heard whether he ever got out of it,- for when I found they had to go outside to find another passage up to Rotterdam, I did not think it prudent to trust myself any longer in the hands of such artists, and, taking leave of the sleeper, with a last ineffectual shake, I hired a boat to take me through the passage in which we then were.

We started with a stiff fair wind, and the boatman assured me that we should reach Rotterdam in less than five hours (forty miles;) but it soon lulled to a dead calm, which left us to the tedious operation of tiding it up; and, to mend the matter, we had not a fraction of money between us, nor anything to eat or drink. I bore starvation all that day and night, with the most Christian-like fortitude; but, the next morning, I could stand it no longer, and sending the boatman on shore, to a neighbouring house, I instructed him either to beg or steal something, whichever he should find the most prolific; but he was a clumsy hand at both, and the single spoonful of coffee with which he returned, proved that he was but a scurvy beggar-man and a villainous bad thief.

It, however, afforded some relief; and in the afternoon we reached the town of Dort, where, on lodging my baggage in pawn with a French innkeeper, he advanced me the means of going on to Rotterdam, where I got cash for the bill which I had on a merchant there. Once more furnished with the "sinews of war," and my feet on *terra firma*, I lost no time in setting forward to Antwerp, and from thence to Brussels, where I had the happiness of rejoining my battalion, which was then quartered in that city.

Brussels was, at this time, a scene of extraordinary preparation, from the succession of troops who were hourly arriving, and in their formation into brigades and divisions. We had the good fortune to be attached to the brigade of our old and favourite commander, Sir James Kempt, and in the Fifth Division, under Sir Thomas Picton. It was the only division quartered in Brussels, the others being all towards the French frontier, except the Duke of Brunswick's corps, which lay on the Antwerp road.

CHAPTER 19

Battle of Quatre Bras

As our division was composed of crack regiments, under crack commanders, and headed by fire-eating generals, we had little to do the first fortnight after my arrival, beyond indulging in all the amusements of our delightful quarter: but, as the middle of June approached, we began to get a little more on the *qui vive*, for we were aware that Napoleon was about to make a dash at some particular point; and, as he was not the sort of general to give his opponent an idea of the when and the where, the greater part of our army was necessarily disposed along the frontier, to meet him at his own place.

They were of course too much extended to offer effectual resistance in their advanced position; but as our division and the Duke of Brunswick's corps were held in reserve at Brussels, in readiness to be thrust at whatever point might be attacked, they were a sufficient additional force to check the enemy for the time required to concentrate the army.

On the 14th of June it was generally known, among the military circles in Brussels, that Buonaparte was in motion, at the head of his troops; and though his movement was understood to point at the Prussians, yet he was not sufficiently advanced to afford a correct clue to his intentions.

We were, the whole of the 15th, on the most anxious look out for news from the front; but no report had been received prior to the hour of dinner. I went, about seven in the evening, to take a stroll in the park, and meeting one of the Duke's staff, he asked me, *en passant*, whether my pack-saddles were all ready.

I told him that they were nearly so, and added, "I suppose they won't be wanted, at all events, before tomorrow?" to which he replied, in the act of leaving me, "If you have any preparation to make, I would recommend you not to delay so long."

I took the hint, and returning to quarters, remained in momentary expectation of an order to move. The bugles sounded to arms about two hours after.

To the credit of our battalion be it recorded, that, although the greater part were in bed when the assembly sounded, and billeted over the most distant parts of that extensive city, every man was on his alarm-post before eleven o'clock, in a complete state of marching order: whereas it was nearly two o'clock in the morning before we were joined by the others.

As a grand ball was to take place the same night, at the Duchess of Richmond's, the order for the assembling of the troops was accompanied by permission, for any officer who chose, to remain for the ball, provided that he joined his regiment early in the morning. Several of ours took advantage of it.

Brussels was, at that time, thronged with British temporary residents, who, no doubt, in the course of the two last days, must have heard, through their military acquaintance, of the immediate prospect of hostilities. But accustomed, on their own ground, to hear of those things as a piece of news in which they were not personally concerned, and never dreaming of danger in streets crowded with the gay uniforms of their countrymen, it was not until their defenders were summoned to the field that they were fully sensible of their changed circumstances; and the suddenness of the danger multiplying its horrors, many of them were now seen running about in the wildest state of distraction.

Waiting for the arrival of the other regiments, we endeavoured to snatch an hour's repose on the pavement; but we were every instant disturbed, by ladies as well as gentlemen; some stumbling over us in the dark—some shaking us out of our sleep to be told the news—and not a few conceiving their immediate safety depending upon our standing in place of lying. All those who applied for the benefit of my advice, I recommended to go home to bed, to keep themselves perfectly cool, and to rest assured that, if their departure from the city became necessary, (which I very much doubted,) they would have at least one whole day to prepare for it, as we were leaving some beef and potatoes behind us, for which I was sure we would fight, rather than abandon!

The whole of the division having at length assembled, we were put in motion about three o'clock on the morning of the 16th, and advanced to the village of Waterloo, where, forming in a field adjoining the road, our men were allowed to prepare their breakfasts. I succeeded in getting mine in a small inn, on the left hand side of the village.

Lord Wellington joined us about nine o'clock; and, from his very particular orders to see that the roads were kept clear of baggage, and everything likely to impede the movements of the troops, I have since been convinced that his Lordship had thought it probable that the position of Waterloo might, even that day, have become the scene of action; for it was a good broad road, on which there were neither the quantity of baggage nor of troops moving at the time, to excite the slightest apprehension of confusion. Leaving us halted, he galloped on to the front, followed by his staff; and we were soon after joined by the Duke of Brunswick, with his corps of the army.

His highness dismounted near the place where I was standing, and seated himself on the roadside, along with his adjutant-general. He soon after despatched his companion on some duty; and I was much amused to see the vacated place immediately filled by an old beggar-man, who, seeing nothing in the black hussar uniform beside him denoting the high rank of the wearer, began to grunt and scratch himself most luxuriously!

The duke showed a degree of courage which few would, under such circumstances, for he maintained his post until the return of his officer, when he very jocularly said, "Well, O———n, you see that your place was not long unoccupied!" How little idea had I, at the time, that the life of the illustrious speaker was limited to three short hours!

About twelve o'clock an order arrived for the troops to advance, leaving their baggage behind; and though it sounded warlike, yet we did not expect to come in contact with the enemy, at all events, on that day. But, as we moved forward, the symptoms of their immediate presence kept gradually increasing; for we presently met a cart load of wounded Belgians; and, after passing through Genappe, the distant sound of a solitary gun struck on the listening ear, But all doubt on the subject was quickly removed; for, on ascending the rising ground, where stands the village of Quatre Bras, we saw a considerable plain in our front, flanked on each side by a wood; and on another acclivity beyond, we could perceive the enemy descending towards us, in most imposing numbers.

Quatre Bras, at that time, consisted of only three or four houses; and, as its name betokens, I believe, stood at the junction of four roads, on one of which we were moving; a second, inclined to the right; a third, in the same degree to the left; and the fourth, I conclude, must have gone backwards; but, as I had not an eye in that direction, I did not see it.

The village was occupied by some Belgians, under the Prince of Orange, who had an advanced post in a large farmhouse, at the foot of the road which inclined to the right; and a part of his division also occupied the wood on the same side.

Lord Wellington, I believe, after leaving us at Waterloo, galloped on to the Prussian position at Ligny, where he had an interview with Blücher, in which they concerted measures for their mutual co-operation. When we arrived at Quatre Bras, however, we found him in a field near the Belgian outpost; and the enemy's guns were just beginning to play upon the spot where he stood, surrounded by a numerous staff.

We halted for a moment on the brow of the hill; and as Sir Andrew Barnard galloped forward to the head-quarter group, I followed, to be in readiness to convey any orders to the battalion. The moment we approached, Lord Fitzroy Somerset, separating himself from the Duke, said, "Barnard, you are wanted instantly; take your battalion and endeavour to get possession of that village," pointing to one on the face of the rising ground, down which the enemy were moving; "but if you cannot do that, secure that wood on the left, and keep the road open for communication with the Prussians."

We instantly moved in the given direction; but, ere we had got half way to the village, we had the mortification to see the enemy throw such a force into it, as rendered any attempt to retake, with our numbers, utterly hopeless; and as another strong body of them were hastening towards the wood, which was the second object pointed out to us, we immediately brought them to action, and secured it. In moving to that point, one of our men went raving mad, from excessive heat. The poor fellow cut a few extraordinary capers, and died in the course of a few minutes.

While our battalion reserve occupied the front of the wood, our skirmishers lined the side of the road, which was the Prussian line of communication. The road itself, however, was crossed by such a shower of balls, that none but a desperate traveller would have undertaken a journey on it. We were presently reinforced by a small battalion of foreign light troops, with whose assistance we were in hopes to have driven the enemy a little further from it; but they were a raw body of men, who had never before been under fire; and as they could not be prevailed upon to join our skirmishers, we could make no use of them whatever.

Their conduct, in fact, was an exact representation of Mathews's ludicrous one of the American militia, for Sir Andrew Barnard repeatedly pointed out to them which was the French, and which our side; and, after explaining that they were not to fire a shot until they joined our skirmishers, the word "March!" was given; but march, to them, was always the signal to fire, for they stood fast, and began blazing away, chiefly at our skirmishers too, the officers on each occasion sending back to say that they were shooting at them; until we were at last obliged to be satisfied with whatever advantages their appearance could give, as even that was of some consequence, where troops were so scarce.

Buonaparte's attack on the Prussians had already commenced, and the fire of artillery and musketry, in that direction, was tremendous; but the intervening higher ground prevented us from seeing any part of it.

The plain to our right, which we had just quitted, had likewise become the scene of a sanguinary and unequal contest. Our division, after we left it, deployed into line, and, in advancing, met and routed the French infantry; but, in following up their advantage, they encountered a furious charge of cavalry, and were obliged to throw themselves into squares to receive it. With the exception of one regiment, however, which had two companies cut to pieces, they were not only successful in resisting the attack, but made awful havoc in the enemy's ranks, who nevertheless continued their forward career, and went sweeping past them, like a whirlwind, up to the village of Quatre Bras, to the confusion and consternation of the numerous useless appendages of our army, who were there assembled, waiting the result of the battle.

The forward movement of the enemy's cavalry gave their infantry time to rally; and, strongly reinforced with fresh troops, they again advanced to the attack. This was a crisis in which, according to Buonaparte's theory, the victory was theirs, by all the rules of war, for they held superior numbers, both before and behind us; but the gallant old Picton, who had been trained in a different school, did not choose to confine himself to rules in those matters: despising the force in his rear, he advanced, charged, and routed those in his front, which created such a panic among the others, that they galloped back through the intervals in his division, with no other object in view but their own safety.

After this desperate conflict, the firing on both sides lulled almost to a calm for nearly an hour, while each was busy in renewing their order of battle. The Duke of Brunswick had been killed early in the action, endeavouring to rally his young troops, who were unable to withstand the impetuosity of the French; and, as we had no other cavalry force in the field, the few British infantry regiments present, having to bear the full brunt of the enemy's superior force of both arms, were now considerably reduced in numbers.

The battle, on the side of the Prussians, still continued to rage in an unceasing roar of artillery. About four in the afternoon, a troop of their dragoons came as a *patrole*, to inquire how it fared with us, and told us, in passing, that they still maintained their position. Their day, however, was still to be decided, and indeed, for that matter, so was our own; for, although the firing, for the moment, had nearly ceased, I had not yet clearly made up my mind which side had been the offensive, which the defensive, or which the winning. I had merely the satisfaction of knowing that we had not lost it; for we had met fairly in the middle of a field, (or, rather unfairly, considering that they had two to one), and after the scramble was over, our division still held the ground they fought on.

All doubts on the subject, however, began to be removed about five o'clock. The enemy's artillery once more opened; and, on running to the brow of the hill, to ascertain the cause, we perceived our old light division general, Count Alten, at the head of a fresh British division, moving gallantly down the road towards us. It was indeed a joyful sight; for, as already mentioned, our division had suffered so severely that we could not help looking forward to a renewal of the action, with such a disparity of force, with considerable anxiety; but this reinforcement gave us new life, and as soon as they came near enough to afford support, we commenced the offensive, and, driving in the skirmishers opposed to us, succeeded in gaining a considerable portion of the position originally occupied by the enemy, when darkness obliged us to desist.

In justice to the foreign battalion, which had been all day attached to us, I must say that, in this last movement, they joined us cordially, and behaved exceedingly well. They had a very gallant young fellow at their head; and their conduct, in the earlier part of the day, can therefore only be ascribed to its being their first appearance on such a stage.

Leaving General Alten in possession of the ground which we had assisted in winning, we returned in search of our division, and reached them about eleven at night, lying asleep in their glory, on the field where they had fought, which contained many a bloody trace of the day's work.

The firing, on the side of the Prussians, had altogether ceased before dark, but recommenced, with redoubled fury, about an hour after; and it was then, as we afterwards learnt, that they lost the battle.

We lay down by our arms, near the farmhouse already mentioned, in front of Quatre Bras; and the deuce is in it if we were not in good trim for sleeping, seeing that we had been either marching or fighting for twenty-six successive hours.

An hour before daybreak, next morning, a rattling fire of musketry along the whole line of piquets made every one spring to his arms; and we remained looking as fierce as possible until daylight, when each side was seen expecting an attack, while the piquets were blazing at one another without any ostensible cause. It gradually ceased as the day advanced, and appeared to have been occasioned by a *patrole* of dragoons getting between the piquets by accident: when firing commences in the dark it is not easily stopped.

June 17th.—As last night's fighting only ceased with the daylight, the scene, this morning, presented a savage unsettled appearance; the fields were strewed with the bodies of men, horses, torn clothing, and shattered *cuirasses*; and though no movement appeared to be going on on either side, yet, as occasional shots continued to be exchanged at different points, it kept every one wide awake. We had the satisfaction of knowing that the whole of our army had assembled on the hill behind in the course of the night.

About nine o'clock, we received the news of Blücher's defeat, and of his retreat to Wavre. Lord Wellington, therefore, immediately began to withdraw his army to the position of Waterloo.

Sir Andrew Barnard was ordered to remain as long as possible with our battalion, to mask the retreat of the others; and was told, if we were attacked, that the whole of the British cavalry were in readiness to advance to our relief. I had an idea, however, that a single rifle battalion in the midst of ten thousand dragoons, would come but indifferently off in the event of a general crash, and was by no means sorry when, between eleven and twelve o'clock, every regiment had got clear off, and we followed, before the enemy had put anything in motion against us.

After leaving the village of Quatre Bras, and passing through our cavalry, who were formed on each side of the road, we drew up at the entrance of Genappe. The rain, at that moment, began to descend in torrents, and our men were allowed to shelter themselves in the nearest houses; but we were obliged to turn out again in the midst of it, in less than five minutes, as we found the French cavalry and ours already exchanging shots, and the latter were falling back to the more favourable ground behind Genappe. We therefore retired with them, *en masse*, through the village, and formed again on the rising ground beyond.

While we remained there, we had an opportunity of seeing the different affairs of cavalry; and it did one's heart good to see how cordially the Life Guards went at their work: they had no idea of anything but straightforward fighting, and sent their opponents flying in all directions. The only young thing they showed was, in every one who got a roll in the mud, (and owing to the slipperiness of the ground, there were many,) going off to the rear, according to their Hyde Park custom, as being no longer fit to appear on parade; I thought, at first, that they had been all wounded, but, on finding how the case stood, I could not help telling them that theirs was now the situation to verify the old proverb, *the uglier the better soldier!*

The roads, as well as the fields, had now become so heavy, that our progress to the rear was very slow; and it was six in the evening before we drew into the position of Waterloo. Our battalion took post in the second line that night, with its right resting on the Namur road, behind La Haye Sainte, near a small mud cottage which Sir Andrew Barnard occupied as a quarter. The enemy arrived in front, in considerable force, about an hour after us, and a cannonade took place in different parts of the line, which ended at dark, and we lay down by our arms. It rained excessively hard the greater part of the night; nevertheless, having succeeded in getting a bundle of hay for my horse, and one of straw for myself, I secured the horse to his bundle, by tying him to one of the men's swords stuck in the ground, and, placing mine under his nose, I laid myself down upon it, and never opened my eyes again until daylight.

Chapter 20

The End

Battle of Waterloo
June 18th, 1815

When I awoke this morning, at daylight, I found myself drenched with rain. I had slept so long and so soundly, that I had at first but a very confused notion of my situation; but having a bright idea that my horse had been my companion when I went to sleep, I was rather startled at finding that I was now alone; nor could I rub my eyes clear enough to procure a sight of him, which was vexatious enough; for independent of his value as a horse, his services were indispensable; and an adjutant might as well think of going into action without his arms as without such a supporter.

But whatever my feelings might have been towards him, it was evident that he had none for me, from having drawn his sword and marched off. The chances of finding him again, amid ten thousand others, were about equal to the odds against the needle in a bundle of hay; but for once the single chance was gained, as, after a diligent search of an hour, he was discovered between two artillery horses, about half a mile from where he broke loose.

The weather cleared up as the morning advanced; and though everything remained quiet at the moment, we were confident that the day would not pass off without an engagement, and therefore proceeded to put our arms in order, as also to get ourselves dried and made as comfortable as circumstances would permit.

We made a fire against the wall of Sir Andrew Barnard's cottage, and boiled a huge camp kettle full of tea, mixed up with a suitable quantity of milk and sugar, for breakfast; and as it stood on the edge of the high road, where all the big wigs of the army had occasion to pass, in the early part of the morning, I believe almost every one of them, from the Duke downwards, claimed a cupful.

About nine o'clock, we received an order to retain a quantity of spare ammunition in some secure place, and to send everything in the shape of baggage and baggage animals to the rear. It therefore became evident that the Duke meant to give battle in his present position; and it was, at the same time, generally understood that a corps of thirty thousand Prussians were moving to our support.

About ten o'clock, an unusual bustle was observable among the staff officers, and we soon after received an order to stand to our arms. The troops who had been stationed in our front during the night were then moved off to the right, and our division took up its fighting position.

Our battalion stood on what was considered the left centre of the position. We had our right resting on the Namur road, about a hundred yards in the rear of the farmhouse of La Haye Sainte, and our left extending behind a broken hedge, which ran along the ridge to the left. Immediately in our front, and divided from La Haye Sainte only by the great road, stood a small knoll, with a sand-hole in its farthest side, which we occupied as an advanced post with three companies.

The remainder of the division was formed in two lines; the first, consisting chiefly of light troops, behind the hedge, in continuation from the left of our battalion reserve; and the second, about a hundred yards in its rear. The guns were placed in the interval between the brigades, two pieces were in the road-way on our right, and a rocket brigade in the centre.

The road had been cut through the rising ground, and was about twenty or thirty feet deep where our right rested, and which in a manner separated us from all the troops beyond. The division, I believe, under General Alten occupied the ground next to us, on the right, He had a light battalion of the German Legion posted inside La Haye Sainte, and the Household Brigade of Cavalry stood under cover of the rising ground behind him. On our left there were some Hanoverians and Belgians, together with a brigade of British heavy dragoons, the Royals and Scotch Greys.

These were all the observations on the disposition of our army that my situation enabled me to make. The whole position seemed to be a gently rising ground, presenting no obstacle at any point, excepting the broken hedge in front of our division; and it was only one in appearance, as it could be passed in every part.

Shortly after we had taken up our ground, some columns, from the enemy's left, were seen in motion towards Hugomont, and were soon warmly engaged with the right of our army. A cannon ball, too, came from the Lord knows where, for it was not fired at us, and took the head off our right hand man. That part of their position, in our own immediate front, next claimed our undivided attention. It had hitherto been looking suspiciously innocent, with scarcely a human being upon it; but innumerable black specks were now seen taking post at regular distances in its front, and recognising them as so many pieces of artillery, I knew, from experience, although nothing else was yet visible, that they were unerring symptoms of our not being destined to be idle spectators.

From the moment we took possession of the knoll, we had busied ourselves in collecting branches of trees and other things for the purpose of making an abatis to block up the road between that and the farmhouse, and soon completed one, which we thought looked sufficiently formidable to keep out the whole of the French cavalry; but it was put to the proof sooner than we expected, by a troop of our own light dragoons, who, having occasion to gallop through, astonished us not a little by clearing away every stick of it. We had just time to replace the scattered branches, when the whole of the enemy's artillery opened, and their countless columns began to advance under cover of it.

The scene at that moment was grand and imposing, and we had a few minutes to spare for observation. The column destined as our particular friends, first attracted our notice, and seemed to consist of about ten thousand infantry. A smaller body of infantry and one of cavalry moved on their right; and, on their left, another huge column of infantry, and a formidable body of *cuirassiers*, while beyond them it seemed one moving mass.

We saw Buonaparte himself take post on the side of the road, immediately in our front, surrounded by a numerous staff; and each regiment, as they passed him, rent the air with shouts of "*Vive l'Empereur!*" nor did they cease after they had passed; but, backed by the thunder of their artillery, and carrying with them the rubidub of drums, and the tantarara of trumpets, in addition to their increasing shouts, it looked, at first, as if they had some hopes of scaring us off the ground; for it was a singular contrast to the stern silence reigning on our side, where nothing, as yet, but the voices of our great guns, told that we had mouths to open when we chose to use them.

Our rifles were, however, in a very few seconds required to play their parts, and opened such a fire on the advancing skirmishers as quickly brought them to a standstill; but their columns came steadily through them, although our incessant tiralade was telling in their centre with fearful exactness, and our post was quickly turned in both flanks, which compelled us to fall back and join our comrades behind the hedge, though not before some of our officers and theirs had been engaged in personal combat.

When the heads of their columns showed over the knoll which we had just quitted, they received such a fire from our first line, that they wavered, and hung behind it a little; but, cheered and encouraged by the gallantry of their officers, who were dancing and flourishing their swords in front, they at last boldly advanced to the opposite side of our hedge, and began to deploy. Our first line, in the meantime, was getting so thinned, that Picton found it necessary to bring up his second, but fell in the act of doing it. The command of the division, at that critical moment, devolved upon Sir James Kempt, who was galloping along the line, animating the men to steadiness.

He called to me by name, where I happened to be standing on the right of our battalion, and desired "that I would never quit that spot." I told him that "he might depend upon it:" and in another instant I found myself in a fair way of keeping my promise more religiously than I intended; for, glancing my eye to the right, I saw the next field covered with the *cuirassiers*, some of whom were making directly for the gap in the hedge where I was standing. I had not hitherto drawn my sword, as it was generally to be had at a moment's warning; but, from its having been exposed to the last night's rain, it had now got rusted in the scabbard, and refused to come forth! I was in a precious scrape!

Mounted on my strong Flanders mare, and with my good old sword in my hand, I would have braved all the chances without a moment's hesitation; but I confess that I felt considerable doubts as to the propriety of standing there to be sacrificed, without the means of making a scramble for it. My mind, however, was happily relieved from such an embarrassing consideration, before my decision was required; for the next moment the *cuirassiers* were charged by our Household Brigade; and the infantry in our front giving way at the same time, under our terrific shower of musketry, the flying *cuirassiers* tumbled in among the routed infantry, followed by the Life Guards, who were cutting away in all directions.

Hundreds of the infantry threw themselves down, and pretended to be dead, while the cavalry galloped over them, and then got up and ran away. I never saw such another scene in all my life.

Lord Wellington had given orders that the troops were, on no account, to leave the position to follow up any temporary advantage: so that we now resumed our post, as we stood at the commencement of the battle, and with three companies again advanced on the knoll.

I was told, it was very ridiculous at that moment to see the number of vacant spots that were left nearly along the whole of the line, where a great part of the dark dressed foreign corps had stood, intermixed with the British when the action began.

Our division got considerably reduced in numbers during the last attack; but Lord Wellington's fostering hand sent Sir John Lambert to our support, with the Sixth Division; and we now stood prepared for another and a more desperate struggle.

Our battalion had already lost three officers killed, and six or seven wounded; among the latter were Sir Andrew Barnard and Colonel Cameron.

Someone asking me what had become of my horse's ear, was the first intimation I had of his being wounded; and I now found that, independent of one ear having been shaved close to his head, (I suppose by a cannon shot,) a musket ball had grazed across his forehead, and another gone through one of his legs; but he did not seem much the worse for either of them.

Between two and three o'clock we were tolerably quiet, except from a thundering cannonade; and the enemy had, by that time, got the range of our position so accurately that every shot brought a ticket for somebody's head.

An occasional gun, beyond the plain, far to our left, marked the approach of the Prussians; but their progress was too slow to afford a hope of their arriving in time to take any share in the battle.

On our right, the roar of cannon and musketry had been incessant from the time of its commencement; but the higher ground near us, prevented our seeing anything of what was going on.

Between three and four o'clock the storm gathered again in our front. Our three companies on the knoll were soon involved in a furious fire. The Germans, occupying La Haye Sainte, expended all their ammunition, and fled from the post. The French took possession of it; and, as it flanked our knoll, we were obliged to abandon it also, and fall back again behind the hedge.

The loss of La Haye Sainte was of the most serious consequence, as it afforded the enemy an establishment within our position. They immediately brought up two guns on our side of it, and began serving out some grape to us; but they were so very near that we destroyed their artillerymen before they could give us a second round.

The silencing of these guns was succeeded by a very extraordinary scene, on the same spot. A strong regiment of Hanoverians advanced in line, to charge the enemy out of La Haye Sainte; but they were themselves charged by a brigade of *cuirassiers*, and, excepting one officer, on a little black horse, who went off to the rear, like a shot out of a shovel, I do believe that every man of them was put to death in about five seconds.

A brigade of British light dragoons advanced to their relief, and a few on each side began exchanging thrusts: it seemed likely to be a drawn battle between them, without much harm being done, when our men brought it to a crisis sooner than either side anticipated, for they previously had their rifles eagerly pointed at the *cuirassiers*, with a view of saving the perishing Hanoverians; but the fear of killing their friends withheld them, until the others were utterly overwhelmed, when they instantly opened a terrific fire on the whole concern, sending both sides flying; so that on the small space of ground, within a hundred yards of us, where five thousand men had been fighting the instant before, there was not now a living soul to be seen.

It made me mad to see the *cuirassiers*, in their retreat, stooping and stabbing at our wounded men, as they lay on the ground. How I wished that I had been blessed with omnipotent power for a moment, that I might have blighted them!

The same field continued to be a wild one the whole of the afternoon. It was a sort of duelling-post between the two armies, every half hour showing a meeting of some kind upon it; but they never exceeded a short scramble, for men's lives were held very cheap there.

For the two or three succeeding hours there was no variety with us, but one continued blaze of musketry. The smoke hung so thick about us that, although not more than eighty yards asunder, we could only distinguish each other by the flashes of the pieces.

A good many of our guns had been disabled, and a great many more rendered unserviceable, in consequence of the unprecedented close fighting; for in several places, where they had been posted but a very few yards in front of the line, it was impossible to work them.

I shall never forget the scene which the field of battle presented about seven in the evening. I felt weary and worn out, less from fatigue than anxiety. Our division, which had stood upwards of five thousand men at the commencement of the battle, had gradually dwindled down into a solitary line of skirmishers. The Twenty-Seventh Regiment were lying literally dead, in square, a few yards behind us.

My horse had received another shot through the leg, and one through the flap of the saddle, which lodged in his body, sending him a step beyond the pension list. The smoke still hung so thick about us that we could see nothing. I walked a little way to each flank, to endeavour to get a glimpse of what was going on; but nothing met my eye except the mangled remains of men and horses, and I was obliged to return to my post as wise as I went.

I had never yet heard of a battle in which everybody was killed; but this seemed likely to be an exception, as all were going by turns, We got excessively impatient under the tame similitude of the latter part of the process, and burned with desire to have a last thrust at our respective *vis-à-vis*; for, however desperate our affairs were, we had still the satisfaction of seeing that theirs were worse. Sir John Lambert continued to stand as our support, at the head of three good old regiments, one dead (the Twenty-Seventh) and two living ones; and we took the liberty of soliciting him to aid our views; but the Duke's orders on that head were so very particular that the gallant general had no choice.

Presently a cheer, which we knew to be British, commenced far to the right, and made every one prick up his ears;—it was

Lord Wellington's long wished-for orders to advance; it gradually approached, growing louder as it grew near;—we took it up by instinct, charged through the hedge down upon the old knoll, sending our adversaries flying at the point of the bayonet. Lord Wellington galloped up to us at the instant, and our men began to cheer him; but he called out, "No cheering, my lads, but forward, and complete your victory!"

This movement had carried us clear of the smoke, and, to people who had been for so many hours enveloped in darkness, in the midst of destruction, and naturally anxious about the result of the day, the scene which now met the eye conveyed a feeling of more exquisite gratification than can be conceived. It was a fine summer's evening, just before sunset. The French were flying in one confused mass. British lines were seen in close pursuit, and in admirable order, as far as the eye could reach to the right, while the plain to the left was filled with Prussians.

The enemy made one last attempt at a stand on the rising ground to our right of La Belle Alliance; but a charge from General Adam's brigade again threw them into a state of confusion, which was now inextricable, and their ruin was complete. Artillery, baggage, and everything belonging to them, fell into our hands. After pursuing them until dark, we halted about two miles beyond the field of battle, leaving the Prussians to follow up the victory.

This was the last, the greatest, and the most uncomfortable heap of glory that I ever had a hand in; and may the deuce take me if I think that everybody waited there to see the end of it, otherwise it never could have been so trouble-some to those who did. We were, take us all in all, a very bad army. Our foreign auxiliaries, who constituted more than half of our numerical strength, with some exceptions, were little better than a raw militia—a body without a soul, or like an inflated pillow, that gives to the touch, and resumes its shape again when the pressure ceases; not to mention the many who went clear out of the field, and were only seen while plundering our baggage in their retreat.

Our heavy cavalry made some brilliant charges in the early part of the day; but they never knew when to stop, their ardour in following their advantages carrying them headlong on, until many of them "burnt their fingers," and got dispersed or destroyed.

Of that gallant corps, the Royal Artillery, it is enough to say, that they maintained their former reputation—the first in the world—and it was a serious loss to us, in the latter part of the day, to be deprived of their more powerful co-operation, from the causes already mentioned.

The British infantry and the King's German Legion continued the inflexible supporters of their country's honour throughout; and their unshaken constancy under the most desperate circumstances, showed that, though they might be destroyed, they were not to be beaten,

If Lord Wellington had been at the head of his old Peninsular army, I am confident that he would have swept his opponents off the face of the earth immediately after their first attack; but with such a heterogeneous mixture under his command, he was obliged to submit to a longer day.

It will ever be a matter of dispute what the result of that day would have been without the arrival of the Prussians: but it is clear to me that Lord Wellington would not have fought at Waterloo unless Blücher had promised to aid him with thirty thousand men; as he required that number to put him on a numerical footing with his adversary. It is certain that the promised aid did not come in time to take any share whatever in the battle. It is equally certain that the enemy had, long before, been beaten into a mass of ruin, in condition for nothing but running, and wanting but an apology to do it; and I will therefore ever maintain, that Lord Wellington's last advance would have made it the same victory had a Prussian never been seen there.

The field of battle, next morning, presented a frightful scene of carnage: it seemed as if the world had tumbled to pieces, and three-fourths of everything destroyed in the wreck. The ground running parallel to the front of where we had stood, was so thickly strewed with fallen men and horses, that it was difficult to step clear of their bodies; many of the former still alive, and imploring assistance, which it was not in our power to bestow.

The usual salutation on meeting an acquaintance of another regiment after an action, was to ask who had been hit? but on this occasion it was, "Who's alive?" Meeting one next morning, a very little fellow, I asked what had happened to them yesterday?

"I'll be hanged," says he, "if I know anything at all about the matter, for I was all day trodden in the mud and galloped over by every scoundrel who had a horse; and, in short, that I only owe my existence to my insignificance."

Two of our men, on the morning of the 19th lost their lives by a very melancholy accident. They were cutting up a captured ammunition wagon for firewood, when one of their swords striking against a nail, sent a spark among the powder. When I looked in the direction of the explosion, I saw the two poor fellows about twenty or thirty feet up in the air.

On falling to the ground, though lying on their backs or bellies, some extraordinary effort of nature, caused by the agony of the moment, made them spring from that position, five or six times, repeatedly, to an extraordinary height, just as a fish does when thrown on the ground after being newly caught. It appeared to me that of five or six springs made by the two bodies in that manner, that the highest exceeded the height of a man, and the lowest was not less than three or four feet. It was so unlike a scene in real life that it was impossible to witness it without forgetting, for a moment, the horror of their situation.

I ran to the spot along with others, and found that every stitch of clothes had been burnt off, and they were black as ink all over. They were still alive, and told us their names, otherwise we could not have recognised them; and, singular enough, they were able to walk off the ground with a little support, but died shortly after.

Among other officers who fell at Waterloo, we lost one of the wildest youths that ever belonged to the service. He seemed to have a prophetic notion of his approaching end, for he repeatedly told us, in the early part of the morning, that he knew the devil would have him before night. I shall relate one anecdote of him, which occurred while we were in Spain. He went, by chance, to pass the day with two officers, quartered at a neighbouring village, who happened to be that day engaged to dine with the clergyman.

Knowing their visitor's mischievous propensities, they were at first afraid to make him one of the party; but, after schooling him into a suitable propriety of behaviour, and exacting a promise of implicit obedience, they at last ventured to take him. On their arrival, the ceremony of introduction had just been gone through, and their host seated at an open window, when a favourite cat of his went purring about the young gentleman's boots, who, catching it by the tail, and giving it two or three preparatory swings round his head, sent it flying out at the window where the parson was sitting, who only escaped it by suddenly stooping! The only apology the youngster made for his conduct was, "Egad, I think I astonished that fellow"; but whether it was the cat or the parson he meant, I never could learn.

About twelve o'clock, on the day after the battle, we commenced our march for Paris. I shall therefore leave my readers at Waterloo, in the hope that, among the many stories of romance to which that and the other celebrated fields gave birth, the foregoing unsophisticated one of an eyewitness may not have been found altogether uninteresting.

Random Shots from a Rifleman

Contents

Notice	191
Family Pictures	193
Militia Life	198
Goes to the War, and Ends in Love	207
Historical, Comical, and Warlike Tales	214
A Fierce Attack Upon Hairs	231
Reaping Golden Opinions Out of a Dung-Hill	239
Action at Foz d'Aronce	256
A *Caçadore* and His Mounted Followers	268
National Character	278
Burning a Bivouac	298
Cupping	306
Very Short, With a Few Anecdotes	320
Gentle Visitors	326
A Line Drawn Between Man and Beast	337

Notice

When I sent my volume of *Adventures in the Rifle Brigade* into the world, some one of its many kind and indulgent critics was imprudent enough to say that "it had one fault, the rarest fault in books—it was too short;" and while I have therefore endeavoured to acquit myself of such an unlooked-for charge, by sending this additional one, I need only observe that if it also fails to satisfy, they may have "yet another."

Like its predecessor, this volume is drawn solely from memory, and of course open to error,—but of this my readers may feel assured, that it is free from romance; for even in the few soldiers' yarns which I have thought fit to introduce, the leading features are facts.

Lastly, in making my second editorial bow to the public, let me assure them that it is with no greater literary pretensions. I sent forth my first volume contrary to my own judgment; but, rough and unpolished as it was, it pleased a numerous class of readers, and I therefore trust to be forgiven for marching past again to the same tune, in the hope that my reviewing generals may make the same favourable report of me in their orderly books.

Chapter 1

Family Pictures

Every book has a beginning, and the beginning of every book is the undoubted spot on which the historian is bound to parade his hero. The novelist may, therefore, continue to envelop his man in a fog as long as he likes, but for myself I shall at once unfold to the world that I am my own hero; and though that same world hold my countrymen to be rich in wants, with the article of modesty among them, yet do I hope to maintain the character I have assumed, with as much propriety as can reasonably be expected of one labouring under such a national infirmity, for

I am a native of that land, which
Some poets' lips and painters' hands

have pictured barren and treeless. But, to show that these are mere fancy sketches, I need only mention that as long as I remember any thine, there grew a bonny brier and sundry gooseberry bushes in our kail-yard, and it was surrounded by a stately row of pines, rearing their long spinster waists and umbrella heads over the cabbages, as carefully as a hen does her wings over her brood of chickens, so that neither the sun nor moon, and but a very few favoured stars had the slightest chance of getting a peep therein, nor had anything therein a chance of getting a peep out, unless in the cabbages returning the sheep's eyes of their stargazers; for, while the front was protected by a long range of house and offices, with no ingress or egress but through the hall-door, the same duty was performed on the other three sides by a thick quick-set hedge which was impervious to all but the sparrows, do that the wondrous wise man of Islington might there have scratched his eyes out and in again a dozen times without being much the wiser.

My father was the laird and farmed the small property I speak of, in the lowlands of Stirlingshire, but ne was unfortunately cut off in early life, and long before his young family were capable of appreciating the extent of their loss, and I may add, to the universal regret of the community to which he belonged; and in no country have I met, in the same walks of life, a body of men to equal in intelligence; prudence, and respectability, the small lowland Scotch laird.

Marrying and dying are ceremonies which almost everyone has to go through at some period of his life, and from being so common, one would expect that they might cease to be uncommon; but people, nevertheless, still continue to look upon them as important events in their individual histories. And while, with the class I speak of, the joys of the one and the grief at the other was as sensibly and unaffectedly shown as amongst any, yet with them the loss of the head of the house produces no very material change in the family arrangements; for while in some places the proprietary of a sheep confers a sort of patent of gentility upon the whole flock, leaving as a bequest a scramble for supremacy, yet the lowland laird is another manner of man; one in fact who is not afraid to reckon his chickens before they are hatched, and who suffers no son of his to be born out of his proper place.

The eldest, therefore, steps into his father's shoes as naturally as his father steps out of them. The second is destined to be a gentleman; that is, he receives a superior education, and as soon as he is deemed qualified, he is started off with a tolerable outfit and some ha'pence in his pocket to fulfil his destiny in one of the armed or learned professions, while the junior members of the family are put in such other way of shifting for themselves as taste and prudence may point out. And having thus, gentle reader, expounded as much of my family history as it behooveth thee to know, it only remains for me, with all becoming modesty, to introduce myself to you as, by birthright, the gentleman of the family, and without farther ceremony to take you by the hand and conduct you along the path which I found chalked out for myself.

In my native country, as elsewhere, Dame Fortune is to be seen cutting her usual capers, and often sends a man starving for a lifetime as a parson looking for a pulpit, a doctor dining on his own pills, or as a lawyer who has nothing to insert in his last earthly testament, who would otherwise have flourished on the top of a haystack, or as a cooper round a tar-barrel. How far she was indulgent in my case is a matter of moonshine. Suffice it that I commenced the usual process at the usual place, the parish school, under that most active of all teachers—Whipping,

That's Virtue's governess,
Tut'ress of arts and sciences;
That mends the gross mistakes of nature.
And puts new life into dull matter.

And from the first letter in the alphabet I was successively flogged up through a tolerable quantity of English, some ten or a dozen books of Latin, into three or four of French, and there is no saying whether the cat-o'-nine tails, wielded by such a masterly hand, might not eventually have stirred me up as high as the woolsack, had not one of those tides in the affairs of schoolboys brought a Leith merchant to a worthy old uncle of mine (who was one of my guardians) in search of a quill-driver, and turned the current of my thoughts into another channel. *To be or not to be, that was the question*; whether 'twere better to abide more stings and scourges from the outrageous cat, or to take the offer which was made, and end them.

It may readily be believed that I felt a suitable horror at the sight of the leathern instrument which had been so long and so ably administered for my edification, nor had I much greater affection for the learned professions as they loomed in perspective, for I feared the minister, hated the doctor, and had no respect for the lawyer, and, in short, it required but little persuasion to induce me to bind my prospects for the ensuing three years to the desk of a counting-house. I therefore took leave of my indefatigable preceptor, not forgetting to insert on the tablets of my memory, a promissory note to repay him stripe for stripe with legal interest, as soon as I should find myself qualified to perform the operation; but I need not add that the note (as all such notes usually are) was duly dishonoured; for, when I became capable of appreciating his virtues, I found him a worthy excellent man, and one who meant for the best; but I have lived to see that the schoolmaster of that day was all abroad.

The reminiscences of my three years' mercantile life leave me nothing worth recording, except that it was then I first caught a glimpse of my natal star.

I had left school as a schoolboy, unconscious of a feeling beyond the passing moment. But the period at length arrived when Bonaparte's threatened invasion fired every loyal pair of shoulders with a scarlet coat. Mine were yet too slender to fill up a gap in the ranks, and my arm too weak to wield anything more formidable than a drum stick, but in devotion to the cause I would not have yielded to Don Quixote himself.

The pride, pomp, and circumstance of glorious war had in fact set my soul in an unquenchable blaze, and I could think of nothing else. In reckoning up a column of pounds, shillings, and pence, I counted them but as so many soldiers, the rumbling of empty puncheons in the wine cellar sounded in my ears as the thunder of artillery, and the croaking voice of a weasand old watchman at "half-past twelve o'clock," as the hoarse challenge of the sentry from the ramparts.

My prospect of succeeding to the object on which I had placed my affections were at the time but slender, but having somewhere read that if one did but set his eye on anything in reason, and pursued it steadily, he would finally attain it, I resolved to adhere to such an animating maxima and fixing my heart on a captain's commission, I pursued it steadily, and for the encouragement of youth in all times to come, I am. proud to record that I finally did attain it.

I returned to the country on the expiration of my apprenticeship, which (considering the object I had in view) happened at a most auspicious moment; for the ensign or our parochial company of local militia had just received a commission in the line, and I was fortunate enough to step into his vacated commission as well as into his clothing and appointments.

I had by that time grown into a tall ramrod of a fellow, as fat as a whipping-post—my predecessor had been a head and shoulders shorter, so that in marching into his trousers I was obliged to put my legs so far through them that it required the eye of a connoisseur to distinguish whether they were not intended as a pair of breeches. The other end of my arms, too, were exposed to equal animadversion, protruding through the coat-sleeves, to an extent which would have required a pair of gauntlets of the horse-guards blue to fill up the vacancy. Nevertheless, no peacock ever strutted more proudly in his plumage than I did in mine—and when I found myself on a Sunday in the front seat of the gallery of our parish church, exposed to the admiration of a congregation of milkmaids, my delight was without alloy.

Chapter 2

Militia Life

No man can tether time or tide.
The hour approaches Tam maun ride.
And he takes one side step and two front ones on the road to glory.

It was a very fine thing, no doubt, to be an ensign in the local militia, and a remarkably pretty thing to be the admiration of alt the milk-maids of a parish; but while time was jogging, I found myself standing with nothing but the precarious footing of those pleasures to stand upon, and it therefore behooved me to think of sinking the ornamental for the sake of the useful; and a neighbouring worthy, who was an importer and vender of foreign timber, happening at this time to make a proposition to unite our fortunes, and that I should take the charge of a branch establishment in the city of Glasgow, it was arranged accordingly, and my next position therefore was behind my own desk in that Wapping of Glasgow, called the Gorbals.

Mars, however, was still in the ascendant, for my first transaction in the way of business was to get myself appointed to a lieutenancy in one of the volunteer regiments, and, as far as I remember, I think that all my other transactions while I remained there redounded more to my credit as a soldier than as a citizen, and when, at the end of the year, the offer of an ensigncy in the militia enabled me to ascend a step higher on the ladder of my ambition, leaving my partner to sell or burn his sticks (whichever he might find the most profitable,) I cut mine, and joined that finest of all militia regiments, the North York, when I began to hold up my head and to fancy myself something like a soldier in reality.

Our movements during the short period that I remained with them, were confined to casual changes among the different stations on the coasts of Kent and Sussex, where I got gradually initiated into all the mysteries of home service,—learnt to make love to the smugglers' very pretty daughters, and became a dead hand at wrenching the knocker from a door.

The idleness and the mischievous propensities of the officers of that district (of the line as well as the militia) were proverbial at the period I speak of; but, while as usual the report greatly exceeded the reality, there was this to be said in their behalf, that they were almost entirely excluded from respectable society; owing partly, perhaps, to their not being quite so select as at the present time, (those heroes who had a choice of pleasures preferring *Almanac's* to Napoleon's balls,) but chiefly to the numbers of the troops with which those districts were inundated, during the war, and which put it out of the power of individual residents to notice such a succession of military interlopers, unless they happened to be especially recommended to them; so that, as the Irishman. expresses it—he was a lucky cove, indeed, who in those days succeeded in getting his legs under a gentleman's mahogany.

It is not therefore much to be wondered at, if a parcel of wild young fellows thrown on their own resources, when that warlike age required a larking spirit to be encouraged rather than repressed amongst them,—I say, it is not to be wondered at if they did occasionally amuse themselves with a class of persons which, under other circumstances, they would have avoided, and if the consequences were sometimes what they had better not have been—but the accounts between the man and woman of that day having been long since closed, it is not for me to reopen them, yet I remember that even that manner of life was not without its charms.

The only variety in my year's militia life was an encampment on the lines at Chatham, where we did duty on board the hulks, in the Medway. My post was for the greater period with a guard on board the old Irresistible, which was laden with about eight hundred heavy Danes who had been found guilty of defending their property against their invaders, and I can answer for it that they were made as miserable as anybody of men detected in such a heinous crime had a right to be, for of all diabolical constructions in the shape of prisons the hulks claim by right a pre-eminence. However, we were then acting under the broad acknowledged principle, that those who are not for, are against us, and upon that same principle, the worthy Danes with their ships were respectfully invited to repose themselves for a while within our hospitable harbours.

On the breaking up of our encampment at Chatham we marched to Deal, where one of the periodical volunteerings from the militia, (to fill up the ranks of the line,) took place, and I need not add that I greedily snatched at the opportunity it offered to place myself in the position for which I had so long sighed.

On those occasions any subaltern who could persuade a given number of men to follow him, received a commission in whatever regiment of the line he wished, provided there was a vacancy for himself and followers. I therefore chose that which had long been the object of my secret adoration, as well for its dress as the nature of its services and its achievements, the old Ninety-Fifth, now the Rifle Brigade.—"Hurrah for the first in the field and the last out of it, the bloody fighting Ninety-Fifth," was the cry of my followers, while beating up for more recruits—and as glory was their object, a fighting and a bloody corps the gallant fellows found it, for out of the many who followed Captain Strode and me to it, there were, but two sergeants and myself, after the sixth campaign, alive to tell the tale.

I cannot part from the good old North York without a parting tribute to their remembrance, for as a militia regiment they were not to be surpassed.—Their officers were officers as well as gentlemen, and there were few among .them who would not have filled the same rank in the line with credit to themselves and to the service, and several wanted but the opportunity to turn up trumps of the first order,

I no sooner found myself gazetted than I took a ran up to London to get rid of my loose cash, which being very speedily accomplished, I joined the regiment at Hythe barracks.

They had just returned from sharing in the glories and disasters of Sir John Moore's retreat, and were busily employed in organizing again for active service. I have never seen a regiment of more gallant bearing than the first battalion there showed itself, from their brilliant chief, (the late Sir Sidney Beckwith,) downwards; they were all that a soldier could love to look on; and, splendid as was their appearance, it was the least admirable part about them, for the beauty of their system of discipline consisted in their doing everything that was necessary, and nothing that was not, so that every man's duty was a pleasure to him, and the *esprit de corps* was unrivalled.

There was an abundance of Johnny Newcome's, like myself, tumbling in hourly, for it was then such a favourite corps with the militia men, that they received a thousand men over their complement within the first three days of the volunteering, (and before a stop could be put to it,) which compelled the horse-guards to give an additional battalion to the corps.

On my first arrival my whole soul was so absorbed in the interest excited by the service officers that, for a time, I could attend to nothing else—I could have worshipped the different relics that adorned their barrack-rooms—the pistol or the dagger of some gaunt Spanish robber—a string of beads from the Virgin Mary of some village chapel—or the brazen helmet of some French dragoon, taken from his head after it had parted company with his shoulders, and with what a greedy ear did I swallow the stories of their hairbreadth 'scapes and imminent perils, and long for the time when I should be able to make such relics and such tales mine own.

Fate has since been propitious, and enabled me to spin as long a yarn as most folks, but as some of their original stories still dwell with much interest on my memory, I shall quote one or two of them, in the hope that they may not prove less so to my readers, for I am not aware that they have yet been published.

Anecdote the First

Of all the vicissitudes of the late disastrous campaign, I found that nothing dwelt so interestingly on the remembrance of our officers as their affair at Calcabellos—partly because it was chiefly a regimental fight, and partly because they were taken at a disadvantage, and acquitted themselves becomingly.

The regiment was formed in front of Calcabellos covering the rear of the infantry, and on the first appearance of the enemy they had been ordered to withdraw behind the town. Three parts of them had already passed the' bridge, and the remainder were upon it, or in the act of filing through the street with the careless confidence which might be expected from their knowledge that the British cavalry still stood between them and the enemy; but in an instant our own cavalry, without the slightest notice, galloped through and over them, and the same instant saw a French sabre flourishing over the head of every man who remained beyond the bridge—many were cut down in the streets, and a great portion of the rear company were taken prisoners.

The remainder of the regiment, seeing the unexpected attack, quickly drew off among the vineyards to the right and left of the road, where they coolly awaited the approaching assault. The dismounted *voltigeurs* first swarmed over the river, assailing the riflemen on all sides, but they were met by a galling fire, which effectually stopped them. General Colbert next advanced to dislodge them, and passing the river at the head of his dragoons, he charged furiously up the road; but, when within a few yards of our men, he was received with such a deadly fire, that scarcely a Frenchman remained in the saddle, and the general himself was among the slain. The *voltigeurs* persevered in their unsuccessful endeavours to force the post, and a furious fight continued to be waged, until darkness put an end to it, both sides having suffered severely.

Although the principal combat had ceased with the daylight,

the riflemen found that the troubles and the fatigues of twenty-four hours were yet in their infancy, for they had to remain in the position, until ten at night, to give the rest of the army time to fall back, during which they had to sustain several fierce assaults, which the enemy made, with the view of ascertaining whether our army were on the move; but in every attempt they were gallantly repulsed, and remained in ignorance on the subject until daylight next morning. Our people had, in the mean time, been on the move the greater part of the night, and those only who have done a mile or two of vineyard walking in the dark, can form an adequate notion of their twenty-four hours' work.

General Colbert (the enemy's hero of the day) was, by all accounts, (if I may be permitted the expression,) splendid as a man, and not less so as a soldier. From the commencement of the retreat of our army he had led the advance, and been conspicuous for his daring: his gallant bearing had, in fact, excited the admiration of his enemies; but on this day, the last of his brilliant earthly career, he was mounted on a white charger, and had been a prominent figure in the attack of our men in the street the instant before, and it is not, therefore, to be wondered at if the admiration for the soldier was for a space drowned in the feeling for the fallen comrades which his bravery had consigned to death; a rifleman, therefore, of the name of Plunket, exclaiming, "thou, too, shalt surely die!" took up an advanced position, for the purpose of singling him out, and by his hand he no doubt fell, Plunket was not less daring in his humble capacity than the great man he had just brought to the dust. He was a bold, active, athletic Irishman, and a deadly shot; but the curse of his country was upon him, and I believe he was finally discharged, without receiving such a recompense as his merits in the field would otherwise have secured to him.

ANECDOTE THE SECOND

In one of the actions in which our regiment was engaged, in covering the retreat to Corunna, a superior body of the enemy burst upon the post of a young officer of the name of Uniacke, compelling him to give way in disorder, and in the short scramble which followed, he very narrowly escaped being caught by the French officer who had led the advance,—a short stout fellow, with a cocked hat, and a pair of huge jack-boots.

Uniacke was one of the most active men in the army, and being speedily joined by his supporting body, which turned the tables upon his adversary, he resolved to give his friend a sweat in return for the one he had got, and started after him, with little doubt, from his appearance and equipment, that he would have him by the neck before he had got many yards farther; but, to his no small mortification, the stout gentleman .plied his seven-league boots so cleverly that Uniacke was unable to gain an inch upon him.

Anecdote the Third

At Astorga, a ludicrous alarm was occasioned by the frolic of an officer; though it might have led to more serious results.

The regiment was quartered in a convent, and the officers and the friars were promiscuously bundled for the night on mattresses lain in one of the galleries; when, about midnight, Captain —— awaking, and seeing the back of one of the *padres* lodging him full in the face, from under the bedclothes, as if inviting the slap of a fist, he, acting, on the impulse of the moment, jumped up, and with a hand as broad as a coal-shovel, and quite as hard, made it descend on the bottom of the astonished sleeper with the force of a paviour, and then stole back to his couch.

The *padre* roared a hundred murders, and murder was roared by a hundred *padres*, while the other officers, starting up in astonishment, drew their swords and began grappling with whoever happened to be near them. The uproar, fortunately, brought some of the attendants with lights before any mischief happened, when the cause of the disturbance was traced, to the no small amusement of every one.

The offender tried hard to convince the afflicted father that he had been under the influence of a dream; but the four fingers and the thumb remained too legibly written on the offended spot to permit him to swallow it.

Anecdote the Fourth

When the straggling and the disorders of the army on the retreat to Corunna became so serious as to demand an example, Sir Edward Paget, who commanded the reserve, caused two of the plunderers to be tried by a court-martial, and they were sentenced to suffer death. The troops were ordered to parade in front of the town, to witness the execution, bitty while in the act of assembling, a dragoon came galloping in from the front to inform Sir Edward, by desire of his brother (Lord Paget,) that the enemy were on the move, and that it was time for the infantry to retire.

Sir Edward, however, took no notice of the message. The troops assembled, and the square was formed, when a second dragoon arrived, to say that the enemy were advancing so rapidly that if Sir Edward did not immediately retire, his lordship could not be answerable for the consequences. Sir Edward, with his usual coolness and determination, said he cared not, for he had a duty to perform, and were the enemy firing into the square, that he would persevere with it. Dragoon after dragoon, in rapid succession, galloped in with a repetition of the message; still the preparations went on, and by the time they were completed, (and it wanted but the word of command to launch the culprits into eternity,) the clang of the carabines of the retreating dragoons was heard all around.

In the breast of Sir Edward, it is probable, that the door of mercy never had been closed, and that he had only waited until the last possible moment to make it the more impressive; and impressive truly it must have been; nor is it easy to imagine such a moment; for, independently of the solemn and desolate feeling with which one at all times witnesses the execution of a comrade, let his offence be what it may, they had an additional intensity on this occasion, on the score of their own safety; for, brief as the span seemed to be that was allotted to the culprits, the clang of the carabine, and the whistling ball, told that it was possible to be even still more brief on the parts of many of the spectators.

Sir Edward, however, now addressed the troops, with a degree of coolness which would argue that danger and he had been long familiar. He pointed out the enormity of the offence of which the culprits had been guilty, that they deserved not to be saved, and that though the enemy were now upon them, and might lay half their number dead while witnessing the .execution, that only one thing would save them, and that was, "would the troops now present pledge themselves that this should be the last instance of insubordination that would occur in the course of the retreat?"

A simultaneous "Yes," burst from the lips of the assembled thousands, and the next instant saw the necessary measures taken to check the advancing foe, while the remainder resumed their retreat, lightened of a load of care, which a few minutes before had been almost intolerable.

The conduct of these regiments, as compared with others, was very exemplary during the retreat, although their duty, in protecting the stragglers of the army till the last possible moment, was of the most harassing kind. They had no means of punishing those to whom they were indebted for their extra trouble, but by depriving them of their ill-gotten gains; so that whenever a fellow came in with a bag of flour under his arm, (which was no uncommon occurrence,) they made it a rule to empty the bag over his head, to make him a marked man. Napier says of them, that for twelve days these hardy soldiers covered the retreat; during which time they had traversed eighty miles of road in two marches, passed several nights under arms in the snow of the mountains, were seven times engaged with the enemy, and now assembled at the outposts (before Corunna,) having fewer men missing from the ranks, including those who had fallen in battle, than any other division in the army.[1]

I shall now, with the reader's permission, resume the thread of my narrative.

---

1. The foregoing story, I find, has just made its appearance in a volume published by Lieutenant-Colonel Cadell; but as this narrative was publicly noticed, as being in preparation, prior to the publication of his, I have not thought it necessary to expunge it..

CHAPTER 3

Goes to the War, and Ends in Love

In those days, the life of a soldier was a stirring and an active one. I had not joined the regiment above a fortnight when the 1st Battalion received orders for immediate active service, and General Graham was to make his appearance on the morrow, to inspect them prior to their embarkation. Every man destined for service was to appear in the ranks, and as my turn had not yet come, I was ordered, the previous evening, to commence my career as a rifleman, in charge of the guard; and a most unhappy debut I made of it, and one that argued but little in behalf of my chances of future fame in the profession.

My guard was composed of a motley assemblage; for, excepting on the back of the sergeant, I remember that there was not a rag of uniform amongst them. I was too anxious to forget all about them to think of informing myself afterwards; but, from what I have since seen, I am satisfied that they must either have been a recent importation from "the first gem of the sea," or they had been furnished for the occasion by the governor of Newgate;—however, be that as it may, I had some ten or a dozen prisoners handed over to me; and as my eye was not sufficiently practised to distinguish, in such a group, which was the soldier and which the prisoner, I very discreetly left the whole affair to the sergeant, who seemed to be a man of *nous*.

But while I was dozing on the guard-bed, about midnight, I was startled by a scramble in the soldier's room, and the cry of "guard, turn out," and, on running out to ascertain the cause, the sergeant told me that the light in the guard-house had been purposely upset by someone, and, suspecting that a trick was intended, he had turned out the guard; and truly his suspicions were well grounded, although he took an erroneous method of counteracting it; for the sentry over the door, not being a much shrewder fellow than myself in distinguishing characters in the dark, in suffering the guard to turn out, had allowed some of the prisoners to turn out too, and, among the rest, one who had been reserved for an especial example of some sort or other, and whose absence was likely to make a noise in the neighbourhood.

This was certainly information enough to furnish me with food for reflection for the remainder of the night, and, as if to enhance its agreeable nature, the sergeant-major paid me a visit at daylight in the morning, and informed me that such things did sometimes happen;—he enumerated several cases of the kind in different regiments, and left me with the consolatory piece of information that the officer of the guard had . on each occasion been allowed to retire without a court martial!!!

My readers, I am sure, will rejoice with me that in this, as in other cases, there is no rule without an exception, for otherwise they would never have had the pleasure of reading a book of mine.

How I had the good fortune to be excepted on that occasion I never found out; probably, in the hurry and bustle of preparation it was overlooked,—or, probably, because they hoped better things of me thereafter,—but my commanding officer never noticed it, and his kindness in so doing put me more on the alert for the future than if he had written a volume of censure.

Among the other novelties of the aforesaid guard- house on that memorable night, I got acquainted with a very worthy goose, whose services in the Rifle Brigade well merit a chapter in its history. If any one imagines that a goose is a goose, he is very much mistaken: and I am happy in having the power of undeceiving him. for I am about to show that my (or rather our regimental) goose was shrewd, active, and intelligent, it was a faithful public servant, a social companion, and an attached friend, (I wish that every biped could say but half so much.) Its death or its manner of departure from this world, is still clouded in mystery, but while my book lives, the goose's memory shall not die.

It had attached itself to the guard-house several years prior to my appearance there, find all its doings had been as steady as a sentry-box: its post was with the sentry over the guards in fine weather it accompanied him in his walk, and in bad, it stood alongside of him in his box. It marched with the officer of the guard in all his visiting rounds, and it was the first on all occasions to give notice of the approach of any one in authority, keeping a particularly sharp look-out for the captain and field-officer of the day, whether by day or night.

The guard might sleep, the sentry might sleep, but the goose was ever wide awake, it never considered itself relieved from duty, except during the breakfast and dinner-hours, when it Invariably stepped into the guard-house, and partook of the soldiers' cheer, for they were so devotedly attached to it that it was at all times bountifully supplied, and it was not a little amusing, on those occasions, to see how the fellow cackled whenever the soldiers laughed; as if it understood and enjoyed the joke as much as they did.

I did not see *Moore's Almanac* for 1812, and, therefore, know not whether he predicted that Michaelmas would be fatal to many of the tribe that year; but I never saw a comrade more universally lamented than the poor goose was when the news of its mysterious disappearance reached us in Spain.

Our comrades at home, as a last proof of their affection, very magnanimously offered a reward of ten pounds for the recovery of the body, dead or alive; but whether it filled a respectable position in a banquet of that year, or still lives to bother the decayed tooth of some elderly maiden, at Michaelmas next, remains to be solved.

On the 24th of March, 1809, our first battalion received orders to march at midnight for Dover, there to be united with the 43rd and 52nd regiments, as a Light Brigade, under Major-General Robert Crawfurd, and to embark next morning to join the army which was then assembling in the Peninsula.

In marching for embarkation in those stirring times, the feeling of the troops partook more of the nature of a ship's crew about to sail on a roving commission, than a land-crab expedition which was likely to prove eternal, for although one did occasionally see some blubber-headed fellow mourning over his severed affections for a day or two, yet a thorough-going one just gave a kiss to his wife, if he had one, and two to his sweetheart, if he had not, and away he went with a song in his mouth.

I now joined the 2nd Battalion, where we were not permitted to rest long on our oars, for, within a months, we were called upon to join the expedition with which

> The Great Earl of Chatham, and a hundred thousand men.
> Sailed over to Holland, and then sailed back again.

As the military operations of that expedition do not entitle them to a place in such an important history as mine is, I shall pass them over, simply remarking that some of our companies fired a few professional shots, and some of our people got professionally shot, while a great many more visited Death by the doctor's road, and almost all who visited him not, got uncommonly well shaken.

South Beeveland ultimately became our head-quarters. It is a fine island, and very fertile, yielding about forty bushels of frogs an acre, and tadpoles enough to fence it with. We were there under the command of General W. Stewart, whose active mind, continually in search of improvement, led him to try (in imitation of some foreign customs,) to saddle the backs of the officers with knapsacks, by way of adding to their comfort; for he proved to demonstration that if an officer had a clean shirt in his knapsack on his back, that he might have it to put on at the end of his day's march; whereas if he had it not on his own back, it might be left too far back to be of use to him when wanted.

This was a fact not to be disputed, but so wedded were we

to ancient prejudices, that we remained convinced that the shirt actually in wear, with all its additions at the end of an extra day or two, must still weigh less than the knapsack with a shirt in it; and upon those grounds we made a successful kick, and threw them off, not, however, until an experimental field-day had been ordered to establish them.

The order required that each officer should parade in a knapsack, or something answering the same purpose, and it was amusing enough to see the expedients resorted to, to evade, without committing a direct breach of it. I remember that my apology for one on that occasion was slinging an empty black oil-skin haversack knapsack-ways, which looked so much like a newly-lanced blister on my back that it made both the *vraws* and the frogs stare. The attempt was never repeated.

What a singular change did a short residence in that pestiferous place work in the appearance of our army! It was with our regiment as with others; one month saw us embark a thousand men at Deal, in the highest health and spirits, and the next month saw us land, at the same place, with about seven hundred men, carrying to hospital, or staggering under disease.

I cannot shake off that celebrated Walcheren fever, without mentioning what may or may not be a peculiarity in it;—that a brother-officer and I experienced a return of it within a day of each other, after a lapse of five years, and again, within a week, after the lapse of the allowing three years.

As my heart had embarked for the Peninsula with the 1st battalion, although my body (for the reasons given) remained behind for a year, I shall, with the reader's permission, follow the first, as being in the more interesting position of the two; and although, tinder these circumstances, I am not permitted to speak in the first person singular, until the two shall be again united, yet whatever I do speak of, I have heard so often and so well authenticated, that I am enabled to give it with the same confidence as if I had been an eyewitness.

A Lay of Love for Lady Bright.

Lisbon was, doubtless, as rich in abominations now as it was a year after, without any other redeeming virtue, which is a very ugly commencement to a tale of love; but having landed my reader a second time at the same place, I am anxious to relieve him from the fear of being treated to a second edition of the same story, and to assure him that my head-piece has been some time charged with fresh ammunition, and I mean to discharge it now, to prevent its getting rusty. I intend to fight those battles only that I never fought before, galloping over the ground lightly, and merely halting to give a little of my conversation, such as it is, whenever I have anything new to tell; and as I have no idea of enduring the fatigues of the march to Talavera, nor the pleasures of fattening on the dinners of chopped straw which followed it.

I shall leave my regiment to its fate until its return to the north of Portugal, and take advantage of the repose it affords to make my editorial bow with all due deference to my fair and lovely readers, to express my joy that I have been once more enabled to put myself in communion with them, and to assure them of my continued unbounded love and admiration, for I feel and have ever felt that the man who gave frailty the name of woman was a blockhead, and must have been smarting under some unsuccessful bit of the tender, for I have met her in the bower and in the battle, and have ever found her alike admirable in both!

That old fool Shakespeare, too, having only a man's courage to meet a sprite with! Had he but told Macbeth to dare as woman dared, he would have seen the ghost of Banquo vanish into the witches' kettle in the twinkling of a wheelbarrow; for although I have never seen a woman kick the bucket, I have certainly seen her kick everything else, and in fact there is nothing in the heroics that I have not seen her do. See her again when she descends into herself, and it is very odd if I have not seen her there too! for no man has ever been so often or so deep in love as I have—my poor heart has been lacerated, torn, and finally scorched until it is withered up like a roasted potato with scarcely the size of a kiss left.

How it was that I did not find myself dangling at a door-post by the end of a silk handkerchief some odd morning is to me astonishing; but here I am, living and loving still as fondly as ever. Prudence, at this moment, whispers that I have said enough for the present, for if I go on making love so fiercely thus early in the day, I shall be forced to marry the whole sex, and bring my book to a premature conclusion, for which posterity would never forgive me.

I must, therefore, for the present, take a most reluctant leave, with a promise of renewing my courtship from time to time as opportunities offer, if they will but good-naturedly follow me through the various scenes into which I am about to conduct them; and while I do my best to amuse them by the way, should I unintentionally dive so deeply into the pathetic as to beguile them of a tear, let me recommend them to wipe it away, for it is only their smiles I court.

While on the way to join the light division on the northern frontier, I shall take the opportunity of introducing the reader to their celebrated commander, the late Major-General Robert Crawfurd, an officer who, for a length of time, was better known than liked, but like many a gem of purer ray his value was scarcely known until lost.

Chapter 4

Historical, Comical, and Warlike Tales

Crawfurd was no common character. He, like a gallant contemporary of his, was not born to be a great general, but he certainly was a distinguished one,—the history of his division and the position which he held beyond the Coa in 1810, attest the fact. He had neither judgment, temper, nor discretion to fit him for a chief, and as a subordinate he required to be held with a tight rein, but his talents as a general of division were nevertheless of the first order. He received the three British regiments under his command, finished by the hands of a master in the art. Sir John Moore, and, as regiments, they were faultless; but to Crawfurd belonged the chief merit of making them the war brigade which they became, alike the admiration of their friends and foes. How he made them so I am about to show, but how such another is to be made, now that his system has fallen into disrepute, will be for futurity to deter mine.

I think I see a regiment of those writers who are just now taking the cat by the tail, parading for a day's march under that immortal chief—that he furnishes them with an inkbottle for a canteen, fills their knapsacks with foolscap, their mouths with mouldy biscuit, and starts them off with sloped pens. They go along with the buoyancy of a corps of reporters reconnoitring for a memorandum, and they very quickly catch one and a Tartar to the bargain, for the monotony of the road is relieved by the crossing of a fine broad stream, and over the stream is a very fine plank to preserve the polish of Warren's jet on the feet of the pedestrian—they all jump gaily towards the plank, but they are pulled up by a grim gentleman with a drawn sword, who, with a voice of thunder, desires them to keep their ranks and march through the stream.

Well! this is all mighty pleasant, but now that they are up to their middles in the water, there surely can be no harm in stopping half a minute to lave a few handfuls of it. into, their parched mouths. I think I see the astonishment of their editorial nerves when they find a dozen lashes well bestowed *a posteriori* upon each, by way of their farther refreshment and clearing off scores for that portion of the day's work (for the general was a man who gave no credit on those occasions.) He had borrowed a leaf from the history of the land-crabs, and suffered neither mire nor water to disturb the order of his march with impunity.

Now I dare say he would have had to flog an editor a dozen times before he had satisfied him that it was to his advantage; but a soldier is open to conviction, and such was the manner of making one of the finest and most effective divisions that that or any other army ever saw.

Where soldiers are to be ruled, there is more logic in nine tails of a cat than in the mouths of a hundred orators I it requires very little argument to prove, and I'll defy the most eloquent preacher, (with the unknown tongue to boot,) to persuade a regiment to ford a river where there is a bridge to conduct them over dry-shod, or to prevent them drinking when they are- in that river if they happen to feel thirsty, let him promise them what he will as a reward for their obedience. It is like preaching to his own flock on the subject of their eternal welfare (and I make the comparison with all due reverence;) they, would all gladly arrive at the, end he aims at, but at the same time how few' will take the necessary steps to do so, and how many prefer their momentary present enjoyment?

So it was with the soldiers, but with this difference, that Crawfurd's cat forced them to take the right road whether they would or no, and the experiment once made carried conviction with it, that the comfort of every individual in the division materially depended on the rigid exaction of his orders, for he shewed that on every ordinary march he made it a rule to halt for a few minutes every third or fourth mile, (dependent on the vicinity of water,) that every soldier carried a canteen capable of containing two quarts, and that if he only took the trouble to fill it before starting, and again, if necessary, at every halt, it contained more than he would or ought to drink in the interim; and that therefore every pause he made ill a river for the purpose of drinking was disorderly, because a man stopping to drink delayed the one behind him proportionately longer, and so on progressively to the rear of the column.

In like manner the filing past dirty or marshy parts of the road in place of marching, boldly through them or filing over a plank or narrow bridge in place of taking the river with the full front of their column in march, he proved to demonstration on true mathematical principles, that with the numbers of those obstacles usually encountered on a day's march, it made a difference of several hours in their arrival at their bivouac for the night.

That in indulging by the way, they were that much longer labouring under their load of arms, ammunition, and necessaries, besides bringing them to their bivouac in darkness and discomfort; it very likely, too, got them thoroughly drenched with rain, when the sole cause of their delay had been to avoid a partial wetting, which would have been long since dried while seated at ease around their campfires; and if this does not redeem Crawfurd and his cat, I give it up.

The general and his divisional code, as already hinted at, was at first much disliked; probably, he enforced it, in the first instance, with unnecessary severity, and it was long before those under him could rid themselves of that feeling of oppression which it had inculcated upon their minds.

It is due, however, to the memory of the gallant general to say that punishment for those disorders was rarely necessary after the first campaign; for the system, once established, went on like clockwork, and the soldiers latterly became devotedly attached to him; for while he exacted from them the most rigid obedience, he was, on his own part, keenly alive to everything they had a right to expect from him in return, and woe befell the commissary who failed to give a satisfactory reason for any deficiencies in his issues.

It is stated that one of them went to the commander-in-chief to complain that he had been unable to procure bread for the light division, and that General Crawfurd had threatened that if they were not supplied within a given time, he would put him in the guard-house. "Did he?" said his lordship; "then I would recommend you to find the bread, for if he said so, be assured, he'll do it!"

Having in this chapter flogged every man who had any shadow of claim to such a distinction, I shall now proceed and place myself along with my regiment to see that they prove themselves worthy of the pains taken in their instruction.

From the position which the light division then held, their commander must have been fully satisfied in his own mind that their military education had not been neglected, for *certes* it required every man to be furnished with a clear head, a bold heart, and a clean pair of heels—all three being liable to be put in requisition at any hour by day or night. It was no place for reefing topsails and making all snug, but one which required the crew to be constantly at quarters; for, unlike their nautical brethren, the nearer a soldier's shoulders are to the rocks the less liable he is to be wrecked—and there they had more than enough of play in occupying a front of twenty-five miles with that small division and some cavalry. The chief of the 1st German Hussars meeting our commandant one morning, "Well, Colonel," says the gallant German in broken English, "how you do?"

"O, tolerably well, thank you, considering that I am obliged to sleep with one eye open."

"Why," says the other, "I never sleeps at all."

Colonel Beckwith at this time held the pass of Barba del

Puerco with four companies of the Rifles, and very soon experienced the advantage of having an eye alive, for he had some active neighbours on the opposite of the river, who had determined to beat up his quarters by way of ascertaining the fact.

The *padre* of the village, it appeared, was a sort of vicar of Bray, who gave information to both sides so long as accounts remained pretty equally balanced between them, but when the advance of the French army for the subjugation of Portugal became a matter of certainty, he immediately chose that which seemed to be the strongest) and it was not ours.

The *padre* was a famous hand over a glass of grog, and where amusements were so scarce, it was good fun for our youngsters to make a *padre* glorious, which they took every opportunity of doing; and as is not unusual with persons in that state, (laymen as well as Padres) he invariably fancied himself the only sober man of the party, so that the report was conscientiously given when he went over to the French General Ferey, who commanded the division opposite, and staked his reputation as a *padre* that the English officers in his village were in the habit of getting blind drunk every night, and that he had only to march over at midnight to secure them almost without resistance.

Ferey was a bold enterprising soldier, (I saw his body in death after the battle of Salamanca;) he knew to a man the force of the English in the village, and probably did not look upon the attempt as very desperate were they even at their posts ready to receive him; but as the chances seemed to be in favour of every enemy's head being "nailed to his pillow," the opportunity was not to be resisted, and accordingly, at midnight on the 19th of March, he assembled his force silently at the end of the bridge.

The shadows of the rocks which the rising moon had just cast over the place prevented their being seen, and the continuous roar of the mountain torrent, which divided them, prevented their being heard even by our double sentry posted at the other end of the bridge within a few yards of them. Leaving a powerful support to cover his retreat in the event of a reverse, Ferey at the head of six hundred chosen grenadiers burst forth so silently and suddenly, that, of our double sentry on the bridge, the one was taken and the other bayoneted without being able to fire off their pieces.

A sergeant's party higher up among the rocks had just time to fire off as an alarm, and even the remainder of the company on picquet under O'Hare had barely time to jump up and snatch their rifles when the enemy were among them. O'Hare's men, however, though borne back and unable to stop them for an instant, behaved nobly, retiring in a continued hand-to-hand personal encounter with their foes to the top of the pass, when the remaining companies under Sidney Beckwith having just started from their sleep, rushed forward to their support, and with a thundering discharge, tumbled the attacking column into the ravine below, where passing the bridge under cover of the fire of their supporting body, they resumed their former position, minus a considerable number of their best and bravest.

The colonel, while urging the fight, observed a Frenchman within a yard or two, taking deliberate aim at his head. Stooping suddenly down and picking up a stone, he immediately shyed it at him, calling him at the same time a "scoundrel, to get out of that." It so far distracted the fellow's attention, that while the gallant Beckwith's cap was blown to atoms, the head remained untouched. The whole concern was but the affair of a few minutes, but we nevertheless looked upon it as no inconsiderable addition to our regimental feather, for the appointed alarm post of one of the companies had earned it to a place where it happened that they were not wanted, so that there were but three companies actually engaged, and therefore with something less than half their numbers they had beaten off six hundred of the *élite* of the French army. But our chief pride arose from its being the first and last night attempt which the enemy ever made to surprise a British post, in that army.

Of the worthy pastor I never heard more—I know not whether the bold Ferey paid the price of the information he had brought, in sold, or with an ounce of lead; but certain it is that his flock were without ghostly consolation during the remainder of our sojourn—not that it was much sought after at that particular time, for the village damsels had already begun running up a score of *peccadillos*, and it was of little use attempting to wipe it out until the final departure of their heretical visitors.

Among the wounded who were left on the field by the enemy, there was a French sergeant whom I have often heard our officers speak of with much admiration—he was a fine handsome young fellow, alike romantic in his bravery, and in devotion to his emperor and his country—he had come on with the determination to conquer or to die, and having failed in the first, he seemed resolved not to be balked in the other, which a ball through a bad part of the thigh had placed him in the high road for, and he, therefore, resisted every attempt to save him, with the utmost indignation, claiming it as a matter of right to be allowed to die on the field where he had fallen.

Our good, honest, rough diamonds, however, who were employed in collecting the wounded, were equally determined that the point in dispute should only be settled between him and the doctor in the proper place, and accordingly they shouldered him off to the hospital whether he would or no. But even there he continued as untameable as an hyena—his limb was in such a state that nothing but amputation could save his life—yet nothing would induce him to consent to it—he had courage to endure anything, but nothing could reconcile him to receive anything but blows from his enemies.

I forget how, or in what way, the amputation of the limb was at length accomplished. To the best of my recollection death had already laid a hand upon him, and it was done while he was in a state of insensibility. But be that as it may, it was done, and the danger and the fit of heroics having travelled with the departed limb, he lived to thank his preservers for the brotherly kindness he had experienced at their hands, and took a grateful and affectionate farewell of them when his health was sufficiently restored to permit his being removed to the care of his countrymen.

Shortly after this affair at Barba del Puerco, the French army under Massena came down upon Ciudad Rodrigo, preparatory to the invasion of Portugal, and obliged the light division to take up a more concentrated position.

It is not my intention to take notice of the movements of the army farther than is necessary to illustrate the anecdotes I relate; but I cannot, on this occasion, resist borrowing a leaf out of Napier's admirable work, to show the remarkable state of discipline which those troops had been brought to—for while I have no small portion of personal vanity to gratify in recording the (act of my having been for many years after an associate in all the enterprises of that gallant band, I consider it more particularly a duty which every military writer owes to posterity, (be his pretensions great or humble,) to show what may be effected in that profession by diligence and perseverance.

The light division, and the cavalry attached to it, was, at this period, so far in advance of every other part of the army that their safety depended on themselves alone, for they were altogether beyond the reach of human aid—their force consisted of about four thousand infantry, twelve hundred cavalry, and a brigade of horse artillery—and yet with this small force did Crawfurd, trusting to his own admirable arrangements, and the surprising discipline of his troops, maintain a position which was no position for three months, within an hour's march of six thousand horsemen, and two hours' march from sixty thousand infantry, of a brave, experienced, and enterprising enemy, who was advancing in the confidence of certain victory.

Napier says:

> His situation demanded a quickness and intelligence in the troops, the like of which has seldom been known. Seven minutes sufficed for the division to get under arms in the middle of the night, and a quarter of an hour, night or day, to bring it in order of battle to the alarm posts, with the baggage loaded and assembled at a convenient distance m the rear. And this not upon a concerted signal, or as a trial, but at all times, and certain!

In peace love times the shepherd's reed,
In war he mounts the warrior's steed.

And thus, in humble imitation of her master-man, did Mother Coleman, one fine morning, mount her donkey, and join her French lover to war against her lord.

While the troops of the light division, as already noticed, were strutting about with the consciousness of surpassing excellence, menacing and insulting a foe for which their persons, knapsacks and all would barely have sufficed for a luncheon—a dish of mortification was served up for those of our corps, by the hands of their better half, which was not easy of digestion. To speak of the wife of a regiment is so very unusual as to imply that she must have been some very great personage—and without depriving her of the advantage of such a magnificent idea, I shall only say that she was the only wife they had got—for they landed at Lisbon with eleven hundred men and only one woman.

By what particular virtues she had attained such a dignified position among them, I never clearly made out, farther than she had arrived at years of discretion, was what is commonly called a useful woman, and had seen some service. She was the wife of a sturdy German, who plied in the art of shoemaking, whenever his duties in the field permitted him to resort to that species of amusement, so that it appeared that she had beauty enough to captivate a cobbler, she had money enough to command the services of a jackass, and, finally, she proved she had wit enough to sell us all, which she did the first favourable opportunity—for, after plying for some months at the tail of her donkey, at the tail of the regiment, and fishing in all the loose dollars which were floating about in gentlemen's pockets, (by those winning ways which ladies know so well how to use when such favourable opportunities offer,) she finally bolted off to the enemy, bag and baggage, carrying away old Coleman's all and awl.

It was one of those French leave-takings which man is heir to, but we eventually got over it, under the deepest obligation all the time for the sympathy manifested by our friends of the

43rd and 52nd.

The movements of the enemy were, at length, unshackled by the fall of Ciudad Rodrigo, after a desperate defence, .which gave immortal glory to its old governor Herrasti, and his brave Spanish garrison—and although it may appear, that I am saying one word in honour of the Spaniards for the purpose of giving two to the British, yet my feelings are too national to permit me to pass over a fact which redounds so much to the glory of our military history—namely, that, in this, the year 1810, the French were six weeks in wresting from the Spaniards the same fortress which we, in the year 1812, carried, with fire and sword, out of the hands of the French in eleven days!

Now that the enemy's movements were unshackled, the cloud, which for months had been gathering over Portugal, began to burst—and sharp as Crawfurd and his division looked before, it now behooved them to look somewhat sharper. Had he acted in conformity with his instructions, he had long ere this been behind the Coa, but deeply enamoured of his separate command as ever youth was of his mistress, he seemed resolved that nothing but force should part them; and having gradually given ground, as necessity compelled, the 23rd of July found him with his back on the river; and his left resting on the fortress of Almeida, determined to abide a battle, with about five thousand men of all arms to oppose the whole French army.

I shall leave to abler pens the description of the action that followed, and which (as might have been foreseen, while it was highly honourable to the officers and troops engaged) ended m their being driven across the Coa with a severe loss. My business is with a youth who had the day before joined the division. The history of his next day's adventure has beguiled me of many a hearty laugh, and although I despair of being able to communicate it to my readers with anything like the humour with which I received it from an amiable and gallant friend, yet I cannot resist giving it such as it rests on my remembrance.

Mr. Rogers, as already stated, had, the day before, arrived from England, as an officer of one of the civil departments attached to the Light Division, and as might be expected on finding himself all at once up with the outposts of the army, he was full of curiosity and excitement. Equipped in a huge cocked hat, and an hermaphrodite sort of scarlet coat, half military and half civil, he was dancing about with his budget of inquiries, when chance threw him in the way of the gallant and lamented Jock MacCulloch, at the time a lieutenant in the Rifles, and who was in the act of marching off a company to relieve one of the picquets for the night MacCulloch, full of humour, seeing the curiosity of the fresh arrival, said, "Come, Rogers, my boy, come along with me, you shall share my beefsteak, you shall share my boat-cloak, and it will go hard with me but you shall see a Frenchman, too, before we part in the morning."

The invitation was not to be resisted, and away went Rogers on the spur of the moment

The night turned out a regular Tam o'Shanter's night, or, if the reader pleases, a Wellington night, for it is a singular fact that almost every one of his battles was preceded by such a night;— the thunder rolled, the lightning flashed and all the fire-engines in the world seemed playing upon the lightning, and the devoted heads of those exposed to it. It was a sort of night that was well calculated to be a damper to a bolder spirit than the one whose story I am relating; but he, nevertheless, sheltered himself as he best could, under the veteran's cloak, and put as good a face upon it as circumstances would permit.

As usual, an hour before daybreak, MacCulloch, resigning the boat-cloak to his dozing companion, stood to his arms, to be ready for whatever changes daylight might have in store for him: nor had he to wait long, for day had just begun to dawn when the sharp crack from the rifle of one of the advanced sentries announced the approach of the enemy, and he had just time to counsel his terrified bed-fellow to make the best of his way back to the division, while he himself awaited to do battle. Nor had he much time for preparation, for, as Napier says:

Ney, seeing Crawfurd's false dispositions, came down upon them with the stoop of an eagle. Four thousand horsemen, and a powerful artillery, swept the plain, and Loison's division coming up at a charging pace, made towards the centre and left of the position."

MacCulloch, almost instantly, received several bad sabre wounds, and, with five-and-twenty of his men, was taken prisoner.

Rogers, it may be believed, lost no time in following the salutary counsel he had received with as clever a pair of heels as he could muster. The enemy's artillery had by this time opened, and, as the devil would nave it, the cannon-balls were travelling the same road, and tearing up the ground on each side of' him almost as regularly as if it had been a ploughing match. Poor Rogers was thus placed in a situation which fully justified him in thinking, as most young soldiers do, that every ball was aimed at himself.

He was half distracted; it was certain death to stop where he was, neither flank offered him the smallest shelter, and he had not wind enough left in his bellows to clear the tenth part of the space between him and comparative safety; but, where life is at stake, the imagination is fertile, and it immediately occurred to him that by dowsing the cocked hat he would make himself a less conspicuous object; clapping it, accordingly, under his arm, he continued his frightful career, with the feelings of a maniac and the politeness of a courtier, for to every missile that passed he bowed as low as his racing attitude would permit, in ignorance that the danger had passed along with it, performing, to all appearance, a continued rotatory sort of evolution, as if the sails of a windmill had parted from the building, and continued their course across' the plain, to the utter astonishment of all who saw him.

At length, when exhausted nature could not have carried him twenty yards farther, he found himself among some skirmishers of the 3rd Caçadores, and within a few yards of a rocky ridge, rising out of the ground, the rear of which seemed to offer him the long-hoped-for opportunity of recovering his wind, and he sheltered himself accordingly.

This happened to be the first occasion in which tile Caçadores had been under fire; they had the highest respect for the bravery of their British officers, and had willingly followed where their colonel had led; but having followed him into the field, they did not see why they should not follow another out of it, and when they saw a red coat take post behind a rock, they all immediately rushed to take advantage of the same cover. Poor Rogers had not, therefore, drawn his first breath when he found himself surrounded by these Portuguese warriors, nor had he drawn a second before their colonel (Sir George Elder) rode furiously at him with his drawn sword, exclaiming "who are you, you scoundrel, in the uniform of a British officer, setting an example of cowardice to my men? get out of that instantly, or I'll cut you down!"

Rogers's case was desperate—he had no breath left to explain that he had no pretensions to the honour of being an officer, for he would have been cut down in the act of attempting it: he was, therefore, once more forced to start for another heat with the round shot, and, like a hunted devil, got across the bridge,. he knew not how; but he was helm up for England the same day, and the army never saw him more.

General Crawfurd's conduct in the affair alluded to, would argue that his usual soldier-like wits had gone a wool-gathering for the time being—he had, in fact, like a moth, been fluttering so long with impunity around a consuming power that he had at length lost all sense of the danger. But even then it is impossible to conceive upon what principle he took up the position he did— for, in the first place, it was in direct defiance of Lord Wellington's orders; and had the river behind him been flowing with milk and honey, or had the rugged bank on which he was posted been built of loaves and fishes, it would scarcely have justified him in running the risk he did to preserve the sweets; but as the one was flooded with muddy water, and the other only bearing a crop of common stones, and when we consider, too, that the simple passing of the river would have made a hundred of his troops equal to a thousand of the invaders, we must continue lost in wonder.

It is difficult to imagine, however, that he ever contemplated the possibility of stopping the French army but for the moment. Confiding, probably, in the superiority of his troops, he had calculated on successfully repelling their first attack, and that having thus taught them the respect that was due to him, he might then have made a triumphant retreat to the opposite bank, where, for a time, he could safely have offered them farther defiance.

If such was his object, (and it is the only plausible one I can find,) he had altogether overlooked that for a man with one pair of arms to grapple with another who had ten, it must rest with the ten-pair man to say when the play is over, for although the one-pair man may disable an equal number in his front, there are still nine pairs left to poke him in the sides and all round about; and thus the general found it; for having once exposed, himself to such overwhelming numbers, there was no getting out of it but at a large sacrifice—and but for the experience, the confidence, and the devotion of the different individual battalion officers, seconded by the gallantry of the soldiers, the division had been utterly annihilated. Napier, as an eye-witness, states, (what I have often heard repeated by other officers who were there,) that:

> there was no room to array the line, no time for anything but battle, every captain carried off his company as an independent body, and joining as he could with the Ninety-Fifth or Fifty-Second, the whole presented a mass of skirmishers acting in small parties, and under no regular command, yet each confident in the courage and discipline of those on his right and left, and all regulating their movements by a common discretion, and keeping together with surprising vigour.

The result of the action was a loss on the British portion of the division of two hundred and seventy-two, including twenty-eight officers, killed, wounded, and taken.

It is curious to observe by what singular interpositions of

Providence the lives of individuals are spared. One of our officers happening to have a pocket-volume of *Gil Blas*, was in the middle of one of his interesting stories when the action commenced. Not choosing to throw it away, he thrust it into the breast of his jacket for want of a better place, and in the course of the day it received a musket-ball which had been meant for a more tender subject The volume was afterwards, of course, treated as a tried friend.

Having, in one of the foregoing pages, introduced the name of MacCulloch in a prominent part of the action, I must be forgiven for taking this opportunity of following him to the end of his highly honourable earthly career.

John MacCulloch was from Scotland, (a native, I believe, of Kirkudbright;) he was young, handsome, athletic, and active; with the meekness of a lamb, he had the heart of a lion, and was the delight of everyone. At the time I first became acquainted with him he had been several years in the regiment, and had shared in all the vicissitudes of the restless life they then led. I brought him under the notice of the reader in marching off to relieve the advanced picquet on the night prior to the action of the Coa.

For the information of those who are unacquainted with military matters, I may as well mention that the command of an outline picquet is never an enviable one— it is a situation at all times dangerous and open to disgrace, but seldom to honour— for, come what may, in the event of an attack spiritedly made, the picquet is almost sure to go to the wall. From the manner in which the French approached on the occasion referred to, it may readily be imagined that my gallant friend had but little chance of escape—It was, therefore, only left to him to do his duty as an officer under the circumstances in which he was placed.

He gave the alarm, and he gave his visitors as warm a reception as his fifty rifles could provide for them, while he gallantly endeavoured to fight his way back to his battalion; but the attempt was hopeless; the cavalry alone of the enemy ought to have been more than enough to sweep the whole of the division off the face of the earth—and MacCulloch's small party had no chance; they were galloped into, and he himself, after being lanced and sabred in many places, was obliged to surrender.

MacCulloch refused to give his *parole*, in the hope of being able to effect his escape before he reached the French frontier; he was, therefore, marched along with the men a close prisoner as far as Valladolid, where fortune, which ever favours the brave, did not fail him. The escort had found it necessary to halt there for some days, and MacCulloch having gained the good will of his conductor, was placed in a private house under proper security; as they thought; but in this said house there happened to be a young lady, and of what avail are walls of brass, bolts, bars, or iron doors, when a lady is concerned?

She quickly put herself in communion with the handsome prisoner—made herself acquainted with his history, name, and country, and as quickly communicated it, as well as her plans for his escape, to a very worthy countrymen of his, at that time a professor m one of the universities there. Need I say more than that before many hours had passed over his head, he found himself equipped in the costume of a Spanish peasant, the necessary quantity of dollars in his pocket, and a kiss on each cheek burning hot from the lips of his preserver, on the high road to rejoin his battalion, where he arrived in due course of time, to the great joy of everybody—Lord Wellington himself was dot the least delighted of the party, and kindly invited him to dine with him that day, in the costume in which he had arrived.

MacCulloch continued to serve with us until Massena's retreat from Portugal, when, in a skirmish which took place on the evening of the 15th of March, 1811, I, myself, got a crack on the head which laid me under a tree, with my understanding considerably bothered for the night, and I was sorry to find, as my next neighbour, poor MacCulloch, with an excruciatingly painful and bad wound in the shoulder joint, which deprived him of the use of one arm for life, and obliged him to return to England for the recovery of health.

In the meantime, by the regular course of promotion, he received his company, which transferred him to the 2nd Battalion, and, serving with it at the battle of Waterloo, he lost his sound arm by one of the last shots that was fired in that bloody field.

As soon as he had recovered from this last wound he rejoined us in Paris, and, presenting himself before the Duke of Wellington in his usual straight-forward manly way, said, "Here I am, my lord; I have no longer an arm left to wield for my country, but I still wish to be allowed to serve it as I best can!"

The Duke duly appreciated the diamond before him, and as there were several captains in the regiment, senior to MacCulloch, his Grace, with due regard to their feelings, desired the commanding officer to ascertain whether they would not consider it a cause of complaint if MacCulloch were recommended for a brevet majority, as it was out of his power to do it for everyone, and, to the honour of all concerned, there was not a dissentient voice. He, therefore, succeeded to the brevet, and was afterwards promoted to a majority, I think, in a veteran battalion.

He was soon after on a visit in London, living at a hotel, when one afternoon he was taken suddenly ill; the feeling to him was an unusual one, and he immediately sent for a physician, and told him that be cared not for the consequences, but insisted on having his candid opinion on his case.

The medical man accordingly told him at once, that his case was an extraordinary one—that he might within an hour or two recover from it, or within an hour or two he might be no more.

MacCullach, with his usual coolness, gave a few directions as to the future, and calmly awaited the result, which terminated fatally within the time predicted—and thus perished, in the prime of life, the gallant MacCulluch, who was alike an honour to his country and his profession.

CHAPTER 5

A Fierce Attack Upon Hairs

After the action of the Coa the enemy quickly possessed themselves of the fortress of Almeida, when there remained nothing between Massena and his kingdom but the simple article of Lord Wellington's army, of which he calculated he would be able to superintend the embarkation within the time requisite for his infantry to march to Lisbon. He therefore put his legions in motion to pay his distinguished adversary that last mark of respect

The Wellingtonians retired slowly before them, showing their teeth as often as favourable opportunities offered, and several bitter bites they gave before they turned at bay—first on the heights of Busaco, and finally and effectually on those of Torres Vedras.

The troops of all arms composing the rearguard conducted themselves admirably throughout the whole of that retreat, for although the enemy did not press them so much as they might have done, yet they were at all times in close contact, and many times in actual combat, and it was impossible to say which' was the most distinguished—the splendid service of the horse artillery, the dashing conduct of the dragoons, or the unconquerable steadiness and bravery of the infantry.

It was a sort of military academy which is not open for instruction every day in the year, nor was it one which every fond mamma would choose to send her darling boy to, although it was calculated to lead to immortal honours. A youngster (if he did not stop a bullet by the way) might commence his studies in, such a place with nothing but "the soft down peeping through the white skin," and be entitled to the respect due to a beard or a bald head before he saw the end of it

It is curious to remark how fashions change and how the change affects the valour of the man too. The dragoon, since the close of the war, has worn all his hair below the head and none on the top of it, and how fiercely he fought in defence of his whiskers the other day when some of the regiments were ordered to be shaved, as if the debility of Samson was likely to be the result of the operation.

My stars! but I should be glad to know what the old Royal Heavies or Fourteenth and Sixteenth Lights cared about hairs at the period I speak of, when with their bare faces they went boldly in and bearded muzzles that seemed fenced with furze bushes; and while it was "damned be he who first cries hold—enough!" they did hold enough too, sometimes bringing in every man his bird, *mustachoes* and all. In those days they seemed to put more faith in their good right hand than in a cart-load of whiskers, for with it and their open English countenances they carved for themselves a name as British dragoons, which they were too proud to barter for any other.

Every attempt at rearing a moustache among the British in those days was treated with sovereign contempt, no matter how aristocratic the soil on which it was sown. But, to do justice to everybody I must say that, to the best of my recollection, a crop was seldom seen but on the lips of nobodies.

It was in the course of this retreat, as I mentioned in a former work, that I first joined Lord Wellington's army, and I remember being remarkably struck with the order, the confidence, and the daring spirit which seemed to animate all ranks of those among whom it was my good fortune to be cast. Their confidence in their illustrious chief was unbounded, and they seemed to feel satisfied that it only rested with him any day to say to his opponent, "thus far shalt thou come, but no farther;" and, if a doubt on the subject had rested with any one before, the battle of Busaco removed it, for the Portuguese troops having succeeded in beating their man, it confirmed them in their own good opinion, and gave increased confidence to the whole allied army.

I am now treading on the heels of my former narrative, and although it did not include the field of Busaco, yet, as I have already stated, it is foreign to my present purpose to enter into any details of the actions in which we were engaged, farther than they may serve to illustrate such anecdotes, as appear to me to be likely to amuse the reader. I shall therefore pass over the present one, merely remarking that to a military man, one of the most interesting spectacles which took place there, was the light division taking up their ground the day before in the face of the enemy. They had remained too long in their advanced position on the morning of the 25th of September while the enemy's masses were gathering around them; but Lord Wellington fortunately came up before they were too far committed and put them in immediate retreat under his own personal direction. Nor, as Napier says:

"Was there a moment to lose, for the enemy with incredible rapidity brought up both infantry and guns, and fell on so briskly that all the skill of the general and the readiness of the excellent troops composing the rear guard, could scarcely prevent the division from being dangerously engaged. Howbeit, a series of rapid and beautiful movements, a sharp cannonade, and an hour's march, brought everything back in good order to the great position."

On the day of the battle (the 27th) the French General Simon, who led the attack upon our division, was wounded and taken prisoner, and as they were bringing him in he raved furiously for General Crawford, daring him to single combat, but as he was already a prisoner there would have been but little wit in indulging him in his humour.

In the course of the afternoon his baggage was brought in under a flag of truce, accompanied by a charm to sooth the savage breast, in the shape of a very beautiful little Spanish girl, who I have no doubt succeeded in tranquillizing his pugnacious disposition. I know not what rank she held on his establishment, but conclude that she was his niece, for I have observed that in Spain the prettiest girl in every gentleman's house is the niece.

The *padres* particularly are the luckiest fellows in the world in having the handsomest brothers and sisters of any men living,— not that I have seen the brother or the sister of any one of them, but then I have seen nine hundred and ninety-nine *padres*, and each had his niece at the head of his establishment, and I know not how it happened but she was always the prettiest girl in the parish.

It was generally the fate of troops arriving from England, to join the army at an unhappy period—at a time when easy stages and refreshment after the voyage were particularly wanted and never to be had. The marches at this period were harassing and severe, and the company with which I had just arrived were much distressed to keep pace with the old campaigners—they made a tolerable scramble for a day or two, but by the time they arrived at the lines the greater part had been obliged to be mounted.

Nevertheless, when it became Massena's turn to tramp out of Portugal a few months after, we found them up to their work and with as few stragglers as the best. Marching is an art to be acquired only by habit, and one in which the strength or agility of the animal, man, has but little to do. I have seen Irishmen (and all sorts of countrymen) in their own country, taken from the plough-tail—huge, athletic, active fellows, who would think nothing of doing forty or fifty miles in the course of the day as countrymen—see these men placed in the rank as recruits with knapsacks on their backs and a musket over their shoulders, And in the first march they are dead beat before they get ten miles.

I have heard many disputes on the comparative campaigning powers of tall and short men, but as far as my own experience goes I have never seen any difference. If a tall man happens to break down it is immediately noticed to the disadvantage of his class, but if the same misfortune befalls a short one, it is not looked upon as being anything remarkable. The effective powers of both in fact depend upon the nature of the building.

The most difficult and at the same time the most important duty to teach a young soldier on first coming into active service, is how to take care of himself. It is one which, in the first instance, requires the unwearied attention of the officer, but he is amply repaid in the long run, for when the principle is once instilled into him, it is duly appreciated, and he requires no farther trouble. In our battalion, during the latter years of the war, it was a mere matter of form inspecting the men on parade, for they knew too well the advantages of having their arms and ammunition at all times in proper order to neglect them, so that after several weeks marching and fighting, I have never seen them on their first ordinary parade after their arrival in quarters, but they were fit for the most rigid examination of the greatest Martinet that ever looked through the ranks. The only thing that required the officers' attention was their necessaries, for as money was scarce, they were liable to be bartered for strong waters.

On service as everywhere else, there is a time for all things, but the time there being limited and very uncertain, the difficulty is to learn how to make the most of it.

The first and most important part lies with the officer, and he cannot do better than borrow a leaf out of General Crawfurd's book, to learn how to prevent straggling, and to get his men to the end of their day's work with the least possible delay.

The young soldier when he first arrives in camp or bivouac will (unless forced to do otherwise) always give in to the languor and fatigue which oppresses him, and fall asleep. He awakens most probably after dark, cold and comfortless. He would gladly eat some of the undressed meat in his haversack, but he has no fire on which to cook it. He would gladly shelter himself in one of the numerous huts which have arisen around him since he fell asleep, but as he lent no hand in the building he is thrust out.

He attempts at the eleventh hour to do as others have done, but the time has gone by, for all the materials that were originally within reach, have already been appropriated by his more active neighbours, and there is nothing left for him but to pass the remainder of the night as he best can, in hunger, in cold, and in discomfort, and he marches before daylight in the morning without having enjoyed either rest or refreshment. Such is often the fate of young regiments for a longer period than would be believed, filling the hospitals and leading to all manner of evils.

On the other band, see the old soldiers come to their ground. Let their feelings of fatigue be great or small, they are no sooner suffered to leave the ranks than every man rushes to secure whatever the neighbourhood affords as likely to contribute towards his comfort for the night. Swords, hatchets, and bill-kooks are to be seen hewing and hacking at every tree and bush within reach, huts are quickly reared, fires are quickly blazing, and while the camp kettle is boiling, or the pound of beef frying, the tired, but happy souls, are found toasting their toes around the cheerful blaze, recounting their various adventures until the fire has done the needful, when they fall on like men, taking especial care, however, that whatever their inclinations may be, they consume no part of the provision which properly belongs to the morrow.

The meal finished, they arrange their accoutrements in readiness for any emergency, (caring little for the worst that can befall them for the next twenty-four hours,) when they dispose themselves for rest, and be their allowance of sleep long or short, they enjoy it; for it does one's heart good to see "the rapture of repose that's there."

In actual battle, young soldiers are apt to have a feeling, (from which many old ones are not exempt,) namely, that they are but insignificant characters—only an humble individual out of many thousands, and that his conduct, be it good or bad, can have little influence over the fate of the day. This is a monstrous mistake, which it ought to be the duty of every military writer to endeavour to correct; for in battle as elsewhere, no man is insignificant unless he chooses to make himself so.

The greater part of the victories on record, I believe, may be traced to the individual gallantry of a very small portion of the troops engaged; and if it were possible to take a microscopic view of that small portion, there is reason to think that the whole of the glory might be found to rest with a very few individuals.

Military men in battle may be classed under three disproportionate heads,—a very small class who consider themselves insignificant—a very large class who content themselves with doing their duty, without going beyond it—and a tolerably large class who do their best, many of which are great men without knowing it. One example in the history of a private soldier will establish all that I have advanced on the subject

In one of the first smart actions that I ever was in I was a young officer in command of experienced soldiers, and, therefore, found myself compelled to be an observer rather than an active leader in the scene. We were engaged in a very hot skirmish, and had driven the enemy's light troops for a considerable distance with great rapidity, when we were at length stopped by some of their regiments in line, which opened such a terrific fire within a few yards, that it obliged everyone to shelter himself as he best could among the inequalities of the ground and the sprinkling of the trees which the place afforded.

We remained inactive for about ten minutes amidst a shower of balls that seemed to be almost like a hail storm, and when at the very worst, when it appeared, to me to be certain death to quit the cover, a young scampish fellow of the name of Priestly, at the adjoining tree, started out from behind it, saying, "Well! I'll be hanged if I'll be bothered any longer behind a tree, so here's at you," and with that he banged off his rifle in the face of his foes, reloading very deliberately, while everyone right and left followed his example, and the enemy, panic struck, took to their heels without firing another shot. The action requires no comment, the individual did not seem to be aware that he had any merit in what he did, but it is nevertheless a valuable example for those who are disposed to study causes and effects in the art of war.

In that same action I saw an amusing instance of the ruling passion for sport predominating over a soldier: a rifleman near me was in the act of taking aim at a Frenchman when a hare crossed between them, the muzzle of the rifle mechanically followed the hare in preference, and, as she was doubling into our lines, I had just time to strike up the piece with my sword before he drew the trigger, or he roost probably would have shot one of our own people, for he was so intent upon his game that he had lost sight of everything else.

Chapter 6

Reaping Golden Opinions Out of a Dung-Hill

I have taken so many flights from our line of retreat in search of the fanciful, that I can only bring my readers back to our actual position, by repeating the oft told tale that our army pulled up in the lines of Torres Vedras to await Massena's farther pleasure; for, whether he was to persevere in his intended compliment of seeing us on board ship, or we were to return it by seeing him out of Portugal again, was still somewhat doubtful; and, until the point should be decided, we make ourselves as comfortable as circumstances would permit, and that was pretty well.

Every young officer, on entering a new stage in his profession, let him fancy himself ever so acute, is sure to become for a time the butt of the old hands. I was the latest arrived at the time I speak of, and of course shared the fate of others, but as the only hoax that I believe they ever tried upon me, turned out a profitable one, I had less cause for soreness than falls to the lot of green-horns in general. It consisted in an officer, famous for his waggery, coming up to me one morning and mentioning that he had just been taking a ride over a part of the mountain, (which he pointed out,) where he had seen a wild horse grazing, and that he had tried hard to catch him, but lamented that he had been unable to succeed, for that he was a very handsome one!

As the country abounded in wolves and other wild characters, I did not see why there should not also be wild horses, and, therefore, greedily swallowed the bait, for I happened not only to be in especial want of a horse, but of dollars to buy one; and arming myself accordingly with a halter and the assistance of an active rifleman, I proceeded to the place, and very quickly converted the wild horse into a tame one!

It was not until a year after that I discovered the hoax by which I had unwittingly become the stealer of some unfortunate man's horse; but, in the mean time, it was to the no small mortification of my waggish friend, that he saw me mounted upon him when we marched a few days, after, for he had anticipated a very different result.

The saddle which sat between me and the horse on that occasion ought not to be overlooked; for, take it all in all, I never expect to see its like again. I found it in our deserted house at Arruda; the seat was as soft as a pillow, and covered with crimson silk velvet, beautifully embroidered, and gilt round the edges. I knew not for what description of rider it had been intended, but I can answer for it that it was exceedingly comfortable in dry weather, and that in wet it possessed all the good properties of a sponge, keeping the rider cool and comfortable.

While we remained in the lines, there was a small thatched, mud-walled, deserted cottage under the hill near our company's post, which we occasionally used as a shelter from the sun or the rain, and some of our men, in prowling about one day, discovered two massive silver salvers concealed in the thatch. The captain of the company very properly ordered them to be taken care of, in the hope that their owner would come to claim them, while the soldiers in the mean time continued very eager in their researches in the neighbourhood, in expectation of making farther discoveries, in which, however, they were unsuccessful.

After we had altogether abandoned the cottage, a Portuguese gentleman arrived one day and told us that he was the owner of the place, and that he had some plate concealed there which he wished permission to remove. Captain —— immediately desired the salvers to be given to him, concluding that they were what he had come in search of; but on looking at them he said they did not belong to him, that what he wished to remove was concealed under the dunghill, and he accordingly proceeded there and dug out about a cart load of gold and silver articles which he carried off, while our unsuccessful searchers stood by, cursing their mutual understandings which had suffered such a prize to slip through their fingers and many an innocent heap of manure was afterwards torn to pieces in consequence of that morning's lesson.

Massena having abandoned his desolated position in the early part of November, the fifteenth of that month saw me seated on my cloth of crimson and gold, taking a look at the French rear guard, which, under Junot, was in position between Cartaxo and El Valle. A cool November breeze whistled through an empty stomach, which the gilded outside was insufficient to satisfy. Our chief of division was red hot to send us over to warm ourselves with the French fires, and had absolutely commenced the movement when the opportune arrival of Lord Wellington put a stop to it; for, as it was afterwards discovered, we should have burnt our fingers.

While we, therefore, awaited farther orders on the road-side, I was amused to see General Slade, who commanded the brigade of cavalry attached to us, order up his sumpter mule, and borrowing our doctor's medical panniers, which he placed in the middle of the road by way of a table, he, with the assistance of his orderly dragoon, undid several packages, and presently displayed a set-out which was more than enough to tempt the cupidity of the hungry beholders, consisting of an honest-looking loaf of bread, a thundering large tongue, and the fag end of a ham—a bottle of porter, and half a one of brandy.

The bill of fare is still as legibly written on my remembrance as on the day that I first saw it—for such things cannot be, and overcome us like the vision of a Christmas' feast, without especial longings for an invitation; but we might have sighed and looked, and sighed again, for our longings were useless—our doctor, with his usual politeness, made sundry attempts to insinuate himself upon the hospitable notice of the general, by endeavouring to arrange the panniers in a more classical shape for his better accommodation, for which good service he received bow for bow, with a considerable quantity of thanks into the bargain, which, after he had done his best, (and that was no joke,) still left him the general's debtor on the score of civility.

When the doctor had failed, the attempt of any other individual became a forlorn hope; but nothing seems desperate to a British soldier, and two thorough going ones, the commanders of the Twelfth and Fourteenth Light Dragoons, (Colonels Ponsonby and Harvey,) whose olfactory nerves, at a distance of some hundred yards, having snuffed up the tainted air, eagerly followed the scent, and came to a dead point before the general and his panniers.

But although they had flushed their game they did not succeed in bagging it; for while the general gave them plenty of his own tongue, the deuce take the slice did he offer of the bullock's—and as soon as he had satisfied his appetite he very deliberately bundled up the fragments, and shouted to horse, for the enemy had by this time withdrawn from our front, and joined the main body of the army on the heights of Santarem. We closed up to them, and exchanged a few civil shots—a ceremony which cannot be dispensed with between contending armies on first taking up their ground, for it defines their territorial rights, and prevents future litigation.

Daylight next morning showed that, though they had passed a restless night, they were not disposed to extend their walk unless compelled to it, for their position, formidable by nature, had, by their unwearied activity, become more so by art—the whole crest of it being already fenced with an abbatis of felled trees, and the ground turned up in various directions.

One of our head-quarter staff-officers came to take a look at them in the early part of the morning, and, assuming a superior knowledge of all that was passing, said that they had nothing there but a rear-guard, and that we should shove them from it in the course of the day—upon which our brigadier, (Sir Sidney Beckwith,) who had already scanned everything with his practised eye, dryly remarked, in his usual homely but emphatic language, "It was a gay strong rear-guard that built that abbatis last night!" And so it proved, for their whole army had been employed in its construction, and there they remained for the next four months.

The company to which I belonged, (and another,) had a deserted farming establishment turned over for our comfort and convenience during the period that it might suit the French marshal to leave us in the enjoyment thereof. It was situated on a slope of the hill overlooking the bridge of Santarem, and within range of the enemy's sentries, and near the end of it was one of the finest aloes I have ever seen, certainly not less than twelve or fourteen feet high.

Our mansion was a long range of common thatched building—one end was a kitchen—next to it a parlour, which became also the drawing and sleeping-room of two captains, with their six jolly subs—a doorway communicated from thence to the barn, which constituted the greater part of the range, and lodged our two hundred men. A small apartment at the other extremity, which was fitted up for a wine-press, lodged our non-commissioned officers; while in the back- ground we had accommodation for our cattle, and for sundry others of the domestic tribes, had we had the good fortune to be furnished with them.

The doorway between the officers' apartment and that of the soldiers showed, (what is so very common on the seat of war,) when "a door is not a door," but a shovel full of dust and ashes— the hinges had resisted manfully by clinging to the doorpost, but a fiery end had overtaken the timber, and we were obliged to fill up the vacuum with what loose stones we could collect in the neighbourhood; it was, nevertheless, so open, that a hand might be thrust through it in every direction, and, of course, the still small voices on either side of the partition were alike audible to all.

I know not what degree of amusement the soldiers derived from the proceedings on our side of the wall, but I know that the jests, the tales, and the songs, from their side, constituted our greatest enjoyment during the many long winter nights that it was our fate to remain there.

The early part of their evenings was generally spent in witticisms and tales; and, in conclusion, by way of a lullaby, some long-winded fellow commenced one of those everlasting ditties in which soldiers and sailors delight so much—they are all to the same tune, and the subject, (if one may judge by the tenor of the first ninety-eight verses,) was battle, murder, or sudden death; but I never yet survived until the catastrophe, although I have often, to attain that end, stretched my waking capacities to the utmost. I have sometimes heard a fresh arrival from England endeavour to astonish their unpolished ears with "the white blossomed sloe," or some such refined melody, but it was invariably coughed down as instantaneously as if it had been the sole voice of a conservative amidst a select meeting of radicals.

The wit and the humour of the rascals were amusing beyond anything—and to see them next morning drawn up as mute as mice, and as stiff as lamp-posts, it was a regular puzzler to discover on which post the light had shone during the bygone night, knowing as we did, that there were at least a hundred original pages for Joe Miller, incased within the head-pieces then before us.

Their stories, too, were quite unique—one, (an Englishman,) began detailing the unfortunate termination of his last matrimonial speculation. He had got a pass one day to go from Shorncliffe to Folkestone, and on the way he fell in with one of the finest young women "as ever he seed! my eye, as we say in Spain, if she was not a wapper; with a pair of cheeks like cherries, and shanks as clean as my ramrod; she was bounding over the downs like a young colt, and faith, if she would not have been with her heels clean over my head if I hadn't caught her up and demanded a parley.

"O, Jem, man, but she was a nice creature! and all at once got so fond of me too, that there was no use waiting; and so we settled it all that self same night, and on the next morning we were regularly spliced, and I carries her home to a hut which Corporal Smith and I hired, behind the barrack for eighteen pence a week. Well! I'll be blessed if I wasn't as happy as a shilling a day and my wife could make me for two whole days; but the next morning, just before parade, while Nancy was toasting a slice of tommy[1] for our breakfast, who should darken our door but the carcass of a great sea marine, who began blinking his goggle eyes like an owl in a goosebury bush, as if he didn't see nothing outside on them; when all at once Nancy turned, and, my eye, what a squall she set up as she threw the toast in the fire, and upset my tinful of crowdy, while she twisted her arms round his neck like a vice, and began kissing him at no rate, he all the time blubbering, like a bottle-nose in a shoal, about flesh of his flesh, and bones of his bones, and all the like o'that.

"Well! says I to myself, says I, this is very queer anyhow—and then I eyes the chap a bit, and then says I to him, (for I began to feel somehow at peeing my wife kissed all round before my face without saying by your leave,) an' says I to him, (rather angrily,) look ye, Mr. Marine, if you don't take your ugly mouth farther off from my wife, I'll just punch it with the butt end of my rifle! thunder and oons, you great sea lobster that you are, don't you see that I married her only two days ago just as she stands, bones and all, and you come at this time o'day to claim a part on her!"

The marine, however, had come from the wars as a man of peace—he had already been at her father's, and learnt all that had befallen her, and, in place of provoking the rifleman's farther ire, he sought an amicable explanation, which was immediately entered into.

It appeared that Nancy and he had been married some three years before; that (he sloop of war to which he belonged was ordered to the West Indies, and while cruising on that station an unsuccessful night attempt was made to cut out an enemy's craft from under a battery, in the course of which the that in which he was embarked having been sent to the bottom with a thirty-

---

1. Brown loaf.

two pound shot, he was supposed to have gone along with it, and to be snugly reposing in Davy Jones's locker. His present turn up, however, proved his going down to have been a mistake, as he had succeeded in saving his life at the expense of his liberty, for the time being; but the vessel, on her voyage to France, was captured by a British frigate bound for India, and the royal marine became once more the servant of his lawful sovereign.

In the mean while Nancy had been duly apprised of his supposed fate by some of his West Indian shipmates—she was told that she might still hope; but Nancy had no idea of holding on by anything so precarious—she was the wife of a sailor, had been frequently on board a ship, and had seen how arbitrarily everything, even time itself, is made subservient to their purposes, and she determined to act upon the same principle, so that, as the first lieutenant authorizes it to be eight o'clock after the officer of the watch has reported that it is so, in like manner did Nancy, when her husband was reported dead, order that he should be so; but it would appear that her commands had about as much influence over her husband's fate as the first lieutenant's had over time, from his making his untoward appearance so early in her second honey-moon.

As brevity formed no part of the narrator's creed, I have merely given an outline of the marine's history, such as I understood it, and shall hasten to the conclusion in the same manner.

The explanation over, a long silence ensued—each afraid to pop the question, which must be popped, of whose wife was Nancy? and when, at last, it did come out, it was more easily asked than answered, for, notwithstanding all that had passed, they had continued both to be deeply enamoured of their mutual wife, and she of both, nor could a voluntary resignation be extracted from either of them, so that they were eventually obliged to trust the winning or the losing of that greatest of all earthly blessings, (a beloved wife,) to the undignified decision of the toss of a halfpenny.

The marine won, and carried off the prize—while the rifleman declared that he had never yet forgiven himself for being cheated out of his half, for he feels convinced that the marine had come there prepared with a ha'penny that had two tails.

The tail of the foregoing story was caught up by a *Patlander* with—"Well! the devil fetch me if I would have let her gone that way anyhow, if the marine had brought twenty tails with his ha'penny!— but you see I was kicked out of the only wife I never had without ere a chance of being married at all.

"Kitty, you see, was an apprentice to Miss Crump, who keeps that thundering big milliner's shop in Sackville Street, and I was Mike Kinahan's boy at the next door—so you see, whenever it was Kitty's turn to carry out one of them great blue boxes with thingumbobs for the ladies, faiths I always contrived to steal away for a bit, to give Kitty a lift, and the darling looked so kind and so grateful for't that I was at last quite kilt!"

I must here take up the thread of Paddy's story for the same reasons given in the last, and inform the reader that, though he himself had received the finishing blow, he was far from satisfied that Kitty's case was equally desperate, for, notwithstanding her grateful looks, they continued to be more like those of a mistress to an obliging servant than of a sweetheart. As for a kiss, he could not get anything like one even by coaxing, and the greatest bliss he experienced, in the course of his love making, was in the interchange among the fingers which the frequent transfer of the band-box permitted, and which Pat declared went quite through and through him.'

Matters, however, were far from keeping pace with Paddy's inclinations, and feeling convinced at last, that there must be a rival in the case, he determined to watch her very closely, in order to have his suspicions removed, or, if confirmed, to give his rival such a pounding as should prevent his ever crossing his path again. Accordingly, seeing her one evening leave the shop better dressed than usual, he followed at a distance, until opposite the post-office, when he saw her joined, (evidently by appointment,) by a tall well-dressed spalpeen of a fellow, and they then proceeded at a smart pace up the adjoining street—Paddy followed close behind in the utmost indignation, but before he had time to make up his mind as to which of his rival's bones he should begin by breaking, they all at once turned into a doorway, which Paddy found belonged to one of those dancing shops so common in Dublin.

Determined not to be foiled in that manner, and ascertaining that a decent suit of toggery and five tin-pennies in his pocket would ensure him a free admission, he lost no time in equipping in his Sunday's best, and having succeeded in borrowing the needful for the occasion out of his master's till, he sallied forth bent on conquest.

Paddy was ushered, up stairs into the ball-room with all due decorum, but that commodity took leave of him at the door; for the first thing he saw on entering, was his mistress and his rival, within a yard of him, whirling in the mazes of a country dance. Pat's philosophy was unequal to the sight, and throwing one arm round the young lady's waist, and giving her partner a douse in the chops with the other, it made as satisfactory a change in their relative positions as he could have reasonably desired, by sending his rival in a continuation of his waltzing movement, to the extremity of the room to salute the wall at the end of it.

Pat, however, was allowed but brief space to congratulate himself on his successful debut in a ball-room, for in the next instant he found himself most ungracefully propelled through the doorway, by sundry unseen hands, which had grasped him tightly by the scruff of the neck, and on reaching the top of the staircase, he felt as if a hundred feet had given a simultaneous kick which raised him like a balloon for a short distance, and then away he went heels over head towards the bottom.

It so happened at this particular moment, that three gentlemen very sprucely dressed, had just paid their money and were in the act of ascending, taking that opportunity, as gentlemen generally do, of arranging their hair and adjusting their frills to make their *entré* the more bewitching, and it is therefore unnecessary to say that the descent of our aeronaut not only disturbed the economy of their wigs, but carried all three to the bottom with the impetus of three sacks of potatoes.

Paddy's temperament had somewhat exceeded a madman's heat before he commenced his aerial flight, and, as may be imagined, it had not much cooled in its course, so that when he found himself safely landed, and, as luck would have it, on the top of one of the unfortunates, he very unceremoniously began taking the change out of his head for all the disasters of the night, and having quickly demolished the nose and bunged up both eyes, he (seeing nothing more to be done thereabouts) next proceeded to pound the unfortunate fellow's head against the floor, before they succeeded in lugging him off to finish his love-adventure in the watch-house.

That night was the last of Paddy's love and of his adventures in the City of Dublin. His friends were respectable of their class, and on the score of his former good conduct, succeeded in appeasing the aggrieved parties, and inducing them to withdraw from the prosecution on condition that he quitted the city for ever, and, when he had time to reflect on the position in which the reckless doings of the few hours had placed him, he was but too happy to subscribe to it, and, passing over to Liverpool, enlisted with a recruiting party of ours, and became an admirable soldier.

Having given two of the soldiers' stories, it may probably be amusing to my readers to hear one from our side of the wall. It was related by one of our officers, a young Scotchman, who was a native of the place, and while I state that I give it to the best of my recollection, I could have wished; as the tale is a true one, that it had fallen into the hands of the late lamented author of Waverley, who would have done greater justice to its merits.

THE OFFICER'S STORY

On the banks of the river Carron, near the celebrated village of that name, which shows its glowing fields of fiery furnaces, stirred by ten thousand imps of darkness, as if all the devils from the nether world there held perpetual revels, toasting their red hot irons and twisting them into all manner of fantastic shapes—tea-kettles, ten-pounders, and ten penny nails—I say, that near that village—not in the upper and romantic region of it, where old Norval of yore fished up his basketful of young Norvals- but about a mile below where the river winds through the low country, in a bight of it there stands a stately two-story house, dashed with pale pink, and having a tall chimney at each end, sticking up like a pair of asses' ears.

The main building is supported by a brace of wings not large enough to fly away with it, but standing .in about the same proportions that the elbows of an easy chair do to its back. The hall door is flanked on each side by a pillar of stone as thick as my leg, and over it there is a niche in the wall which in the days of its glory might have had the honour of lodging Neptune or Nicodemus, but is now devoted exclusively to the loves of the sparrows.

Viewed at a little distance the mansion still wears a certain air of imposing gentility— -looking like the substantial retreat of one who had well feathered his nest upon the high seas, or as an adventurer in foreign lands. But a nearer approach shows that the day of its glory has long departed, the winds are howling through the glassless casements, the roof is plastered by the pigeons, the pigs and the poultry are galloping at large over the ruins of the garden wall, luxuriating in its once costly shrubbery, and a turkey is most likely seen at the hall-door, staring the visitor impertinently in the face, and blustering as if he would say, "If you want me, you must down with the dust."

Had that same turkey, however, lived some six score years before, in the life-time, or in the death-time of the last of its lairds, he would have found himself compelled to gabble to another tune; for in place of being allowed to insult his guests in his master's hall, he would have been called upon to share his merry-thought for their amusement at the festive board.

That the last laird of Abbots-Haugh had lived like a right good country gentleman all of the olden days, the manner of his death will testify; for though his living history is lost in the depth of time, his death is still alive in the recollections of our existing great grandfathers. He was, to the best of my belief wifeless and relationless, nevertheless, when the time approached that "the old man he must die," he did as all prudent men do, made his temporal arrangements previous to the settling of that last debt which he owed to nature.

The laird, it appeared, was not haunted by the fears of most men, which forbid the inspection of their last testaments, until the last shovelful of earth has secured their remains from the wrath of disappointed expectants, and from a conscious dread, too, that the only tears that would otherwise be shed at their obsequies, would be by the undertaker and his assistants with their six big black horses; but the laird, as before said, was altogether another manner of man, and his last request was, that certain persons should consider themselves his executors, that they should open his will the moment the breath was out of his body, and that they should see his last injunctions faithfully executed as they hoped that he should rest calmly in his grave.

The laird quietly gave up the ghost, and his last wish was complied with; when, to the no small astonishment of the executors, the only bequest which his will decreed was, that every man within a given distance of his residence was to be invited to the funeral, and that they were all to be filled blind drunk before the commencement of the procession!

This was certainly one of the most jovial wills that was ever made by a dying man, and it was acted upon to the letter.

The appointed day arrived, and so did the guests too; and although the invitations had only extended to the men, yet did their wives, like considerate folks as they always are, reflect that a dying man cannot have all his wits about him, and had any one but taken the trouble to remind him that there were such things as angels even in this world, they would no doubt have been included, and with that view of the case they considered it their duty to give their aid in the mournful ceremony.

The duties of the day at length began as was usual on those days, by—

One mile prayers and half mile graces,

to which the assembled multitude impatiently listened with

their

Toom wames and lang wry faces.

That ceremony over, they proceeded with all due diligence to honour the last request of the departed laird.

The droves of bullocks, sheep, and turkeys, which had been sacrificed for the occasion, were served up at mid-day, and as every description of foreign and British wines, spirits, and ales flowed in pailsful, the executors indulged in the very reasonable expectation that the whole party would be sufficiently glorious to authorize their proceeding with their last duty sp as to have it over before dark: but they had grossly miscalculated the capacities of their guests, for even at dusk when they considered themselves compelled to put the procession in motion at all hazards, it was found that many of them were not more than "half seas over."

The distance from Abbots-Haugh to the dormitory of the parish church is nearly two miles, the first half of the road runs still between two broad deep ditches which convey the drainings of these lowlands into the river; the other .half is now changed by the intersection of the great canal, but an avenue formed by two quick-set hedge-rows still marks its former line.

Doctor MacAdam had not in those days begun to disturb the bowels of the harmless earth, by digging for stones wherewith to deface its surface, so that the roads were perfect evergreens, (when nobody travelled upon them,) but at the period I speak of, a series of wet weather and perpetual use had converted them into a sort of hodge-podge, which contributed nothing towards maintaining the gravity of the unsteady multitude now in motion, so that although the hearse started with some five or six hundred followers, all faithful and honest in their purpose, to see the end of the ceremony, there were not above as many dozens who succeeded in following it into the churchyard, which it reached about midnight.

These few, however, went on in the discharge of their duty, and proceeded to remove the coffin from the hearse to its intended receptacle, but to their utter consternation there was no longer a coffin or a corpse there!

Tarn O'Shanter lived a generation later than the period of my history, and I believe that there were few Scotchmen even in his days who were altogether free from supernatural dread, however, well primed with whisky; but certain it is, that on this occasion every bonnet that was not on a bald head rose an inch or two higher, and many of them were pitched off altogether, as they began to reason (where reason there was none) as to the probable flight of the coffin; and though they were unanimously of opinion that it had gone no one knew where, yet they at last agreed that it was, nevertheless, a duty they owed the deceased to go back to Abbots-Haugh and inquire whether the laird had not returned.

They accordingly provided themselves with lanterns, and examined all parts of the road on their way back, which was easily traced by the sleeping and besotted persons of the funeral party which formed a continuous link from the one place to the other—some lying in the road—some stuck fast in the hedges, but the majority three parts drowned in the ditches. When our return party arrived near the site of the present distillery, which happened to be the deepest part of the way, they heard something floundering at a frightful rate at the edge of a pool of water on the roadside, and which, on examination, proved to be a huge old woman who was in the habit of supplying the farmers in that part of the country with loaf bread for their Sunday's breakfasts; she was holding on fiercely by what appeared to be the stump of a tree, while her nether end was immersed in the water; but when they went to pull her out, they found to their delight and astonishment that she was actually holding on by the end of the lost coffin, which had fallen at the edge of the pool.

Old Nelly could give no information as to how it got there, she had some recollection of having been shoved into the hearse at first starting, but knew nothing more until she found herself up to her oxters, in the water, holding fast by something—that she had bawled until she was hoarse, and had now nothing but a kick left to tell the passersby that a poor creature was perishing:. She had most probably been reposing on the coffin as a place of rest, and been jolted a step beyond it when the two fell out

A council was now called to determine the proper mode of farther proceeding, when it was moved and carried that a vote of censure be passed upon the executors for having failed to fulfil the provisions of the laird's will, for in place of being drunk, as they ought to have been, they were all shamefully sober; secondly, that it was in vain to repeat the attempt to bury him until the conditions upon which he died were complied with, for he had pledged himself not to rest quiet in his grave if it was neglected, and it was evident from what he had already done that he was not to be humbugged, but would again slip through their fingers unless justice was done to his memory; and it was therefore finally resolved that the laird be carried back to his own hall, there to lie in state until the terms of his testament were confirmed and ratified beyond dispute.

Back, therefore, they went to Abbots-Haugh, and set themselves again right honestly to work, as good and loyal vassals to obey their master's last behests, and that they at length succeeded in laying the restless spirit may be inferred from the fact that it was the afternoon of the third day from that time before the party felt themselves in a condition to renew the attempt to complete the ceremony; however, it was then done effectually, as for fear of accidents, and not to lose sight of the coffin a second time, as many as there was room for took post on the top of it, provided with the means of finishing, at their destination, what the defunct might have considered underdone on their departure.

And accordingly when they had at last succeeded in depositing the coffin within the family vault, and had set the bricklayers to work, they renewed their revels in the churchyard, until they finally saw the tomb closed over one of the most eccentric characters that ever went into it.

I shall now take leave of tales, and recommence the narration of passing events by mentioning that while we remained at Valle, one of our officers made an amusing attempt to get up a pack of hounds. He offered a dollar a head for anything in the shape of a dog that might be brought to him, which in a very short time furnished his kennel with about fifteen couple, composed of poodles, sheep-dogs, curs, and every species but the one that was wanted.

When their numbers became sufficiently formidable to justify the hope that there might be a few noses in the crowd gifted with the sense of smelling something more game than their porridge-pots; the essay was made; but they proved a most ungrateful pack, for they were no sooner at liberty than everyone went howling away to his own home, as if a tin kettle had been tied to his tail. (A prophetic sort of feeling of what would inevitably have befallen him, had he remained a short time longer.)

Scotchmen are generally famed for the size of their noses, and I know not whether it is that on service they get too much crammed with snuff and gunpowder, or from what other cause, but certain it Is that they do not prove themselves such useful appendages to the countenance there as they do in their own country, in scenting out whatever seemeth good unto the wearer; for I remember one day, while waging war against the snipes on the flooded banks of the Rio Maior, in passing by the rear of a large country house which was occupied by the commander-in-chief of the cavalry, (Sir Stapleton Cotton,) I was quite horrified to find myself all at once amidst the ruins of at least twenty dozen of sheep's heads, unskinned and unsinged, to the utter disgrace of about two thousand highland noses belonging to the Forty- Second and Seventy-Ninth regiments, which had, all the while of their accumulation, been lodged within a mile, and not over and above well provided with that national standing dish.

I will venture to say, that had such a deposite been made any evening on the North Inch of Perth in the days of their great grandfathers, there would have been an instinctive gathering of all the clans between the Tay and Cairngorum before daylight next morning.

CHAPTER 7

Action at Foz d'Aronce

Blood and destruction shall be so in use,
And dreadful objects so familiar.
That mothers shall but smile when they behold
Their infants quartered with the hands of war.

The month of March, eighteen hundred and eleven, showed the successful workings of Lord Wellington's admirable arrangements. The hitherto victorious French army, which, under their "spoilt child of fortune," had advanced to certain conquest, were now obliged to bundle up their traps and march back again, leaving nearly half their numbers to fatten the land which they had beggared. They had fallen, too, on nameless ground, in sickness and in want, and without a shot, by which their friends and relatives might otherwise have proudly pointed to the graves they filled,

Portugal, at that period, presented a picture of sadness and desolation which it is sickening to think of—its churches spoliated, its villages fired, and its towns depopulated.

It was no uncommon sight, on entering a cottage, to see m one apartment some individuals of the same family dying of want, some perishing under the brutal treatment of their oppressors, and some (preferring death to dishonour) lying butchered upon their own hearths.

These were scenes which no Briton could behold without raising his voice in thanksgiving to the Author of all good, that the home of his childhood had been preserved from such fearful visitations; and yet how melancholy it is to reflect that even in that cherished home there should be many self-styled patriots, who not only grumble at, but would deny their country's pittance to those who devoted the best part of their lives, sacrificed their health, and cheerfully scattered their limbs in rolling the tide of battle from its door.

I lament it feelingly, but not selfishly, for as far as I am individually concerned, my country and I are quits. I passed through the fiery ordeal of these bloody times and came out scatheless. While I parted from its service on the score of expediency, it is to me a source of pride to reflect (may I be pardoned the expression) that we parted with mutual regret. That she may never again require a reunion with such an humble individual as myself may Heaven in its infinite mercy forfend; but if she does, I am happy in the feeling that I have still health and strength, and a heart and soul devoted to her cause.

Massena's retreat having again called the sword from its scabbard, where it had slumbered for months, it was long ere it had another opportunity of running to rust through idleness, seeing that it was not only in daily communication with the heads of the enemy's corps in the course of their return through Portugal, but wherever else these same heads were visible, and for a year and a half from that date they were rarely out of sight.

On the 9th, we came up with their rear-guard on a table land near Pombal. We had no force with which to make any serious attack upon it, so that it was a day's dragooning, "all cry and little wool." We had one company mixed among them from daylight until dark, but they came back to us without a scratch.

On the morning of the 11th, finding that the enemy had withdrawn from the scene of the former day's skirmish, we moved in pursuit towards the town, which they still occupied as an advanced post. Two of our companies, with some *Caçadores* and a squadron of the Royal Dragoons, made a dash into it, driving the enemy out, and along with a number of prisoners captured the baggage of young Soult.

I know not whether young Soult was the son of old Soult or

only the son of his father; all I know is, that by the letters found in his portmanteau, he was the colonel of that name.

His baggage, I remember, was mounted on a stately white horse with a Roman nose and a rat tail, which last I believe is rather an unusual appendage in a horse of that colour, but he was a waggish looking fellow, and probably had shaken all the hairs out of his tail in laughing at the contents of the portmanteau of which he was the bearer.

He and his load were brought to the hammer the same day by his captors, and excited much merriment among us. I wish that I felt myself at liberty to publish an inventory of the contents of a French officer's portmanteau, but as they excited such excess of laughter in a horse I fear it would prove fatal to my readers—not to mention (as I see written on some of the snug corners of our thoroughfares) that "decency forbids." Suffice it that it abounded in luxuries which we dreamt not of.

Next day, the 12th, in following the retiring foe we came to the field of Redinha. I have never in the course of my subsequent military career seen a more splendid picture of war than was there shown. Ney commanded the opposing force, which was formed on the table land in front of the town in the most imposing shape. We light folks were employed in the early part of the action m clearing the opposing lights from the woods which flanked his position, and in the course of an hour about thirty thousand British, as if by magic, were seen advancing, on the plain in three lines, with the order and precision of a field day: the French disappeared before them like snow under the influence of a summer's sun. The forces on both sides were handled by masters in the art.

A late lady writer (Miss Pardoe) I see has now peopled Redinha with *banditti*, and as far as my remembrance goes, they could not have selected a more favourable position, with this single but important professional drawback, that there can be but few folks thereabout worth robbing.

I know not what class of beings were its former tenants, but at the time I speak of, the curse of the MacGregors was upon them, for the retiring enemy had given

Their roofs to the flames and their flesh to the eagles,

and there seemed to be no one left to record its history.

After the peace, in 1814, 1 met, at a ball in Castel Sarrazin, the colonel who commanded the regiment opposed to us in the wood on that occasion. He confessed that he had never been so roughly handled, and had lost four hundred of his men. He was rather a rough sort of a diamond himself, and seemed anxious to keep his professional hand in practice, for he quarrelled that same night with one of his countrymen and was bled next morning with a small sword.

From Redinha we proceeded near to Condeixa, and passed that day and night on the roadside in comparative peace. Not so the next, for at Casal Nova, on the 14th, we breakfasted, dined, and supped on powder and ball.

Our general of division was on leave of absence in England during this important period, and it was our curse in the interim to fall into the hands successively of two or three of the worthiest and best of men, but whose only claims to distinction as officers was their sheet of parchment The consequence was, that whenever there was anything of importance going on, we were invariably found leaving undone those things which we ought to have done, and doing that which we ought not to have done.

On the occasion referred to we were the whole day battering our brains out against stone walls at a great sacrifice of life, whereas, had we waited with common prudence until the proper period, when the flank movements going on under the direction of our illustrious chief had begun to take effect, the whole of the loss would have been on the other side; but as it was, I am afraid that although we carried our point we were the greatest sufferers. Our battalion had to lament the loss of two very valuable officers on that occasion. Major Stewart and Lieutenant Strode.

At the commencement of the action, just as the mist of the

morning began to clear away, a section of our company was thrown forward among the skirmishers, while the other three remained in reserve behind a gentle eminence, and the officer commanding it, seeing a piece of rising ground close to the left, which gave him some uneasiness, he desired me to take a man with me to the top of it, and to give him notice if the enemy attempted any movement on that side.

We got to the top; but if we had not found a couple of good sized stones on the spot, which afforded shelter at the moment, we should never have got anywhere else; for I don't think they expended less than a thousand shots upon us in the course of a few minutes. My companion, John Rouse, a steady sturdy old rifleman, no sooner found himself snugly covered, than he lugged out his rifle to give them one in return, but the slightest exposure brought a dozen balls to the spot in an instant, and I was amused to see old Rouse, at every attempt, jerking back his head with a sort of knowing grin, as if it were only a parcel of schoolboys, on the other side, threatening him with snowballs; but seeing, at last, that his time for action was not yet come, he withdrew his rifle, and, knowing my inexperience in those matters, he very good-naturedly called to me not to expose myself looking out just then; for, said he, "there will be no moving among them while this shower continues."

When the shower ceased we found that they had also ceased to hold their formidable post, and, as quickly as may be, we were to be seen standing in their old shoes, mixed up with some of the Forty-Third, and among them the gallant Napier, the present historian of the Peninsular War, who there got a ball through his body which seemed to me to have reduced the remainder of his personal history to the compass of a simple paragraphs it nevertheless kept him but a very short while in the background.

I may here remark that the members of that distinguished family were singularly unfortunate in that way, as they were rarely ever in any serious action in which one or all of them did not get hit

The two brothers in our division were badly wounded on

this occasion, and, if I remember right, they were also at Busaco; the naval captain, (the present admiral of that name,) was there as an amateur, and unfortunately caught it on a spot where he had the last wish to be distinguished; for, accustomed to face broadsides on his native element, he had no idea of taking in a ball in any other direction than from the front, but on shore we were obliged to take them just as they came !

This severe harassing action closed only with the daylight, and left the French army wedged in the formidable pass of Miranda de Corvo.

They seemed so well in hand that some doubt was entertained whether they did not intend to burst, forth, upon us; but, as the night closed in, the masses were seen to melt, and at daylight next morning they were invisible.

I had been on picquet that night in a burning village, and the first intimation we had of their departure was by three Portuguese boys, who had been in the service of French officers, and who took the opportunity of the enemy's night march to make their escape—they seemed well fed, well dressed, and got immediate employment in our camp, and they proved themselves very faithful to their new masters. One of them continued as a servant to an officer for many years after the peace.

In the course of the morning we passed the brigade of General Nightingale, composed of Highlanders, if I remember right, who had made a flank movement to get a slice at the enemy's rear guard; but he had arrived at the critical pass a little too late.

In the afternoon we closed up to the enemy at Fez d'Aronce, and, after passing an hour in feeling for their different posts, we began to squat ourselves down for the night on the top of a bleak hill. but soon found that we had other fish to fry. Lord Wellington, having a prime nose for smelling out an enemy's blunder, no sooner came up than he discovered that Ney had left himself on the wrong side of the river, and immediately poured down upon him with our division, Picton's and Pack's Portuguese, and, after a sharp action, which did not cease until after dark, we drove him across the river with great loss.

I have often lamented in the course of the war that battalion officers, on occasions of that kind, were never intrusted with a peep behind the curtain. Had we been told before we advanced that there was but a single division in our front, with a river close behind them, we would have hunted them to death, and scarcely a man could have escaped; but, as it was, their greatest loss was occasioned by their own fears and precipitancy in taking to the river at unfordable places— for we were alike ignorant of the river, the localities, or the object of the attack; so that when we carried the position, and exerted ourselves like prudent officers to hold our men in hand, we were, from want of information, defeating the very object which had been intended, that of hunting them on to the finale.

When there is no object in view beyond the simple breaking of the heads of those opposed to us, there requires no speechification; but, on all occasions, like the one related, it ought never to be lost sight of—it is easily done—it never, by any possibility, can prove disadvantageous, and I have seen many instances in which the advantages would have been incalculable.

I shall mention as one—that three days after the battle of Vittoria, in following up the retreating foe, we found ourselves in a wood, engaged in a warm skirmish, which we concluded was occasioned by our pushing the enemy's rear guard faster than they found it convenient to travel; but, by and by, when they had disappeared, we found that we were near the junction of two roads, and that we had all the while been close in and engaged with the flank of another French division, which was retiring by a road running parallel with our own.

The road (and that there was a retiring force upon it) must, or ought to have been known to some of our staff officers, and had they only communicated their information, there was nothing to have prevented our dashing through their line of march, and there is little doubt, too, but the thousands which passed us, while we stood there exchanging shots with them, would have fallen into our hands.

The day after the action at Foz d'Aronce was devoted to repose, of which we stood much in want, for we had been marching and fighting incessantly from daylight until dark for several consecutive days, without being superabundantly provisioned; and our jackets, which had been tolerably tight fits at starting, were now beginning to sit as gracefully as sacks upon us. When wounds were abundant, however, we did not consider it a disadvantage to be low in flesh, for the poorer the subject the better the patient!

A smooth ball or a well polished sword will slip through one of your transparent gentlemen so gently that he scarcely feels it, and the holes close again of their own accord. But see the smash it makes in one of your turtle or turkey fed ones! the hospital is ruined in finding materials to reduce his inflammations, and it is ten to one if ever he comes to the scratch again.

On descending to the riverside next morning to trace the effects of the preceding night's combat, we were horrified and disgusted by the sight of a group of at least five hundred donkeys standing there hamstrung. The poor creatures looked us piteously in the face, as much as to say, "Are you not ashamed to call yourselves human beings?"

And truly we were ashamed to think that even our enemy could be capable of such refinement in cruelty, I fancy the truth was, they were unable to get them over the river, they had not time to put them to death, and, at the same time, they were resolved that we should not have the benefit of their services. Be that as it may, so disgusted and savage were our soldiers at the sight, that the poor donkeys would have been amply revenged, had fate, at that moment, placed five hundred Frenchmen in our hands, for I am confident that every one of them would have undergone the same operation.

The French having withdrawn from our front on the 16th, we crossed the sierra, at dawn of day, on the 17th; the fords were still so deep, that, as an officer with an empty haversack on my back, it was as much as I could do to flounder across it without swimming. The soldiers ballasted with their knapsacks, and the sixty rounds of ball cartridge were of course in better fording trim. We halted that night in a grove of cork trees, about half a league short of the Alva.

Next morning we were again in motion, and found the enemy's rear-guard strongly posted on the opposite bank of that river.

The Alva was wide, deep, and rapid, and the French had destroyed the bridge of Murcella, and also the one near Pombeira. Nevertheless, we opened a thundering cannonade on those in our front, while Lord Wellington, having, with extraordinary perseverance, succeeded in throwing three of his divisions over it higher up, threatening their line of retreat—it obliged those opposed to us to retire precipitately, when our staff corps, with wonderful celerity, having contrived to throw a temporary bridge over the river, we passed in pursuit and followed until dark; we did not get another look at them that day, and bivouacked for the night in a grove of pines, on some swampy high lands, by the roadside, without baggage, cloaks, or eatables or any kind.

Who has not passed down Blackfriars-road of an evening? and who has not seen, in the vicinity of Rowland Hill's chapel, at least half a dozen gentlemen presiding each over his highly polished tin case, surmounted by variegated lamps, and singing out that most enchanting of all earthly melodies to an empty stomach, that has got a sixpence in its clothly casement, "hot, all hot!" The whole concern is not above the size of a drum, and, in place of dealing in its empty sounds, rejoices in mutton-pies, beef-steaks, and kidney-puddings, "hot, all hot!" If the gentlemen had but followed us to the wars, how they would have been worshipped in such a night, even without their lamps.

In these days of invention, when every suggestion for ameliorating the condition of the soldier is thank- fully received, I, as one, who have suffered severely by outward thawings and inward gnawings, beg to found my claim to the gratitude of posterity, by proposing that, when a regiment is ordered on active service, the drummers shall deposite their sheepskins and their cat-o'-nine tails in the regimental store- room, leaving one cat only in the keeping of the drum major. And, in lieu thereof, that each drummer be armed with a tin drum full of "hot, all hot!" and that whenever the quarter-master fails to find the cold, the odd cat in the keeping of the drum-major shall be called upon to remind him of his duty.

If the simple utterance of the three magical monosyllables already mentioned did not rally a regiment more rapidly round the given point than a tempest of drums and trumpets, I should be astonished, and as we fought tolerably well on empty stomachs, I should like to see what we would not do on kidney puddings, "hot, all hot!"

On the 19th, we were again in motion at daylight, and both on that day and the next, although we did not come into actual contact with the enemy, we picked up a good many stragglers. We were obliged, however, to come to a halt for several days from downright want, for the country was a desert, and we had outmarched our supplies. Until they came up, therefore, we remained two days in one village, and kept creeping slowly along the foot of the sierra, until our commissariat was sufficiently reenforced to enable us to make another dash.

I was amused at that time, in marching through those towns and villages which had been the head-quarters of the French army, to observe the falling off in their respect to the Marquess d'Alorna, a Portuguese nobleman, who had espoused their cause, and who, during Massena's advance, had been treated like a prince among them. On their retreat, however, it was easily seen that he was considered an incumbrance. Their names were always chalked on the doors of the houses they occupied, and were remarked that the one allotted to the unfortunate marquis grew gradually worse as we approached the frontier, and I remember that in the last village before we came to Celerico, containing about fifty houses, only a cow's share of the buildings had fallen to his lot.

We halted one day at Mello, and seeing a handsome-looking new church on the other side of the Mondego, I strolled over in the afternoon to look at it. It had all the appearance of having been magnificently adorned in the interior, but the French had left the usual traces of their barbarous and bloody visits. The doors were standing wide open, the valuable paintings destroyed, the statues thrown down, and mixed with them on the floor, lay the bodies of six or seven murdered Portuguese peasants.

It was a cruel and a horrible sight, and yet, in the midst thereof, was I tempted to commit a most sacrilegious act; for round the neck of a prostrate marble female image, I saw a bone necklace of rare and curious workmanship, the only thing that seemed to have been saved from the general wreck, which I very coolly transferred to my pocket and in due time to my portmanteau. But a day of retribution was at hand, for both the portmanteau and the necklace went from me like a tale that is told, and I saw them no more.

It was the 28th before we again came in contact with the enemy at the village of Frexadas. Two companies of ours and some dragoons were detached to dislodge them, which they effected in gallant style, sending them off in confusion and taking a number of prisoners; but the advantage was dearly purchased by the death of our adjutant, Lieutenant Stewart He imprudently rode into the main street of the village, followed by a few riflemen, before the French had had time to withdraw from it, and was shot from a window.

One would imagine that there is not much sense wrapped up in an ounce of lead, and yet it invariably selects our best and our bravest, (no great compliment to myself by the way, considering the quantity of those particles that must have passed within a yard of my body at different times, leaving all standing. Its present victim was a public loss, for he was a shrewd, active, and intelligent officer; a gallant soldier, and a safe, jovial and honourable companion.

I was not one of the party engaged on that occasion, but with many of my brother officers, watched their proceedings with my spy-glass from the churchyard of Alverca, Our rejoicings on the flight of the enemy were quickly turned into mourning by observing in the procession of our returning victorious party, the gallant adjutant's well-known bay horse with a dead body laid across the saddle. We at first indulged in the hope that he had given it to the use of some more humble comrade; but long ere they reached the village we became satisfied that the horse was the bearer of the inanimate remains of his unfortunate master, who but an hour before had left us in all the vigour of health, hope, and manhood. At dawn of day on the following morning the officers composing the advanced guard, dragoons, artillery, and riflemen, were seen voluntarily assembled in front of Sir Sidney Beckwith's quarters, and the body, placed in a wooden chest, was brought out and buried there amid the deep but silent grief of the spectators.

Brief, however, is the space which can be allotted to military lamentations in such times, for within a quarter of an hour we were again on the move in battle array, to seek laurels or death in another field.

Our movement that morning was upon Guarda, the highest standing town in Portugal, which is no joke, as they are rather exalted in their architectural notions—particularly in convent-building—and, were even a thunder-charged cloud imprudent enough to hover for a week within a league of their highest land, I verily believe that it would get so saddled with monks, nuns, and their accompanying iron bars, that it would be ultimately unable to make its escape.

Our movement, as already said, was upon Guarda, and how it happened, Wellington only knows, but even in that with mountainous region the whole British army arriving from all fronts of the compass were seen to assemble there at the same instant, and the whole French army were to be seen at the same time in rapid retreat within gunshot through the valley below us.

There must have been some screws loose among our minor departments, otherwise such a brilliant movement on the part of our chief would not have gone for nothing. But notwithstanding that the enemy's masses were struggling through a narrow defile for a considerable time, and our cavalry and horse artillery were launched against them, three hundred prisoners were the sole fruits of the day's work.

CHAPTER 8

A *Caçadore* and His Mounted Followers

In one of the first chapters of this book I not only pledged my constancy to my fair readers, but vowed to renew my addresses from time to time as opportunities offered. As my feet, however, have since trodden from one extremity of a kingdom to the other, and many months have, in the mean while, rolled away without giving me an opportunity of redeeming the pledge, I fear that my fidelity might be doubted if I delayed longer in assuring them that the spirit has all along been willing, but the subject fearfully wanting; for wherever I have wandered the angel of death has gone before, and carefully swept from the female countenance all lines of beauty, leaving nothing for the eye to dwell on but the hideous ruins of distress.

The only exceptions were our fellow travellers, for the country on our line of march, as already said, was reduced to a desert, and no one remained in it who had either wealth or strength to remove, and our regimental wife had deserted, out our gallant associates, the 43rd and 52nd regiments, had one each, who had embarked with them, and remained true to the brigade until the end of the war.

One of them was remarkable pretty, and it did one's heart good to see the everlasting sweets that hung upon her lovely countenance, assuring us that our recollections of the past were not ideal, which they would otherwise have been apt to revolve themselves into from the utter disappearance of reality for so long a period.

The only addition to them which our division could boast, were two smart substantial-looking Portuguese angels, who followed our two *Caçadore* regiments, and rode on mule-back under the especial protection of their regimental chaplain. These two were a continual source of amusement to us. on the march whenever we found ourselves at liberty to indulge in it.

The worthy father himself was quite a lady's man, (Portuguese,) he was a short stout old fellow, with a snuff-coloured coat buttoned up to the throat, which was quite unnecessary with him, seeing that he shaves and put on a clean shirt sometimes as often as once a fortnight. The round mealy-faced ball which he wore as a head was surmounted by a tall cocked hat, and when mounted on his bay pony in his Portuguese saddle, which is boarded up like a bucket, (the shape of his seat and thighs,) he was exactly like some of the cuts I have seen of Hudibras starting on his erratic expedition.

It was our daily amusement whenever we could steal away from our regiment a short time, for two or three of us to start with some design against the *padre* and his dark-eyed wards. One of us would ride quietly up alongside of him and another on that of the ladies as if we wished to pass, but in wishing them the compliments of the season we of course contrived to get ourselves entangled in conversation, while a third officer of our party rode some distance in the rear in readiness to take advantage of circumstances.

The *padre* was a good-natured old fellow, fond of spinning yarn, and as soon as one of us had got him fairly embarked in his story, the other began gradually to detach one or both of the damsels from his side, according as the inequalities of the road favoured the movement. They entered into the frolic merrily, but still he was so much alive that we rarely succeeded in stealing one out of sight; but if we did by any accident, it was a grand scene to see the scramble which he and his pony made after the fugitives, and on recovering the one, his rage on his return to find that the other had also disappeared.

After one of these successful expeditions we found it prudent never to renew the attack until his wrath was assuaged, and it never abode with him long, so that week after week and year after year we continued to renew the experiment with various success.

It is amusing to think to what absurdities people will have recourse by way of amusement when subjects for it are scarce. It was long a favourite one with us to hunt a *Caçadore* as we called it. Their officers as well as our own were always mounted, and when their corps happened to be marching in our front, any officer who stopped behind, (which they frequently had occasion to do,; invariably, in returning to rejoin his regiment, passed ours at a full gallop; and on those occasions he had no sooner passed our first company than the officers of it were hard at his heels, the others following in succession as he cleared them, so that by the time he had reached the head of the regiment the whole of our officers had been in full chase.

We never carried the joke too far, but made it a point of etiquette to stop short of our commanding officer, (who was not supposed to see what was going on,) and then fell quietly back to our respective places.

I have often seen the hunted devil look round in astonishment, but I do not think he ever saw the wit of the thing, and for that matter I don't know that my readers will feel that they are much wiser, but it was nevertheless amusing to us; and not without its use, for the soldiers enjoyed the joke, which, though trifling, helped to keep op that larking spirit among them, which contributed so much towards the superiority and the glory of our arms. In times of hardship and privation the officer cannot be too much alive to the seizing of every opportunity, no matter how ridiculous, if it serves to beguile the soldier of his cares.

On the 1st of April we again closed up with the enemy on the banks of the Coa, near Sabugal. It was a wet muggy afternoon near dusk when we arrived at our ground), and I was sent, with the company which I had charge of, on picquet to cover the left front of our position.

The enemy held an opposite post on our side of the river, and I was ordered if they were civil to me not to interfere with then; but in the event of the reverse, to turn them over to their own side. My stomach was more bent upon eating than fighting that evening, and I was glad to find that they proved to be gentlemen and allowed me to post my sentries as close as I pleased without interruption.

I found one of our German hussar *videttes* on a rising ground near me, and received an order from my brigadier to keep him there until he was relieved, and I accordingly placed a rifleman alongside of him for his better security, but after keeping him an hour or two in the dark and no relief appearing, I was forced to let him go or to share my slender allowance with him, for the poor fellow (as well as his horse) was starving. I have seen the day, however, that I would rather have dispensed with my dinner (however sharp set) than the services of one of those thoroughbred soldiers; for they were as singularly intelligent and useful on outpost duty, as they were effective and daring in the field.

The First regiment of Hussars were associated with our division throughout the war, and were deserved favourites. In starting from a swampy couch and bowling along the road long ere dawn of day, it was one of the romances of a soldier's life to hear them chanting their national war songs—some three or four voices leading and the whole squadron joining in the chorus. As I have already said, they were no less daring in the field than they were surpassingly good on outpost duty.

The hussar was at all times identified with his horse, he shared his bed and his board, and their movements were always regulated by the importance of their mission. If we saw a British dragoon at any time approaching in full speed, it excited no great curiosity among us, but whenever we saw one of the First Hussars coming on at a gallop it was high time to gird on our swords and bundle up.

Their chief, too, was a perfect soldier, and worthy of being the leader of such a band, for he was to them what the gallant

Beckwith was to us—a father, as well as a leader.

He was one who never could be caught napping. They tell a good anecdote of him after the battle of Toulouse, when the news arrived of the capture of Paris and Bonaparte's abdication. A staff officer was sent to his out-post quarter to apprize him of the cessation of hostilities—it was late when the officer arrived, and after hearing the news, the colonel proceeded to turn into bed as usual, "all standing," when the officer remarked with some surprise, "Why, colonel, you surely don't mean to sleep in your clothes tonight, when you know there is an armistice?"

"Air mistress or no air mistress," replied the veteran, "I sleeps in my breeches!"

We remained another day in front of Sabugal, and as it was known that Reynier held that post with his single corps unsupported, Lord Wellington resolved to punish him for his temerity.

The day dawned on the morning of the 3rd of April, however, rather inauspiciously. Aurora did not throw off her nightcap at the usual hour, and when she could no longer delay the ceremony she shed such an abundance of dewy tears that Sabugal, with its steel clad heights, remained invisible to the naked eye at the distance of a few hundred yards, which interfered materially with that punctuality in the combined movements so necessary to ensure the complete success of our enterprise. Leaving, therefore, to those concerned to account for their delays, my object in renewing this battle is to pay a last tribute to the memory of Sir Sidney Beckwith, the hero of that day. He, as he had been directed, moved his brigade to a ford of the Coa, and was there waiting farther orders, when a staff officer rode up, and hastily demanded why he had not attacked?

Beckwith was an actor of the immortal Nelson's principle—that if a commander is in doubt he never can do wrong in placing himself alongside of the enemy. We instantly uncorked our muzzle-stoppers, off with our lock-caps, and our four companies of riflemen, led through the river, (which was deep and rapid,) followed by the 43rd, driving in the enemy's picquet which defended it The officer commanding, left his sky-blue cloak fluttering in the breeze on the top of a furze bush, and I felt a monstrous inclination to transfer it to my own shoulders, for it was an article of which I happened, at that moment, to be in especial want; but as it was the beginning of a battle in place of the end of one, and I had an insurmountable objection to fight under false colours, I passed it by.

As soon as we gained the summit of the hill it became as clear as the mist that we were regularly in for it. Beckwith, finding himself alone and unsupported, in close action, with only hundreds to oppose to the enemy's thousands, at once saw and felt all the danger of his situation; but he was just the man to grapple with any odds, being in his single person a host—of a tall commanding figure and noble countenance, with a soul equal to his appearance—he was as Napier says, "a man equal to rally an army in flight."

Our four companies had led up in skirmishing order, driving in the enemy's light troops; but the summit was defended by a strong compact body, against which we could make no head; but opening out and allowing the 43rd to advance, they, with a tearing volley and a charge, sent the enemy rolling into the valley below, when the rifles again went to work in front, sticking to them like leeches.

The hill we had just gained became our rally-post for the remainder of the day, and, notwithstanding the odds on the side of the enemy, they were never able to wrest it from us. Our force was as well handled as theirs was badly, so that in the successive and desperate encounters which took place, both in advance and in retreat, we were as often to be seen in their position as they were in ours.

Beckwith himself was the life and soul of the fray: he had been the successful leader of those who were then around him in many a bloody field, and his calm, clear, commanding voice was distinctly heard amid the roar of battle, and cheerfully obeyed. He had but single companies to oppose to the enemy's battalions; but, strange as it may appear, I saw him twice lead successful charges with but two companies of the 43rd, against an advancing mass of the enemy. His front, it is true, was equal to theirs, and such was his daring, and such the confidence which these hardy soldiers had in him, that they went as fiercely to work single-handed as if the whole army had been at their heels.

Beckwith's manner of command on those occasions was nothing more than a familiar sort of conversation with the soldier. To give an idea of it I may as well mention that in the last charge I saw him make with two companies of the 43rd, he found himself at once opposed to a fresh column in front, and others advancing on both flanks, and, seeing the necessity for immediate retreat, he called out, "Now, my lads, we'll just go back a little if you please."

On hearing which every man began to run, when he shouted again, "No, no, I don't mean that—we are in no hurry—we'll just walk quietly back, and you can give them a shot as you go along." This was quite enough, and was obeyed to the letter—the retiring force keeping up a destructive fire, and regulating their movements by his, as he rode quietly back in the midst of them, conversing aloud in a cheerful encouraging manner—his eye all the while intently watching the enemy to take advantage of circumstances.

A musket-ball had, in the meantime, shaved his forehead, and the blood was streaming down his countenance, which added not a little to the exciting interest of his appearance. As soon as we had got a little way up the face of our hill, he called out, "Now, my men, this will do—let us show them our teeth again!" This was obeyed as steadily as if the words halt, front, had been given on parade, and our line was instantly in battle array, while Beckwith, shaking his fist in the faces of the advancing foe, called out to them, "Now, you rascals, come on here if you dare!"

Those he addressed showed no want of courage, but, for awhile, came boldly on to the tune of old trousers,[1] notwith-

---

1. Old trousers was a name given by our soldiers to the point of war which is beat by the French drummers in advancing to the charge. I have, when skirmishing in a wood, and a French regiment coming up to the relief of the opposing skirmishers, often heard the drum long before we saw them, (continued next page)

standing the fearful havoc we were making in their ranks; but they could not screw themselves up the long disputed hill—the 52nd (two battalions) had, by this time, come into the line of battle, and were plying them hard on the right, while our rifles were peppering them on their front and left, and, as soon as they came near enough, another dash by Beckwith, at the head of the 43rd, gave them the *coup de grace*.

The fate of the day was now decided— the net which had been wove in the morning, and which the state of the weather had prevented being brought to a crisis as soon as was intended, now began to tighten around them—the 5th Division crossed by the bridge of Sabugal, and the 3rd, (I believe,) by a ford to the right—and Reynier, seeing no hopes of salvation but by immediate flight, very speedily betook himself to it, and, I believe, saved all that did not fall on the field of battle—a piece of good fortune of which his conduct that day showed him undeserving; for, had not the extraordinary state of the weather caused the delays and mistakes which took place on our side, he could scarcely hare taken a man out of the field.

While standing in our last position, awaiting the attack in our front, I was much amused in observing, on the opposite height, the approach of our 3rd division, unnoticed by the enemy—a French column occupied the top of what seemed to be almost a precipice overlooking the river; but I observed some of the 60th Rifles clambering up the face of it on all fours, and, to see their astonishment, when they poked their heads over the brink, to find themselves within a couple of yards of a French column!

They, of course, immediately concealed themselves under the bank; but it was curious to observe that they were unseen by the enemy, who were imprudent enough either to consider themselves secure on that side, or to give all their attention to the fight going on between their comrades and us; but certain it is they allowed the riflemen to leather there in formidable numbers. As we advanced immediately, the intervening rising

---

and, on those occasions, our riflemen immediately began calling to each other, from behind the different bushes, "Holloa there! look sharp! for here comes old trousers?"

ground prevented my seeing what took place, but on crowning the opposite height, which the French had just evacuated, we found, by the bodies on the ground, that they had just received a volley from a part of the Third Division—and one of the most deadly which had been fired that day.

Our cavalry had been astray during the fight, but they afterwards made two or three ineffectual attempts to break in upon the enemy's line of retreat.

Immediately after the action, we drew up behind an old cowshed, which Lord Wellington occupied for a short time, while it poured torrents of rain. Sir William Erskine, with some of his horsemen, joined us there, and I heard him say to the commander-in-chief that he claimed no merit for the victory, as it belonged alone to Sidney Beckwith! I believe his lordship wanted no conjurer to tell him so, and did ample justice to the combatants, by stating in his despatch that "this was one of the most glorious actions that British troops were ever engaged in."

To those accustomed to the vicissitudes of warfare it is no less curious to remark the many miraculous escapes from wounds than the recovery from them. As an instance of the former, I may observe, that, in the course of the action just related, I was addressing a passing remark to an officer near me, who, in turning round to answer, raised his right foot, and I observed a grape shot tear up the print which it had but that instant left in the mud.

As an instance of the latter I shall here relate, (though rather misplaced,) that, at the storming of Badajos, in April, 1812, one of our officers got a musket-ball in the right ear, which came out at the back of the neck, and, though after a painful illness, he recovered, yet his head got a twist, and he was compelled to wear it, looking over the right shoulder. At the battle of Waterloo, in 1815, (having been upwards of three years with his neck awry,) he received a shot in the left ear, which came out within half an inch of his former wound in the back of the neck, and it set his head straight again!

This is an anecdote which I should scarcely have dared to relate, were it not that, independent of my personal knowledge of the facts, the hero of it still lives to speak for himself, residing on his property, in Nottinghamshire, alike honoured and respected as a civilian, as he was loved and esteemed as a gentleman and a gallant soldier.[2]

After the action at Sabugal our brigade was placed under cover in the town, and a wild night it proved—the lightning flashed—the winds howled—and the rains rained. The house occupied by my brother sub and myself was a two-story one, and floored after the manner of some of our modern piers, with the boards six inches apart, and transferable, if necessary, to a wider range, without the trouble of extracting or unscrewing nails.

The upper floor, as the most honoured portion, was assigned to us, while the first was reserved for the accommodation of some ten or a dozen well-starved inmates.

We had scarcely proceeded to dry our clothes, and to masticate the few remaining crumbs of biscuit, when we received a deputation from the lower regions, craving permission to join the mess; but, excepting the scrapings of our haversacks, we had literally nothing for ourselves, and were forced to turn a deaf ear to their entreaties, for there was no making them believe we were as destitute ad we seemed. It was one of those cruel scenes to which the seats of war alone can furnish parallels, for their wan and wasted countenances showed that they were wildly in want.

The following day saw Portugal cleared of its invaders, and the British standard once more unfurled within the Spanish boundary.

The French army retired behind the Agueda, and our division took possession of a portion of its former quarters, Fuentes d'Onor, Gallegos, and Espeja. There we enjoyed a few days' repose, of which we stood in much need, it having been exactly a month since we broke up in front of Santarem, and, as the foregoing pages show, it was not spent in idleness.

---

2. Lieutenant Worsley.

CHAPTER 9

National Character

Fuentes, which .was our first resting place, was a very handsome village, and every family so well known to the Light Division, that no matter into which quarter the billet fell, the individual was received as an old and approved friend.

The change from Portugal into Spain, as alluded to in my first work, was very striking. In the former the monkish cowl seemed even on ordinary occasions to be drawn over the face of nature; for though their sun was a heavenly one, it shone over a dark and bigoted race; and though they were as ripe for mischief as those of more enlightened nations, yet even in that they were woefully defective, and their joys seemed often sadly miscalled. But at the time I speak of, as if to shroud everything in unfathomable gloom, the ravages of the enemy had turned thousands of what (to them) were happy homes, into as many hells—their domestic peace ruined—their houses and furniture fired, and every countenance bearing the picture of melancholy and wan despair.

Their damsels' cheeks wore no roses, yet did they wear soil enough on which to rear them. But at the same time be it remarked that I quarrel not with the countenance, but with the soil, for I am a pale lover myself.

In Spain, on the contrary, health and joy seemed to beam on every countenance, and comfort in every dwelling. I have observed some writers quarrel with. my former statement on this subject, and maintain that though the difference in appearance was remarkable, that so far as regards the article of cleanliness, the facts were not so. With these, however, I must still differ after giving everything due consideration. The Portuguese did not assume to be a cleanly race, and they were a filthy one in reality.

The Spaniards did affect to be the former, and I do think that they approached it as nearly as may be. I allude to the peasantry, for the upper and middling classes sink into immeasurable contempt in the comparison, but their peasantry I still maintain areas fine and as cleanly a class as I ever saw. Their dress is remarkably handsome, and though I can give no opinion as to the weekly value of soap expended on their manly countenances, yet, in regard to the shirt, which is their greatest pride, and neatly embroidered in the bosom, according to the position of the wearer in the minds of those on whom that portion of the ornamental devolves, I can vouch for their having shown a clean one as often as need be.

And though I do not feel myself at liberty to enter into the details of the dress of their lovely black-eyed damsels, I may be permitted to say that it is highly becoming to them; and, in short, I should have some dread of staking our national credit by parading the inmates of any chance village of our own against a similar one of theirs.

Their houses too are remarkably neat and cleanly, and would be comfortable were it not for those indefatigable villainous insects that play at a perpetual hop, skip, and jump, giving occasional pinches to the exposed parts of the inmate; and yet what warm country is exempt from them, or something worse. Go into boasted America, and so great is the liberty of all classes there, that what with the hum of the mosquito above, and the bug below the blanket, the unfortunate wight, as I can testify, is regularly humbugged out of his natural repose. As I have taken a trip across the Atlantic for the foregoing example, I cannot resist giving an anecdote to show that our brethren on that side of the water sometimes have a night's rest sacrificed to inexpressible causes as well as natural ones.

A gentleman at the head of the law there, (not the hangman,) told me that in his early days, while the roads were jet in their infancy, he was in the habit of going his circuit on horseback, with nothing but a change of linen tacked to his crupper—that one day he had been overtaken by a shower of rain before he could reach the lonely cottage, which he had destined for his night's repose—and that it interfered materially with the harmony which had hitherto existed between him and his leathern breeches,. for he felt uncomfortable in them, and he felt uncomfortable out of them, arising from the dread that he might never be able to get into them again.

His landlady, however, succeeded in allaying his fears for the moment; and having lent him one of her nether garments for present use, she finally consigned him to bed, with injunctions to sleep undisturbed, for that she would take especial care, while they underwent the necessary fiery ordeal; that she would put that within which should preserve their capacities undiminished.

Notwithstanding the satisfactory assurance on the part of the dame, a doubt continued still to hang on the mind of the man in the petticoat; and as *the mind disturbed denies the body rest*, so was every attempt of his to close an eye, met by the vision of a pair of shrivelled leathers, until at length in a fit of feverish excitement he started from his couch determined to know the worst; and throwing open the door of the kitchen, he to his no small astonishment, beheld his leathers not only filled; but well filled too, by the landlady herself, who there stood in them, toasting and turning round and round; neither so gracefully nor so fast as Taglioni, perhaps, but still she kept turning all the same; and it, most probably, was the smoke arising from the lawyer's wet leathers which Tom Moore saw curling so gracefully above the green elms when he wrote the *Woodpecker*.

But to return to the Peninsula. While it. must be admitted that the *hidalgo's* evil is the lesser, I could, nevertheless, wish that the good old Spaniard would march a little more with the spirit of the times; for by the ordinary use of a small-tooth comb, he might be enabled to limit his hair hunting to the sports of the field.

The day after our arrival at Fuentes I was amused to hear one of our soldiers describing to a comrade his last night's fare in the new quarter. Soon after his taking possession of it, three days' rations had been served out to him, and his landlady, after reconnoitring it for awhile with a wistful eye; at length proposed that they should mess together while he remained in their house, to which he readily assented; and, by way of making a fair beginning, he cut off about a pound of the beef, which he handed over to her, but at the same time allowing her about as much play with it as a cat does to a mouse—a precaution which he had reason to rejoice in; for he presently found it transferred into a kettle then boiling on the fire, containing, as he said, thirteen buckets of water, in which his pound of beef was floating about like a cork in the middle of the ocean!

"Hilloah, my nice woman," says I, " if you and I are to mess together, I'll just trouble you to take out twelve buckets and a half of that water, and in place thereof, that you will be pleased to put in a pound of beef for every month which you intend shall keep mine in company—and if you choose to give some butter or a slice or two of bacon in addition, I shall not object to it, but I'll have none of your gammon!" The dispute ended in the rifleman's being obliged to fish out his pound of beef and keep it under his own protection.

Our repose in Fuentes was short. The garrison of Almeida was blockaded with a fortnight's provision only, and two companies of ours under Colonel Cameron were immediately despatched to shoot their bullocks while grazing on the ramparts, which still farther contract their means of subsistence.

Lord Wellington had in the mean time hurried off to the south, in consequence of the pressing importance of the operations of the corps under Marshal Beresford, leaving the main army, for the time being, under the command of Sir Brent Spencer. In the afternoon of the 16th of April we were hastily ordered under arms, and passing through Gallegos we were halted behind a hill on the banks of the Agueda, when we found that the movement had been occasioned by the passing of a convoy of provisions which the enemy were attempting to throw into Ciudad Rodrigo, and which was at that moment with its escort of two hundred men shut up in some enclosures of stone walls within half a mile of us, surrounded by our dragoons.

I don't know how it happened, but we were kept there inactive for a couple of hours with eight thousand men sending in summonses for them to surrender, when a couple of our idle guns would have sent the loose wall about their ears and made them but too happy to be allowed to do so. But as it was, the garrison of Ciudad Rodrigo came out and carried them off triumphantly from under our noses.

There's nae luck about the houses
There's nae luck ava;
There's nae luck about the house,
When our gude man's awa.

This was the most critical period of the whole war; the destinies not only of England but of Europe hung upon it, and all hinged on the shoulders of one man,—that man was Wellington! I believe there were few even of those who served under him capable of knowing, still less of appreciating, the nature of the master-mind which there, with God's assistance, ruled all things; for he was not only the head of the army, but obliged to descend to the responsibility of every department in it. In the different branches of their various duties, he received the officers in charge, as ignorant as schoolboys, and, by his energy and unwearied perseverance, he made them what they became—the most renowned army that Europe ever saw.

Wherever he went at its head, glory followed its steps—wherever he was not—I will not say disgrace, but something near akin to it ensued; for it is singular enough to remark that, of all the distinguished generals who held separate commands in that army throughout the war, Lord Hill alone (besides the commander-in-chief) came out of it with his fame untarnished by any palpable error. In all his battles, Lord Wellington appeared to us never to leave anything to chance. However desperate the undertaking—whether suffering under momentary defeat, or imprudently hurried on by partial success—we ever felt confident that a redeeming power was at hand, nor were we ever deceived.

Those only, too, who have served under such a master-mind, and one of inferior calibre, can appreciate the difference in a physical as well as a moral point of view—for when in the presence of the enemy, under him,, we were never deprived of our personal comforts until prudence rendered it necessary, and they were always restored to us again at the earliest possible moment. Under the temporary command of others we have been deprived of our baggage for weeks through the timidity of our chief, and without the shadow of necessity; and it is astonishing in what a degree the vacillation and want of confidence in a commander descends into the different ranks.

Of all the commanders in that army at the period I speak of, none stood more distinguished than he who was for the moment our head (the gallant Spencer;) and yet, singularly enough, the moment he was left to himself, not only his usual daring, but all spirit of enterprise seemed to have forsaken him. Witness the escape of the French detachment as just related, as well as the various subsequent movements under him; whereas, within a few days, when in the field of Fuentes under Wellington, he was himself again.

While halted behind the hill already mentioned, I got my first look at the celebrated guerrilla chief, Don Julian Sanchez. He was a middling-sized thick-set fellow, with a Spanish complexion, well whiskered and moustached, with glossy black hair, and dressed in a hussar uniform. The peasantry of that part of the country used to tell rather a romantic story of the cause which induced him to take up arms,—namely, that the French had maltreated and afterwards murdered his wife and family before his face, besides firing his house, (cause enough in all conscience,) and for which he amply revenged himself; for he became the most celebrated throat-cutter in that part of the world.

His band, when he first took the field, did not exceed fifty men, but about the period I speak of his ranks had swelled to about fifteen hundred.

They were a contemptible force in the field; but brave, enterprising, and useful in their mountain fastnesses—in cutting off supplies and small detachments. I did not see his troops until sometime after, when his heavy dragoons one day crossed our line of march. They afterwards cut a more respectable figure; but at that period they looked a regular set of ragamuffins, wearing cocked hats with broad white lace round the edges, yellow coats, with many more than buttonholes, and red facings; breeches of various colours and no stockings, bat a sort of shoe on the foot with a spur attached, and their arms were as various as their colours; some with lances, some with carabines, and, in short, everyone seemed as if he had equipped himself in whatever the fortune of war had thrown in his way.

As the battle of Fuentes approached, our life became one of perpetual motion, and when I raised my head from its stone pillow in the morning, it was a subject of speculation to guess within a league of its next resting-place, although we were revolving within a very limited space. Nothing clings so tenaciously to my mind as the remembrance of the different spots on which I have passed a night. Out of six years' campaigning it is probable that I slept at least half the period under the open canopy of heaven, (barring latterly a sheet of canvass,) and though more than twenty years have since rolled over my head, I think I could still point out my every resting-place.

On the night of the 1st of May I was sent from Alameida with thirty riflemen and six dragoons to watch a ford of the Agueda. The French held a post on the opposite side—but at daylight in the morning I found they had disappeared. Seeing a Spanish peasant descending on the opposite bank—and the river not being fordable to a person on foot, while its continuous roaring through its rugged course drowned every other voice—I detached one of the dragoons, who brought him over behind him, and as he told me that the French were, at that moment, on the move to the left, I immediately transmitted the information to head-quarters.

I was soon after ordered to join my battalion, which I found lodged in a stubble field about half way between Gallegos and Alameida, on a piece of rising ground which we had christened Kraüchenberg's hill, in compliment to that gallant captain of German hussars, who, with his single troops had made a brilliant and successful charge from it the year before on the enemy's advancing horsemen.

The following night we had gone to bed in the village of Espeja, but were called to arms in the middle of it, and took post in the wood behind.

With the enemy close upon us, our position was anything but a safe one; but, as it included a conical hill, which commanded a view of their advance. Lord Wellington was anxious to retain it until the last possible moment.

The chief of the German hussars, who covered the reconnoitring party, looked rather blank when he found, next morning, that the infantry were in the act of withdrawing, and tried hard to persuade Beckwith to leave two companies of riflemen as a sup- port, assuring him that all the cavalry in the world were unable to harm them in such a cover; but as the cover was, in reality, but a sprinkling of the Spanish oaks, our chief found it prudent to lend his deaf ear to the request. However, we all eventually reached the position of Fuentes unmolested—a piece of good luck which we had no right to expect, considering the military character of our adversaries and the nature of the ground we had to pass over.

Having been one of the combatants in that celebrated field, and having already given a history of the battle such as the fates decreed, it only remains with me, following the example of other historians, to favour the public with my observations thereon.

In the course of my professional career several events have occurred to bother my subaltern notions en the principles of the art of war, and none more than the battle of Fuentes; but to convey a just idea of what I mean to advance, it is necessary that I should describe the ground, and while those who choose, may imagine that they see it sketched by one who never before drew anything but the cork out of a bottle, or a month's pay out of the hands of the pay-master, others, whose imaginations are not so lively, must be contented in supposing themselves standing, with an army of thirty thousand men, between the streams of the Tourones and Dos Casas, with our right resting on Nava d'Aver, and our left on Fort Conception, a position extending seven miles.

The French advanced from Rodrigo with forty-five thousand men to relieve their garrison, which we had shut up in Almeida, which is in rear of our left—and in place of going the straight road to it, through Alameida and Fort Conception, Massena spreads his army along our whole front, and finally attacks the most distant part of it, (Nava d'Aver.)

That, I believe, was all strictly according to rule, for the purpose of preserving his base of operations; but I am labouring to show that it was an occasion on which Massena might and ought to have set every role at defiance, for, in possession of a strong fortress under his own lee, and another under that of his adversary, with an army in the field exceeding ours by a fourth, he ought to have known that no possible cast of the dice could have enabled us to do more than maintain the blockade—that, if we gave him a defeat it was impossible for us to follow it up, and if he defeated us our ruin was almost inevitable—in short, had I been Prince of Essling, I would have thrust everything but my fighting men under the protection of the suns of Rodrigo, and left myself, free and unfettered, to go where I liked, do what £ could, and, if need be, to change bases with my adversary; and it is odd to me if I would not have cut such capers as would have astonished the great Duke himself.

From Fuentes to Alameida, a distance of between two and three miles, trusting to the ruggedness of the banks of the Dos Casas, the position was nearly altogether unoccupied on our side, and had Massena but taken the trouble to wade through that stream as often as I had, sometimes for love and sometimes for duty, he would have found that it was passable in fifty places—and, as the ground permitted it, had he assembled twenty thousand infantry there, to be thrust over at daylight, and held the rest of his army in readiness to pounce upon the wing to be attacked—and, had he prayed too, as did the Scottish knight of old, (who had more faith in his good sword than in the justice of his cause,) in these words—

O Lord, we all know that the race is not to the swift nor the battle to the strong, and that, whichever side you take, will be sure to win; but if you will, for this once, stand aside, and leave us two to fight it out, I shall be forever obliged to you

—he might then have commenced the day's work with a tolerable prospect of success—for, if half the twenty thousand men, on reaching the top of the hill, remained to keep the one wing in check, and the remainder turned against the flank of the devoted one, while his main army took it in front, they would have had good cause to feel ashamed of themselves if they did not dispose of it long before human aid could have reached, and odd would it have been if the others had not then considered it high time to be off.

What alterations Lord Wellington would have made in his dispositions had he found himself opposed to one who held such fighting views as I do, it is not for me to say; but it is evident that he estimated Massena at his full value when he persisted in holding such an extended position with an inferior army, while the other, with his superior force, was satisfied with battering a portion of his best regimental[3] brains out against the stone walls about Fuentes, and retiring, at last, without attaining the object of his advance.

The foregoing reflections will no doubt, to many, appear wild; but, with a tolerable knowledge of the ground, and of the

---

3. The most formidable attack there on the 5th was made by his most choice troops, and they succeeded in penetrating to the high ground behind the church, where they were met by a brigade of the 3rd division, and routed with great slaughter. One of the wounded prisoners pointed out to me the body of a captain of grenadiers, (whose name I forget,) who was renowned in their army for his daring.

comparative strength, I am not the less satisfied that my plan may be often tried with success.

In speaking of distance, however, it must not be forgotten that in war the opposing bodies come together with wonderful celerity; for, although soldiers do not see so far as severed lovers, who, by transmitting their looks at each other through the moon or some favoured star, contrive to kill space more quickly, yet the soldier, who has no great stomach for the battle, and sees his enemy in the morning almost out of sight, begins to reckon himself secure for that day, must be rather astonished when he finds how soon a cannon-ball makes up the difference between them!

Packenham, (the gallant Sir Edward,) who was then adjutant-general, led the brigade of the Third Division, which restored the battle in the village. He came to us immediately after, faint with excitement, where we were standing in reserve, and asked if any officer could oblige him with some wine or brandy—a calabash was unslung for his use, and after taking a small sip out of it, and eulogizing, in the handsomest manner, the conduct of the troops, he left us to renew his exertions wherever they might be wanted. He was as gallant a spirit as ever went into afield!

Lord Wellington, in those days, (as he was aware,) was always designated among the soldiers by the name of Old Douro. The morning after the battle, the celebrated D. M. of the guards, rode up to a group of staff officers, and demanded if any of them had seen Beau Douro this morning? His Lordship, who was there reclining on the ground in his boat cloak, started up, and said, "Well! I never knew I was a *beau* before!"

The same morning that officer came galloping to us with an order—our chief, (Sidney Beckwith,) who was never on horseback except when his duty required it, had the greatest horror of the approach of a stair officer, who generally came at full speed until within a yard or two—seeing M. coming on as usual on his fiery dark chesnut, he began waving his hand for him to stop before he had got within fifty yards, and calling out, "Ay, ay, that will do! we'll hear all you have got to say quite well enough!"

Among the great and goodly names of general officers which the army list furnished, it was lamentable to see that some were sent from England, to commands in that army, who were little better than old wives,[4] and who would have been infinitely more at home in feeding the pigs and the poultry of a farmyard than in furnishing food for powder in the field; yet so it was:—the neglect of such a one to deliver an order with which he had been intrusted, lost us the fame and the fruits of our victory; it prevented a pliant regiment from occupying the important post intended for it, and it cost that regiment its gallant chiefs whose nice sense of honour could see no way of removing the stain which the neglect of his superior had cast upon his reputation, than by placing a pistol to his own head. His fate was sadly and deeply deplored by the whole army.

As this particular period furnished few occurrences to vary the monotony of the hammer-and-tongs sort of life we led, I shall take advantage of the opportunity it affords to fire a few random shots for the amusement of my readers.

Shot the First
The Duel

On reaching Paris, after the battle of Waterloo, we found Johnny Petit in very bad humour; and that three out of every four of the officers in each army were not disposed of by private contract, with pistols, and small swords, must be ascribed to our ignorance alike of their language and their national method of conveying offence; for, in regard to the first, although we were aware that the *sacre bœuftake* and *sacre pomme de terre*, with which we were constantly saluted, were not applied complimentarily, jet as the connecting offensive links were lost to most of us, these words alone were not looked upon as of a nature requiring satisfaction; and, with regard to practical insults, a favourite one of theirs, as we afterwards discovered, was to tread, as if by accident, on the toe of the person to be insulted.

Now, as the natural impulse of the Englishman, on having his

---
4. No allusion to the last mentioned officer, who was one of another stamp.

toe trodden on, is to make a sort of apology to the person who did it, by way of relieving him of a portion of the embarrassment which he expects to be the attendant of such awkwardness, many thousand insults of the kind passed unnoticed:—the Frenchman flattering himself that he had done a bold thing,—the Englishman a handsome one; whereas, had the character of the tread been distinctly understood, it would, no doubt, have been rewarded on the spot by our national method—a douse on the chops! However, be that as it may, my business is to record the result of one in which there was no misunderstanding; and, as someone has justly remarked, *when people are all of one mind, it is astonishing how well they agree.*

It occurred at an early hour in the morning, at one of those seminaries for grown children so common in Paris, and the parties (a French officer and one of ours) agreed to meet at daylight, which left them but brief space for preparation, so that when they arrived on the ground, and their fighting irons were paraded, the Frenchman's were found to consist of a brace of pocket-pistols, with finger-sized barrels,—while our officer had a huge horse pistol, which he had borrowed from the quarter-master, and which looked, in the eyes of the astonished Frenchman, like a six-pounder, the bore of it being large enough to swallow the stocks, locks, and barrels of his brace, with the ball-bag and powder-horn into the bargain; and he, therefore, protested vehemently against the propriety of exposing himself to such fearful odds, which being readily admitted on the other side, they referred the decision to a halfpenny Whether they should take alternate shots with the large, or one each with the small.

The Fates decreed in favour of the small arms; and, the combatants having taking their ground, they both fired at a given signal, when the result was that the Frenchman's pistol burst, and blew away his finger, while our man blew away his ramrod; and as they had no longer the means of continuing the fight, they voted that they were a brace of good fellows, and after shaking the Frenchman by his other three fingers, our officer accompanied him home to breakfast.

Shot the Second
Cannon-Law.

While stationed, in the province of Artois, with the Army of Occupation, one of our soldiers committed a most aggravated case of highway-robbery upon a Frenchwoman, for which he was tried by a court-martial, condemned, and suffered death within three days. About a fortnight after, when the whole affair had nearly been forgotten by us, the French report of the outrage, after having gone through its routine of the different official functionaries, made its appearance at our head-quarters, describing the atrocious nature of the offence, and cabling for vengeance on the head of the offender. The commander-in-chief's reply was, as usual, short, but to the purpose:—The man was hanged for it ten days ago.

Shot the Third
Civil Law.

Whilst on the station mentioned in the foregoing anecdote, two of our medical officers went in a gig, on a short tour, in the neighbourhood of our cantonments, and having unconsciously passed the line of demarkation, they were pulled up on their entrance into the first town they came to, for the payment of the usual toll; but they claimed a right to be exempted from it on the score of their being officers of the Army of Occupation. The collector of the customs, however, being of a different opinion, and finding his oratorical powers thrown away upon them, very prudently called to his aid one of those, men-at-arms with which every village in France is so very considerately furnished.

That functionary, squaring his cocked hat, giving his *mustachoes* a couple of twists, and announcing that he was as brave as a lion, as brave as the devil, and sundry other characters of noted courage, he, by way of illustration, drew his sword, and making half-a-dozen furious strokes at the paving stones, made the sparks fly from them like lightning. Seeing that the first half dozen had failed to extract the requisite quantity of *sous*, he was proceeding to give half-a-dozen more, but his sword broke at the first, and our two knights of the lancet, having fewer scruples about surrendering to him as an unarmed than an armed man, made no farther difficulty in accompanying him to the municipal magistrate.

That worthy, after hearing both sides of the case with becoming gravity, finally sentenced our two travellers to pay for the repairs of the sword which had been so courageously broken in defence of their civic rights.

Shot the Fourth

Sword Law

At the commencement of the battle of Waterloo, three companies of our rifleman held a sand bank, in front of the position, and abreast of La Haye Saint, which we clung to most tenaciously, and it was not until we were stormed in front and turned in both flanks that we finally left it. Previous to doing so, however, a French officer rushed out of their ranks and made a dash at one of ours, but neglecting the prudent precaution of calculating the chances of success before striking the first blow, it cost him his life.

The officer he stormed happened to be a gigantic highlander about six feet and it half—and, like most big men, slow to wrath, but a fury when roused. The Frenchman held that in his hand which was well calculated to bring all sizes upon a level—a good small sword—but as he had forgotten to put on his spectacles, his first (and last) thrust passed by the body and lodged in the highlander's left arm. Saunders' blood was now up (as well as down) and with our then small regulation half-moon sabre, better calculated to shave a lady's maid than a Frenchman's head, he made it descend on the pericranium of his unfortunate adversary with a force which snapped it at the hilt.

His next dash was with his fist (and the hilt in it) smack in his adversary's face, which sent him to the earth; and though I grieve to record it, yet as the truth must be told, I fear me that the chivalrous Frenchman died an ignominious death, *viz*, by a kick. But where one's own life is at stakes we must not be too particular.

Shot the Fifth
Love Law

Of all the evils with which a sober community can be cursed, there is none so great as a guard-house; for while the notable housewife is superintending the scouring of her kitchen coppers, and the worthy citizen is selling his sweets, the daughters are as surely to be found lavishing theirs upon their gaudy neighbour, while the nursery-maid, standing a story higher, is to be seen sending her regards a step lower—into the sentry-box.

Though many years have now passed away, I remember as if but yesterday, my first guard mountings is a certain garrison town which shall be nameless. After performing the first usual routine of military duties, my next was, as a matter of course, to reconnoitre the neighbourhood; for if a house happened to be within range of the officer's beat, he seldom had to look for an adventure in vain,—nor had I on the occasion alluded to. The station was in the centre of a populous city, the *purlieus* were genteel, and at the window of one of the opposite houses I soon descried a bevy of maidens who seemed to be regarding me with no small curiosity.

Eyes met eyes which looked again, and as all seemed to go merry as a marriage bell, I took oat my pencil and motioned as if I would write, which meeting with an approving smile, I straightway indited an epistle suitable to the occasion, and showing it to them when ready, I strolled past the door, where, as I expected, I found a fair hand, which seemed to belong to nobody, in readiness to receive it.

In the course of a few minutes I received a note from the same mysterious hand, desiring to be informed for which of the group my last effusion was intended; and though the question was rather a puzzler to a person who had never seen them before, and, even then, too far off to be able to distinguish whether their eyes were green or yellow, yet I very judiciously requested that my correspondent would accept it on her own account. It was arranged accordingly, and her next epistle, while it preached prudence and discretion, desired that I should come to the door at eleven at night, when she would have an opportunity of speaking to me.

It may be imagined that time flew on leaden wings until the arrival of the appointed hour, when proceeding as directed, I found the door ajar, and the vision of the hand, now with a body in the back ground, beckoning me to enter. Following the invitation, the door was gently closed, and I was soon in a large dimly lighted hall, by the side of my fair *incognita*, with my hand clasped in hers. But ah me! I had barely time to unburden myself of a hurricane of sighs (enough to have blown a fire out) and to give one chaste salute, when papa's well-known knock was heard at the door, and dissolved the charm.

In an agony of affright my fair friend desired me to run up stairs to the first landing, and as I valued my life, not to stir from it until she should come to fetch me.

Misfortunes, they say, seldom come single, and so I found it; for I had scarcely reached the desired place when the voice of the sentry thundered, "Guard, turn out!" and conveyed to me the very pleasant information that the grand rounds approached, while I, the officer of the guard, was absent, the captive. of a damsel.

I was in a precious scrape; for, prior to the arrival of the other evil, I held it to be somewhat more than doubtful whether I was reserved for a kiss or a kick, but the odds were now two to one in favour of the latter; for, if I did not find my way outside the walls within three quarters of a minute, it was quite certain that if I failed to receive what was due to me inside the house I should catch it outside, by getting kicked from the service. My case was therefore desperate; and as the voice of papa was still heard at the stair-foot and precluded the possibility of bolting undetected by the door, my only alternative was the stair window..

The field officer was passing under it as I threw up the sash, and though the distance to the ground loomed fearfully long there was no time for deliberation; but bundling out, and letting myself down by the hands as far as I could, I took my chance of the remainder, and came down on the pavement with such a tremendous clatter that I thought I had been shivered to atoms.

The noise fortunately startled the field officer's horse, so that it was as much as he could do to keep his seat for the moment, which gave me time to gather myself up; when, telling him that in my hurry to get to my place before him, I had stumbled against a lamp post and fallen, the affair passed away without farther notice; but my aching bones, for many an after-day, would not permit me to forget the adventure of that night.

In my next turn for guard at the same place I got a glimpse of my fair friend, and but for once. I saw on my arrival that the family were in marching order, and my old acquaintance, the hand, soon after presented me with a billet, announcing their immediate departure for the season, to a distant watering places She lamented the accident which she feared had befallen me, and as she thought it probable that we would never meet again, she begged that I would forgive and look upon it merely as the badinage of a giddy girl.

SHOT THE SIXTH
At a Sore Subject

They who can feel for others' woes should ne'er have cause to mourn their own!' so sayeth the poet, and so should I say if I saw them feeling; but I have found such a marvellous scarcity of those tender hearted subjects on the field of battle, that, in good sooth, if the soldier had not a tear to shed for his own woes, he stood a very good chance of dying unwept, which may either be considered a merry or a dreary end, according to the notion of the individual.

In taking a comparative view of the contorts at- tending a sea and land fight, I know not what evils our nautical brethren may have to contend against, which we have not; but they have this advantage over us—that, whatever may be the fate of the day, they have their bed and breakfast, and their wounds are promptly attended to. This shot, be it observed, is especially fired at the wounded.

When a man is wounded the corps he belongs to is generally in action, and cannot spare from the ranks the necessary assistance; so that he is obliged to be left to the tender mercies of those who follow after; and they generally pay him the attention due to a mad dog, by giving him as wide a berth as they possibly can—so that he often lies for days in the field without assistance of any kind.

Those who have never witnessed such scenes will be loath to believe that men's hearts can get so steeled; but so it is—the same chance befalls the officer as the soldier, and one anecdote will illustrate both.

At the battle of Vittoria one of our officers was disabled by a shot through the leg, but having contrived to drag himself to a roadside, he laid himself down there, in the hope that, among the passing thousands, some good Samaritan might be found with compassion enough to bind up his wound, and convey him to a place of shelter.

The rear of a battle is generally a queer place—the day is won and lost there a dozen times, unknown to the actual combatants—fellows who have never seen an enemy in the field, are there to be seen flourishing their drawn swords, and "cutting such fantastic tricks before high Heaven, as make angels weep," while others are flying as if pursued by legions of demons; and, in short, while everything is going on in front with the order and precision of a field-day, in rear everything is confusion worse confounded.

When my wounded friend took post on the roadside, it was in the midst of a panic amongst the followers of the army, caused by an imaginary charge of cavalry—he tried in vain, for a length of time, to attract the notice of somebody, when his eyes were at length regaled by a staff surgeon of his acquaintance, who approached amid the crowd of fugitives, and, having no doubt but he would at length receive the requisite attention, he hailed him by name as soon as he came within reach. The person hailed, polled up, with "Ah! my dear fellow, how do you do? I hope you are not badly hit?"

"I can't answer for that," replied my friend, "all I know is, that my leg is bleeding profusely, and until some good-natured person dresses it and assists me to remove, here I must lie!"

"Ah! that's right," returned the other, "keep yourself quiet—this is only an affair of cavalry—so that you may make yourself quite comfortable," and, clapping spurs to his horse, he was out of sight in a moment!

The next known character who presented himself was a volunteer, at that time attached to the regiment—an eccentric sort of a gentleman, but one who had a great deal of method in his eccentricity—for, though he always went into battle with us, I know not how it happened, but no one ever saw him again until it was all over—he must have been an especial favourite of the fickle goddess—for, by his own showing, his absence from our part of the battle was always occasioned by his accidentally falling in with some other regiment which had lost all its offices, and, after rallying and leading them on to the most brilliant feat of the day, he, with the modesty becoming a hero, left them alone in their glory—in ignorance of the person to whom they owed so much, while he retired to his humble position as a volunteer!

On the occasion referred to, however, in place of being at the head of a regiment, and leading them on to the front, he was at the head of half a dozen horses, which he bad contrived to scrape together in the field, and was leading them the other road. As soon as he had descried my wounded friend he addressed him as did the doctor—was remarkably glad to see him, and hoped he was net badly hit—and, having received a similar reply, he declared that he was. very sorry to hear it—very—"but," added he, "as you are lying there, at all events, perhaps you will be good, enough to hold these horses for me until I return, for I know where I can get about as many more!"

Patience had not then ceased to be a virtue—and lest my readers should think that I am drawing too largely on theirs, I shall resume the thread of my narrative.

CHAPTER 10

Burning a Bivouac

Soon after the battle of Fuentes Lord Wellington was again called to the south, leaving us with a burning desire to follow, which was eventually gratified; for, after various coquettish movements between us and the enemy, which carried us in retreat near to Sabugal, we, at length, received an order for the south; and, leaving our adversaries to do that which might seem best unto them, we were all at once helm up for the other side of the Tagus.

On our way there we halted a night at Castello, Branco, and hearing that the Bishop's garden was open for inspection, and well worth the seeing, I went with a brother-officer to reconnoitre it.

Throughout the country which we had been traversing for a season, the ravages of the contending armies had swept the fruits, flowers, and even the parent stems, from the face of the earth, as if such things had never been; and it is, therefore, difficult to convey an idea of the gratification we experienced in having our senses again regaled with all that was delightful in either, and in admirable order.

Beauty, in whatever shape it comes before us, is almost irresistible, and the worthy prelate's oranges proved quite so; for they looked so brightly yellow—so plumply ripe—and the trees groaned with their load, as if praying for relief, that with hearts framed as ours, so sensitively alive to nature's kindlier feelings, it was impossible to refuse the appeal.

Stolen kisses, they say, are the sweetest, and besides, as there might have been some impropriety in pressing the oranges to our lips so publicly, we were at some loss to provide for their transfer to a suitable place, as our dress was pocketless, and fitted as tight as a glove; but we contrived to stow away about a dozen each in our then sugar-loaf-shaped regimental caps, and placing them carefully on the head, we marched off as stiffly as a brace of grenadiers.

As the devil would have it, however, in traversing the palace-hall, we encountered the Bishop himself, and as it was necessary that the compliments of the reason should pass between us, it was rather an awkward meeting; I was myself alive to the consequences of having more brains above the head than in it, and, therefore, confined myself to the stiff soldier's salute; but my companion, unluckily, forgot his load, and in politely returning the prelate's bow, sent his cap and oranges rolling at his feet, while his face shone as a burnt offering at the same shrine! The Bishop gave a benevolent smile, and after very good-naturedly assisting the youth to collect the scattered fruit, he politely wished us a good looming, leaving us not a little ashamed of ourselves, and deeply impressed with a sense of his gentleman-like demeanour and amiable disposition.

Our third march from Castello Branco brought us to Portalegrè, where we halted for some days.

In a former chapter, I have given the Portuguese national character, such as I found it generally,—but in nature there are few scenes so blank as to have no sunny side, and throughout that kingdom the romantic little town of Portalegrè still dwells the greenest spot on memory's waste.

Unlike most other places in that devoted land, it had escaped the vengeful visit of their ruthless foe, and having, therefore, no fatal remembrance to cast its shade over the future, the inhabitants received us as if we had been beings of a superior order, to whom they were indebted for all the blessings they enjoyed, and showered their sweets upon us accordingly.

In three out of four of my sojourns there, a friend and I had the good fortune to be quartered in the same house. The family consisted of a mother and two daughters, who were very good-looking and remarkably kind. Our return was ever watched for with an tense interest, and when they could not command sufficient influence with the local authorities to have the house reserved, they, nevertheless, contrived to squeeze us in; for when people are in a humour to be pleased with each other, small space suffices for their accommodation.

Such uniform kindness on their part, it is unnecessary to say, did not fail to meet a suitable return on ours. We had few opportunities of falling in with things that were rich and rare, (if I except such jewels as those just mentioned,) yet were we always stumbling over something or. other; which was carefully preserved for our next happy meeting; and whether they were gems or gew-gaws, they were alike valued for the sake of the donors.

The kindness shown by one family to. two particular individuals goes, of course, for nothing beyond its value; but the feeling there seemed to be universal.

Our usual morning's amusement was to visit one or other of the convents, and having ascertained the names of the different pretty nuns, we had only to ring the bell, and request the pleasure of half an hour's conversation with one of the prettiest amongst them, to have it indulged; and it is curious enough that I never yet asked a nun, or an attendant of a nunnery, if she would elope with me, that she did not immediately consent,— and that, too, unconditionally.

My invitations to that effect were not general, but, on the contrary, remarkably particular; and to show that in accepting it they meant no joke, they invariably pointed out the means, by telling me that they were strictly watched at that time, but if I returned privately, a week or two after the army had passed, they could very easily arrange the manner of their escape.

I take no credit to myself for any preference shown, for if there be any truth in my looking-glass—and it was one of the most flattering I could find— their discriminating powers would entitle them to small credit for any partiality shown to me individually; and while it was no compliment, therefore, to me, or to the nunnery, it must necessarily be due to nature, as showing that the good souls were overflowing with the milk of human kindness, and could not say nay while they possessed the powers of pleasing: for, as far as I have compared notes with my companions, the feeling seemed to have been general.

On quitting Portalegrè, we stopped, the next night, at Aronches, a small miserable walled town, with scarcely a house in it that would entitle the holder to vote on a ten shilling franchise; and on the night following we went into bivouac, on Monte Reguingo, between Campo Mayor and the Caya, where we remained a considerable time. We were there, as our gallant historian (Napier) tells us, in as judicious, but, at the same time, in as desperate a position as any that Lord Wellington had held during the war; yet, I am free to say, however, that none of us knew anything at all about the matter, and cared still less.

We there held, as we ever did, the most unbounded confidence in our chief, and a confidence in ourselves, fed by continued success, which was not to be shaken; so that we were at all times ready for anything, and reckless of everything. The soldiers had become so inured to toil and danger that they seemed to have set disease, the elements, and the enemy alike at defiance. Headaches and heartaches were unknown amongst them, and whether they slept under a roof, a tent, or the open sky, or whether they amused themselves with a refreshing bath in a stream, or amused the enemy with a shot, was all a matter of indifference. I do not eulogize our own men at the expense of others, for although the light division stood on that particular post alone, our chief confidence originated in the hope and belief that every division in the army was animated by the same spirit.

The day after our taking post at Reguingo, notwithstanding my boasted daring, we were put to the rout by an unlooked-for enemy, namely, a fire in the bivouac;—a scorching sun had dried up the herbage, and some of the campfires communicated with the long grass on which we were lodged; the fresh summer-breeze wafted the ground flame so rapidly through the bivouac that before all the arms and accoutrements could be removed, many of the men's pouches were blown up, and caused some accidents.

I believe it is not generally, and cannot be too well known to military men, that this is a measure which is very often had recourse to by an enemy, (when the wind favours,) to dislodge a post from a field of standing corn or long grass; and the only way to counteract it is, for the officer commanding the post to fire the grass immediately behind him, so that by the time the enemy's fire has burnt up, his own will have gone away in proportion, and left a secure place for him to stand on, without losing much ground.

Our bivouac at Monte Reguingo abounded in various .venomous reptiles, and it is curious enough to think that amongst the thousands of human beings sleeping in the same bed and at their mercy, one rarely or never heard of an injury done by them.

A decayed tree full of holes, against which the officers of our company had built their straw hut, was quite filled with snakes, and I have often seen fellows three feet long winding their way through the thatch, and voting themselves our companions at all hours; but the only inconvenience we experienced was in a sort of feeling that we would rather have had the hut to ourselves.

One morning, in turning over a stone, on which my head had rested all night, I saw a scorpion with the tail curled over his back looking me fiercely in the face; and though not of much use, I made it a rule thereafter to take a look at the other side of my pillow before I went to sleep, whenever I used a stone one.

An officer, in putting on his shoe one morning, found that he had squeezed a scorpion to death in the toe of it. That fellow must have been caught napping, or he certainly would have resisted the intruder.

The only thing in the shape of an accident from reptiles that I remember ever having occurred in our regiment was to a soldier who had somehow swallowed a lizard. He knew not when or how, and the first hint he had of the tenement being so occupied, was in being troubled with internal pains and spitting of blood, which continued for many months, in spite of all the remedies that were administered. But a powerful emetic eventually caused him to be delivered of as ugly a child of the kind as one would wish to look at about three inches long. I believe that Dr. Burke, late of the Rifles, has it still preserved.

In that neighbourhood I was amused in observing the primitive method adopted by the farmers in thrashing their corn,— namely, in placing it on a hard part of the public road and driving some bullocks backwards and forwards through it; and for winnowing, they tossed it in a sieve and trusted to the winds to do the needful. Notwithstanding the method, however, they contrived to show us good looking bread in that part of the world—as white as a confectioner's seed cake—and though the devil take such seeds as these tons of cows had contrived to grind up with the flour, yet it was something like the cooking on board ships we ought to have been thankful for the good which the gods provided, and asked no questions.

In July, the breaking up of the assembled armies, which had so long menaced us, sent our division again stretching off to the north in pursuit of fresh game. The weather was so intensely hot, that it was thought advisable to perform the greater part. of our marches during the night. I can imagine few cases, however, in which a night march can prove in any way advantageous; for unless the roads are remarkably good, it requires double time to perform them.

The men go stumbling along half asleep, and just begin to brighten up when their permitted hour of repose arrives. The scorching sun, too, murders sleep, and of our ten or twelve days' marching on that occasion, I scarcely ever slept at all. I have always been of opinion that if men who are inured to fatigue are suffered to have a decent allowance of repose during the night, that you may do what you like with them during the day, let the climate or the weather be what it may.

I remember having been at that time in possession of a small black pony, and like the old man and his ass, it might have admitted of a dispute among the spectators which of us ought to have carried the other, but to do myself justice I rarely put him to the inconvenience of carrying anything beyond my boat-cloak, blanket, &c.; but one morning before daylight, in stumbling along through one of those sleepy marches, my charger, following at the length of the bridle-rein, all at once shot past me as if he had been fired out of a mortar, and went heels over head, throwing a complete somerset and upsetting two of the men in his headlong career.

I looked at the fellow in the utmost astonishment to see whether he was in joke or earnest, thinking that I had by accident got hold of one of Astley's cast-off's, who was showing me some of his old stage tricks; but when he got up, he gave himself a shake and went quietly on as usual, so that it must have been nothing beyond a dreaming caper, seeing that he was not much given to the exhibition of feats of agility in his waking moments.

On reaching our destination in the north, our division took up a more advanced position than before, and placed the garrison of Ciudad Rodrigo under blockade.

In the first village we occupied (Mortiago) the. only character worthy of note was a most active half-starved curate, whose duty it was to marry and to bury everybody within a wide range, besides performing the usual services in sundry chapels in that and the adjoining villages. He was so constantly at a gallop on horseback in pursuit of his avocations, that we dubbed him the *padre volante* (the flying parson.) We did there, as in all the Spanish villages the moment we took possession, levelled the ground at the end of the church, and with wooden bats cut out in the shape of rackets, got up something like an apology for that active and delightful game.

Our greatest enjoyment there was to catch the *padre* in one of his leisure moments and to get him to join in the amusement, of which he was remarkably fond, and he was no sooner enlisted, than it became the malicious aim of every one to send the ball against his lank ribs. Whenever he saw that it was done intentionally, however, he made no hesitation in shying his bat at the offender; but he was a good-natured soul, as were also his tormentors, so that everything passed off as was intended.

The *padre* in addition to his other accomplishments was a sportsman, and as he was possessed of a pointer dog, (a companion which, as we had more mouths than food, we were obliged to deny ourselves,) his company in the field on that account was in great request; whatever his feats might have been there, however, he generally came off but second best.

I remember that two of our gentlemen accompanied him the first day, and when they sprung the first covey, the *padre's* bird, out of the three shots, was the only one that came to the ground; but notwithstanding, one of the. officers immediately ran up and very coolly placed it in his own bag. The *padre* ran up too, and stood gaping open-mouthed thinking he had pocketed the bird in joke; however, the other went on deliberately loading as if all had been right. Meanwhile, the other officer coming up, said, "Why, S. that was not your bird; it is the *padre's*!"

"My dear sir," he replied, "I know it is not my bird, but do you suppose that I would allow a fellow like that to think that he had killed a bird? My good sir, I would not allow him to suppose for one moment that he had even fired at it!"

Chapter 11

Cupping

When we next changed our quarter we found the new one peopled exclusively by old wives and their husbands, and, as the enemy were at a distance, we should certainly have gone defunct through sheer *ennui*, had not fortune sent us a fresh volunteer—a regular "broth of a boy," from the Emerald Isle, who afforded ample scope for the exercise of our mischievous propensities during our hours of idleness.

A volunteer—be it known to all who know it not—is generally a young man with some pretensions to gentility—and while, with some, those pretensions are so admirably disguised as to be scarcely visible to the naked eye, in others they are conspicuous; but, in either case, they are persons who, being without the necessary influence to obtain a commission at home, get a letter of introduction to the commander of the forces in the field, who, if he approves, attaches them to regiments, and, while they are treated as gentlemen out of the field, they receive the pay, and do the duty of private soldiers in it. In every storming party or service of danger, in which any portion of a regiment is engaged, if a volunteer is attached to it, he is expected to make one of the number, and, if a bullet does not provide for him in the mean time, he eventually succeeds to the commission of some officer who has fallen in action.

Tommy Dangerfield, the hero of my tale, was, no doubt, (as we all are,) the hero of his mother—in stature he was middle-sized—rather bull shouldered, and walked with bent knees—his face was a fresh good-natured one, but with the usual sinister cast in. the eye worn by common Irish country countenances—in short. Tommy was rather a good-looking, and, in reality, not a bad, fellow, and the only mistake which he seemed to have made, was in the choice of his profession, for which his general appearance and his ideas altogether disqualified him—nevertheless, had he fallen into other hands, it is possible that he might have passed muster with tolerable repute until the termination of the war; but I don't know how it was, nor do I know whether we differed from other regiments in the same respect, but our first and most uncharitable aim was to discover the weak points of every fresh arrival, and to attack him through them. If he had redeeming qualities, he, of course, came out scatheless, but, if not, he was dealt with most unmercifully. Poor Tommy had none such—he was weak on all sides; and therefore, went to the wall.

At the time he joined, we were unusually situated with regard to the enemy, for, on ordinary occasions, we had their sentries opposite to ours within a few hundred yards; but, at that period, we had the French garrison of Ciudad Rodrigo behind us, with the 52nd Regiment between; while the nearest enemy in our front was distant, some ten or twelve miles—nevertheless, our first essay was to impress Tommy with a notion that our village was a fortified place, and that we were closely blockaded on all sides—and it became our daily amusement to form a reconnoitring party to endeavour to penetrate beyond the posts—which posts, be it remarked, were held by a few of our own men, disguised for the purpose, and posted at the outskirts of the village-wood. Tommy, though not a desperate character, showed no want of pluck—wherever we went he followed, and wherever we fled he led the way!

On the first occasion of the kind we got him on horseback, and conducting him through the wood until we received the expected volley, we took to our heels in the hope that he would get unseated in the flight, but he held on like grim death, and arrived In the village with the loss of his cap only. It was, however, brought to him in due time by an old rifleman of the name of Brotherwood, who had commanded the enemy on that occasion, but who claimed peculiar merit in its recovery; and, having taken the opportunity of cutting a hole in it as if a ball had passed through, he got a dollar for the cut!

Poor Tommy, from that time, led the life of the devil—he could not show his nose outside his own house that he was not fired at—and whenever we made up a larger party to show him more of the world it was only to lead him into farther mischief.

I was some time after this removed into the left wing of our regiment, which belonged to a different brigade, so that I ceased to be a daily witness of his torments, though aware that they went on as theretofore.

Tommy continued to rub on for a considerable time. Death had become busy in our ranks—first, by the siege and storming of Ciudad Rodrigo, and immediately after, by that of Badajos. I had heard little or nothing of him during those stirring events of real war—and it was not until the morning after the storming of Badajos that he again came under my notice—from having heard that he had been missing the night before. I there saw him turn up, like a half-drowned rat, covered with mud and wet, which looked very much as if he had passed the night in the inundation, adjoining the breach, up to his neck in the water, and probably a little deeper at times, when the fire-balls were flying thickest!

He, nevertheless, contrived to hold on yet a little longer—one day, (agreeably to order,) taking post in the middle of a river, with his face towards Ispahan, to watch the enemy in that direction—and the next day, in conformity with the same orders, applying to the quarter-master-general for a route for himself and party to go to Kamskatcha to recruit, he got so bewildered that he could not distinguish between a sham and a real order, and, at last, when in the face of the enemy, in front of Salamanca, he absolutely refused to take the duty for which he had been ordered, and was consequently obliged to cut.

It was the best thing that could have happened both for him and the service; for, as I said before, he had mistaken his profession, and as he was yet but a youth, it is to be hoped that he afterwards stumbled upon the right one.

Atalya, which we now occupied, is a mountain village about half a league in front of the Vadillo. The only amusing characters we found in it were the pigs. I know not whether any process was resorted to in the mornings to entice them from their homes to grub up the falling acorns from the beautiful little evergreen oaks which adorned the hills above, but it was a great scene every evening at sunset to go to the top of the village, and see about five hundred of them coming thundering down the face of the mountain at full speed, and each galloping in to his own door.

We had been a considerable time there before we discovered that the neighbourhood could furnish metal more attractive, but a shooting excursion at last brought us acquainted with the Quinta Horquera (I think it was called,) a very respectable farmhouse, situated on a tongue of land formed by the junction of another mountain stream with the Vadillo.

The house itself was nothing out of the common run, but its inmates were, for we found it occupied by the chief magistrate of Ciudad Rodrigo, with his wife and daughter, and two young female relatives. He himself was a stanch friend of his country, and when the fortress of Rodrigo fell into the hands of the French, rather than live in communion with them, he retired with his family to that remote property, in the hope that as it was so much out of the way he might rest there in peace and security until circumstances enabled him to resume his position in society as a true and loyal Spaniard; but as the sequel will show, he had reckoned without his host, for with a British regiment in the neighbourhood, and his house filled with young ladies he was an unreasonable man to expect peace there, and the enemy also by and by came down upon him, as if to prove that his notions of security were equally fallacious.

Don Miguel himself was a splendid ruin of a man of three

score, of a majestic figure, regular features, and stern dark Castilian countenance. He was kind and amusing withal, for though his own face was forbidden to smile, yet he seemed to enjoy it in others, and did all in his power to promote amusement, that is, as much as a Spaniard ever does.

His wife was very tall and very slender—the skin of her pale fleshless face fitting so tight as to make it look like a pin-head. She was very passive and very good-natured, her other day having long passed by.

Their only daughter was a woman about twenty-eight years of age, with rather a dull pock-pitted countenance, and a tall, stout, clumsy figure. She had very little of the Spaniard in her composition, but was nevertheless a kind good-natured gin. Her relatives, however, were metal of another sort: the eldest was a remarkably well made plump little figure, with a fair complexion, natural curly hair, and a face full of dimples which showed eternal sunshine; while her sister, as opposite as day from night, showed the flashing dark eye, sallow complexion, and the light sylph-like figure for which her country-women are so remarkable. To look at her was to see a personification of that beautiful description of Byron's in his first canto of Childe Harold—

Yet are Spain's maids no race of Amazon,
But formed for all the witching arts of love!

Their house, under the circumstances in which we were placed, became an agreeable lounge for many of us for a month or two: for though the sports of the field, with the limited means at our disposal, formed our daily amusement, we always contrived that it should terminate somewhere in the neighbourhood of the Quinta, where we were sure of three things—a hearty welcome, a dish of conversation, and another of chestnuts fried in hog's lard, with a glass of *aguadente* to wind up with; which, after the fatigues of the day, carried us comfortably home to our more substantial repast, with a few little pleasing recollections to dream about.

The French marshal, as if envious of our enjoyments, meagre

as they were, put a sudden stop to them. His advance, however, was not so rapid but that we were enabled to give our first care towards providing for the safety of our friends of the Quinta, by assisting them with the means of transporting themselves to a more remote glen in the mountains, before it was necessary to look to our own, and

Although the links of love that mom
Which War's rude hands had asunder torn

had not been patent ones, yet did it savour somewhat of chivalric times when we had been one evening in the field in the front of the Quinta sporting with the young and the lovely of" the land, as if wars and rumours of wars were to be heard of no more.

I say I felt it rather queerish or so, to be spreading down my boat-cloak for a bed in the same field the next night, with an enemy in my front, for so it was, and to find myself again before daylight next morning, from. my cold clay couch, gazing at the wonderful comet of 1811, that made such capital claret, and wishing that he would wag his fiery tail a little nearer to my face, for it was so stiff with hoar frost that I dared neither to laugh nor cry for fear of breaking it.

We passed jet another night in the same field hallowed by such opposite recollections; but next day, independently of the gathered strength of the enemy in our front, we found a fight of some magnitude going on behind us, the combat of Elbodon; and our major-general, getting alarmed at last at his own temerity, found a sleeping place for us, some distance in the rear, in a hollow, where none but the comet and its companions might be indulged with a look.

Our situation was more than ticklish—with an enemy on three sides and an almost impassable mountain on the fourth—but starting with the lark next morning and passing through Robledillo, we happily succeeded in joining the army in front of Guinalao in the afternoon, to the no small delight of his Grace of Wellington, whose judicious and daring front with half the enemy's numbers, had been our salvation. And it must no doubt have been a mortifying reflection to our divisional chief, to find that his obstinacy and disobedience of orders had not only placed his own division, but that of the whole army in such imminent peril.

Marmont had no doubt a laurel-wreath in embryo for the following day, but he had allowed his day to go by; the night was ours and we used it, so that when daylight broke, he had nothing but empty field-work to wreak his vengeance on. He followed us along the road, with some sharp partial fighting at one or two places, and there seemed a probability of his coming on to the position in which Lord Wellington felt disposed to give him battle; but a scarcity of provisions forced him to retrace his steps, and break up to a certain extent for the subsistence of his army, while our retreat terminated at Soita, which it appeared was about the spot on which Lord Wellington had determined to make a stand.

I shall ever remember our night at Soita for one thing. The commissariat had been about to destroy a cask of rum in the course of that day's retreat, when at the merciful intercession of one of my brother officers, it was happily spared and turned over to his safe keeping, and he showed himself deserving of the trust, for by wonderful dexterity and management, he contrived to get it wheeled along to our resting-place, when establishing himself under the awning of a splendid chestnut-tree, he hung out the usual emblem of its being the head-quarters of a highland chief—not for the purpose of scaring way-fairers as erst did his forefathers of yore, to exclude the worthy Baillie Nicol Jarvie from the clachan of Aberfoyle—but for the more hospitable one of inviting them to be partakers, thereof; and need I add that among the many wearers of empty calabashes which the chances of war had there assembled around him, the call was cheerfully responded to, and a glorious group very quickly assembled.

The morrow promised to be a bloody one; but we cared not for the morrow:—"sufficient for the day is the evil thereof:"—

the song and the jest went merrily round, and, if the truth must be told, I believe that though we carried our cups to the feast, we all went back in them, and with the satisfaction of knowing that we had relieved our gallant chieftain of all farther care respecting the contents of the cask.

The enemy having withdrawn the same night, we retracted our steps, next day, to our former neighbourhood; and though we were occasionally stirred up and called together by the menacing attitudes of our opponents, yet we remained the unusually long period of nearly three months without coming again into actual contact with them.

No officer during that time had one fraction to rub against another; and when I add that our paunches were nearly as empty as our pockets, it will appear almost a libel upon common sense to say that we enjoyed it; yet so it was,—our very privations were a subject of pride and boast to us, and there still continued to be an *esprit de corps*,—a buoyancy of feeling animating all, which nothing could quell; we were alike ready for the field or for frolic, and when not engaged in the one, went headlong into the other.

Ah me! when I call to mind that our chief support in those days of trial was the anticipated delight of recounting those tales in after years, to wondering and admiring groups around our domestic hearths, in merry England; and when I find that so many of these after years have already passed, and that the folks who people these present years, care no more about these dear-bought tales of former ones than if they were spinning-wheel stories of some *auld wife ayont the fire*; I say it is not only enough to make me inflict them with a book, as I have done, but it makes me wish that I had it all to do over again; and I think it would be very odd if I would not do exactly as I have done, for I knew no happier times, and they were their own reward!

It is worthy of remark that Lord Wellington, during- the time I speak of, had made his arrangements for pouncing upon the devoted fortress of Ciudad Rodrigo, with such admirable secrecy, that his preparations were not even known to his own army.

I remember, about a fortnight before the siege commenced, hearing that some gabions and fascines were being made in the neighbourhood, but it was spoken of as a sort of sham preparation, intended to keep the enemy on the *qui vive*, as it seemed improbable that he would dare to invest a fortress in the face of an army which he had not force enough to meet in the field, unless on some select position; nor was it until the day before we opened the trenches that we became quite satisfied that he was in earnest

The sieges, stormings, and capture of Ciudad Rodrigo and Badajos followed hard on each other's heels; and as I gave a short detail of the operations in my former volume, it only remains for me now to introduce such anecdotes and remarks as were there omitted.

The garrison of Ciudad was weak in number, but had a superabundant store of ammunition, which was served out to us with a liberal hand; yet, curious enough, except what was bestowed on the working parties, (and that was plenty in all conscience,) the greater portion of what was intended for the supporting body was expended in air, for they never seemed to have discovered the true position of the besieging force; and though some few of us, in the course of each night, by chance-shots, got transferred from natural to eternal sleep, yet their shells were chiefly employed in the ploughing-up of a hollow way between two hills, where we were supposed to have been, and which they did most effectually at their own cost.

When our turn of duty came for the trenches, however, we never had reason to consider ourselves neglected, but, on the contrary, could well spare what was sent at random.

I have often heard it disputed whether the most daring deeds are done by men of good or bad repute, but I never felt inclined to give either a preference over the other, for I have seen the most desperate things done by both. I remember one day during the siege that a shell pitched in the trenches within a few yards of a noted bad character of the 52nd Regiment, who, rather than take the trouble of leaping out of the trench until it had exploded, went very deliberately up, took it in his arms, and pitched it outside, obliging those to jump back who had there taken shelter from it.

A wild young officer, whose eccentricities and death, at Waterloo, were noticed in my former volume, was at that time at variance with his father on the subject of pecuniary matters, and in mounting the breach, at Ciudad, sword in hand, while both sides were falling thick and fast, he remarked to a brother officer alongside of him, in his usual jocular way, "Egad, if I had my old father here now, I think I should be able to bring him to terms!"

Nothing shows the spirit of daring and inherent bravery of the British soldier so much as in the calling for a body of volunteers for any desperate service. In other armies, as Napier justly remarks, the humblest helmet may catch a beam of glory; but in ours, while the subaltern commanding the forlorn hope may look for death or a company, and the field-officer commanding the stormers an additional step by brevet, to the other officers and soldiers who volunteer on that desperate service, no hope is held out—no reward given; and yet there were as many applicants for a place in the ranks as if it led to the highest honours and rewards.

At the stormings of Badajos and St. Sebastian I happened to be the adjutant of the regiment, and had the selection of the volunteers on those occasions, and I remember that there was as much anxiety expressed, and as much interest made by all ranks to be appointed to the post of honour, as if it had been sinecure situations, in place of deathwarrants, which I had at my disposal.

For the storming of St. Sebastian, the numbers from our battalion were limited to twenty-five; and in selecting the best characters out of those who offered themselves, I rejected an Irishman of the name of Burke, who, although he had been on the forlorn hope both at Ciudad and Badajos, and was a man of desperate bravery, I knew to be one of those wild untameable animals that, the moment the place was carried, would run into every species of excess.

The party had been named two days before they were called for, and Burke besieged my tent night and day, assuring me all the while that unless he was suffered to be of the party, the place would not be taken! I was forced at last to yield, after receiving an application in his behalf from the officer who was to command the party; and he was one of the very few of that gallant little band who returned to tell the story.

Nor was that voracious appetite for fire-eating confined to the private soldier, for it extended alike to all ranks. On the occasion just alluded to, our quota, as already stated, was limited to a subaltern's command of twenty-five men; and as the post of honour was claimed by the senior lieutenant, (Percival,) it in a manner shut the mouths of all the juniors; yet were there some whose mouths would not be shut,—one in particular (Lieutenant H.) who had already seen enough of fighting to satisfy the mind of any reasonable man, for he had stormed and bled at Ciudad Rodrigo, and he had stormed at Badajos, not to mention his having had his share in many, and not nameless battles, which had taken place in the interim; yet nothing would satisfy him but that he must draw his sword in that also.

Our colonel was too heroic a soul himself to check a 'feeling of that sort in those under him, and he very readily obtained the necessary permission to be a volunteer along with the party. Having settled his temporal affairs, namely, willing away his pelisse, jacket, two pairs of trousers, and sundry nether garments—and however trifling these bequests may appear to a military youth of the present day, who happens to be reconnoitring a merchant tailor's settlement in St James's Street, yet let me tell him that, at the time I speak of, they were valued as highly as if they had been hundreds a year in reversion.

The prejudice against will-making by soldiers on service is so strong, that had H. been a rich man in place of a poor one, he must have died on the spot for doing what was accounted infinitely more desperate than storming a breach; but his poverty seemed to have been his salvation, for he was only half killed,—a ball entered under his eye, passed down the roof of the mouth, through the palate, entered again at the collar-bone, and was cut out at the shoulder-blade.

He never again returned to his regiment, but I saw him some years after, in his native country, (Ireland,) in an active situation, and, excepting that he had gotten an ugly mark on his countenance, and his former manly voice had dwindled into a less commanding one, he seemed as well as ever I saw him.

Will-making, as already hinted at, was, in the face of the enemy, reckoned the most daring of all daring deeds, for the doer was always considered a doomed man, and it was but too often verified—not but that the same fatality must have marked him out without it; but so strong was the prejudice generally on that subject that many a goodly estate has, in consequence, passed into what, under other circumstances, would have been forbidden hands.

On the subject of presentiments of death in going into battle, I have known as many instances of falsification as verification. To the latter the popular feeling naturally clings as the more interesting of the two;. but I am inclined to think that the other would preponderate if the account could be justly rendered. The officer alluded to may be taken as a specimen of the former—he had been my messmate and companion at the sieges and stormings of both Ciudad and Badajos—and on the morning after the latter, he told me that he had had a presentiment that he would have fallen the night before, though he had been ashamed to confess it sooner—and yet, to his credit be it spoken, so far from wishing to avoid, he coveted the post of danger—as his duty for that day would have led him to the trenches, but he exchanged with another officer, on purpose to ensure himself a place in the storm.

Of my own feelings on the point in consideration, I am free to say that, while I have been engaged in fifty actions, in which I have neither had the time, nor taken the trouble to ask myself any questions on the subject, but encountered them in whatever humour I happened to be—yet, in many others, (the eve of pitched battles,) when the risk was imminent, and certain that one out of every three must go to the ground, I have asked myself the question, "Do I feel like a dead man?" but I was invariably answered point blank, "No!" And yet must I still look like a superstitious character, when I declare that the only time that I ever went into action, labouring under a regular depression of spirits, was on the evening on which the musket ball felt my head at Foz d'Aronce.

But to return to the storming of Ciudad. The moment which is the most dangerous to the honour and the safety of a British army is that in which they have won the place they have assaulted. While outside the walls, and linked together by the magic hand of discipline, they are heroes—but once they have forced themselves inside they become demons or lunatics—for it is difficult to determine which spirit predominates.

To see the two storming divisions assembled in the great square that night, mixed up in a confused mass, shooting at each other, and firing in at different doors and windows, without the shadow of a reason, was enough to drive any one, who was in possession of his senses, mad. The prisoners were formed in a line on one side of the square—unarmed, it is true—but, on my life, had they made a simultaneous rush forward, they might have made a second Bergen-op-Zoom of it—for so absolute was the sway of the demon of misrule, that half of our men, I verily believe, would have been panicstruck and thrown themselves into the arms of death, over the ramparts, to escape a danger that either did not exist or might have been easily avoided.

After calling, and shouting, until I was hoarse in endeavouring to restore order, and when my voice was no longer audible, seeing a soldier raising his piece to fire at a window, I came across his shoulders with a musket-barrel which I had in my hand, and demanded, "What the devil, sir, are you firing at?" to which he answered, "I don't know, sir! I am firing because everybody else is!"

The storming of a fortress was a new era to the British army of that day, and it is not to be wondered at if the officers were not fully alive to the responsibility which attaches to them on such an occasion—but on their conduct everything hinges—by judgement and discretion men may be kept together—but once let them loose and they are no longer redeemable.

I have often lamented that speechifying was at such a discount in those days, for, excepting what was promulgated in Lord Wellington's orders, which were necessarily brief, the subordinates knew nothing of the past, present, or the future, until the glimpse of an English newspaper some months after served to enlighten their understandings; but there were every day occasions, in which the slightest hint from our superiors, as to the probable results, would have led to incalculable advantages, and in none more so than in the cases now quoted. So far from recommending caution, the chief of one of the storming divisions is grievously belied if he did not grant some special licenses for that particular occasion, though I am bound to say for him that he did all he could to repress them when he found the advantage taken.

Ciudad, being a remote frontier fortress, could boast of few persons of any note within its walls—our worthy friends of Horquera, (the *alcalde*, with his family,) were probably the best, and he returned and resumed his official functions as soon as he found that the place had reverted to its legal owners—his house had been a princely one, but was, unfortunately, situated behind the great breach, and was blown to atoms—so that, for me time being, he was obliged to content himself with one more humble—though, if I may speak as I have felt, I should say not less comfortable, for I contrived to make it my home as often as I could find an excuse for so doing—and, as the old Proverb goes, *where there is a will there is a way*, it was as often as I could.

One portion of the ceremony of Spanish hospitality was their awaking me about five in the morning to make a cup of chocolate, made so thick that a teaspoon might stand in it, which, with a little crisp brown toast, was always administered by the fair hands of one of the damsels, and *certes* I never could bring myself to consider it an annoyance, however unusual it may seem in this cold land of ours.

Chapter 12

Very Short, With a Few Anecdotes

After the fall of Ciudad Rodrigo, our battalion took possession for a time of Ituera, a pretty little village on the banks of the Azava.

It was a delightful coursing country, abounding in hares; and as the chase in those days afforded a double gratification—the one present, and the other in perspective, (the dinner hour,) it was always followed with much assiduity. The village, too, happened to be within a short ride of Ciudad, so that frequent visits to our friends formed an agreeable variety, and rendered our short sojourn there a season of real enjoyment.

I was much struck, on first entering Spain, in observing what appeared to be a gross absurdity in their religious observances; for whenever one of those processions was heard approaching, the girls, no matter how they had been employed, immediately ran to the window, where, kneeling down, they continued repeating their *aves* until it had passed, when they jumped up again and were ready for any frolic or mischief.

Such was the effect produced inwardly by the outward passage of the *Hoste* but it was not until I went to Ituera that I had an opportunity of witnessing the fatal results of a more familiar visit from those gentlemen bearing torches and dark lanterns, for they certainly seemed to me to put several souls topflight before they were duly prepared for it. One happened to be the landlady of the house in which I was quartered, a woman about three score, and blind; but she was, nevertheless, as merry as a cricket, and used to amuse us over the fire-side in the evening, while "twisting her rock and her wee pickle tow" in chaunting Malbrook and other ditties equally interesting, with a voice which at one time might have had a little music in it, but had then degenerated into the squeak of a penny trumpet.

In her last evening on earth, she had treated as with her usual serenade, and seemed as likely to live a dozen years longer as any one of the group around her; but on my return from a field-day next forenoon, I met the *padre*, the sexton, and their usual accompaniments, marching out of the house to the tune of that grave air of theirs; and I saw that farther question was needless, for the tears of the attendant damsels told me the tale of woe.

Her sudden departure was to me most unaccountable, nor could I ever obtain an explanation beyond that she was very aged; that they had sent for the Father to comfort her, and now she was happy in the keeping of their blessed Virgin.

There was much weeping and wailing for a day or two, and her granddaughter, a tall thin lath of a girl, about eleven or twelve years of age, seemed the most distressed of the group. It so happened that a few days after, an order was promulgated authorizing us to fill up our ranks with Spanish recruits, to the extent of ten men for each company, and I started off to some of the neighbouring villages, where we were well-known, in the hope of being able to pick up some good ones. On my return I was rather amused to find that the damsel already mentioned, whom I had left ten days before bathed in tears, was already a blushing bride in the hands of a strapping muleteer.

While on the subject of those Spanish recruits, I may here remark that we could not persuade the countrymen to join us, and it was not until we got to Madrid that we succeeded in procuring the prescribed number for our battalion. Those we got, however, were a very inferior sample of the Spaniard, and we therefore expected little from them, but to their credit be it recorded, they turned out admirably well—they were orderly and well-behaved in quarters, and thoroughly good in the field; and they never went into action that they had not their full portion of casualties.

There were fifty of them originally, and at the close of the war, (about a year and a half after,) I think there were about seventeen remaining, and there had not been a single desertion from among them. When we were leaving the country they received some months' gratuitous pay and were discharged, taking with them our best wishes, which they richly merited.

Lord Wellington during the whole of the war kept a pack of fox-hounds, and while they contributed not a little to the amusement of whatever portion of the army happened to be within reach of head-quarters, they were to his Lordship valuable in many ways; for while he enjoyed the chase as much as any, it gave him an opportunity of seeing and conversing with the officers of the different departments, and other individuals, without attracting the notice of the enemy's emissaries; and the pursuits of that manly exercise, too, gave him a better insight into the characters of the individuals under him, than he could possibly have acquired by years of acquaintance under ordinary circumstances.

It is not unusual to meet, in the society of the present day, some old Peninsular trump, with the rank very probably of a field officer, and with a face as polished, and its upper story as well furnished as the figure-head of his sword hilt, gravely asserting that all the merit which the Duke of Wellington has acquired from his victories was due to the troops! And having plundered the commander-in-chief of his glory, and divided it among the followers, he, as an officer of those same followers, very complacently claims a field officer's allowance in the division of the spoil.

I would stake all I have in this world that no man ever heard such an opinion from the lips of a private soldier—I mean a thorough good service one—for the ideas of such men are beyond it; and I have ever found that their proudest stories relate to the good or gallant deeds of those above them. It is impossible, therefore, to hear such absurdities advanced by one in the rank of an officer, without marvelling by what fortuitous piece of luck he, with the military capacity of a baggage animal, had contrived to hold his commission, for he must have been deeply indebted to the clemency of those above, and take's the usual method of that class of persons, to show his sense thereof, by kicking down the ladder by which he ascended.

Our civil brethren in general are of necessity obliged to swallow a considerable portion of whatever we choose to place before them, nut when they meet with such a one as I have described they may safely calculate that whenever the items of his services can be collected, it will be found that his Majesty has had a hard bargain! For, knowing, as everyone does, what the best ship's crew would be afloat in the wide world of waters without a master, they may, on the same principle, bear in mind that there can no more be an efficient army without a good general, than there can be an efficient general without a good army, for the one is part and parcel of the other they cannot exist singly!

The touching on. the foregoing subject naturally obliges me to wander from my narrative to indulge in a few professional observations, illustrative not only of war, but of its instruments.

Those unaccustomed to warfare, are apt to imagine that a field of battle is a scene of confusion worse confounded, but that is a mistake, for, except on particular occasions, there is in general no noise or confusion anything like what takes place on ordinary field days in England. I have often seen half the number of troops put to death, without half the bluster and confusion which takes place in a sham fight in the Phoenix-Park of Dublin.

The man who blusters at a field day is not the man who does it on the field of battle: on the contrary, his thoughts there are generally too his for utterance, and he would gladly squeeze himself into a nutshell if he could. The man who makes a noise on the field of battle is generally a good one, but. all rules have their exceptions, for I have seen one or two thorough good ones, who were blusterers in both situations, but it, nevertheless, betrays a weakness in any officer who is habitually noisy about trifles, from the simple fact that when anything of importance occurs to require an extraordinary exertion of lungs, nature cannot supply him with the powers requisite to make the soldiers understand that it is the consequence of an occurrence more serious, than the trifle he was in the habit of making a noise about.

In soldiering, as in everything else, except Billingsgate and ballad singing, the cleverest things are done quietly.

At the storming of the heights of Bera, on the 8th of October, 1813, Colonel, now Sir John Colbourne, who commanded our second brigade, addressed his men before leading them up to the enemy's redoubt, with, "Now, my lads, we'll just charge up to the edge of the ditch, and if we can't get in, we'll stand there and fire in their faces."

They charged accordingly, the enemy fled from the works, and in following them up the mountain. Sir John, in rounding a hill, accompanied only by his brigade-major and a few riflemen, found that he had headed a retiring body of about 300 of the French, and whispering to his brigade-major to get as many men together as he could, he without hesitation rode boldly up to the enemy's commander, and demanded his sword! The Frenchman surrendered it with the usual grace of his countrymen, requesting that the other would bear witness that he had conducted himself like a good and valiant soldier! Sir John answered the appeal with an approving nod; for it was no time to refuse bearing witness to the valour of 300 men, while they were in the act of surrendering to half a dozen.

If a body of troops is under fire, and so placed as to be unable to return it, the officer commanding should make it a rule to keep them constantly on the move, no matter if it is but two side steps to the right or one to the front, it always makes them believe they are doing something, and prevents the mind from brooding over a situation which is the most trying of any.

The coolness of an officer in action, if even shown in trifles, goes a great way towards maintaining the steadiness of the men. At the battle of Waterloo, I heard Sir John Lambert call one of his commanding officers to order for repeating his (the general's) word of command, reminding him that when the regiments were in contiguous close columns, they ought to take it from himself! As the brigade was under a terrific fire at the time, the notice of such a trifling breach of rule showed, at all events, that the gallant general was at home!

In the course of the five days' fighting which took place near Bayonne, in December, 1813, a singular change of fate, with its consequent interchange of civilities, took place between the commanding officer of a French regiment and one of ours; I forget whether it was the 4th or 9th, but I think it was one of the regiments of that brigade—it had been posted amongst some enclosures which left both its flanks at the mercy of others.

The fighting at that place had been very severe, with various success, and while the regiment alluded to was hotly engaged in front, a French corps succeeded in getting in their rear; when the enemy's commandant advancing to the English one, apologised for troubling him, but begged to point out that he was surrounded, and must consider himself his prisoner!

While the British colonel was listening to the mortifying intelligence, and glancing around to see if no hope of escape was left, he observed another body of English in the act of compassing the very corps by which he had been caught; and, returning the Frenchman's salute, begged his pardon for presuming to differ with him in opinion, but that he was labouring under a mistake, for he (the Frenchman) was, on the contrary, his prisoner, pointing in his turn to the movement that had taken place while they had been disputing the point. As the fact did not admit of a doubt, the Frenchman giving a shrug of the shoulders, and uttering a lament over the fickleness of the war-goddess, quietly surrendered.

CHAPTER 13

Gentle Visitors

Pass we on to Badajos—to that last, that direful, but glorious night—the 6th of April—"so fiercely fought, so terribly won, so dreadful in all its circumstances, that posterity can scarcely be expected to credit the tale."

Anyone who has taken the trouble to read and digest what Napier has said in vindication of the measures adopted by Lord Wellington for the subjugation of those fortresses in the manner in which it was done, must feel satisfied that their propriety admits of no dispute. But as the want of time rendered it necessary to set the arts and sciences at defiance—and that, if carried at all, it must have been done with an extra sacrifice of human life, it will forever remain a matter of opinion at what period of the siege the assault should have been made with the best prospect of success, and with the least probable loss—and such being the case it must be free to every writer to offer his own ideas.

Lord Wellington, at is well known, waited on each occasion for open breaches, and was each time successful—so far he did well, and they may do better who can. Colonel Lamarre would have attacked Badajos the first night of the siege with better hopes of success than on the last, as the garrison, he says, would have been less prepared, and the defences not so complete.

But I differ from him on both positions, for, depend upon it, that every garrison is excessively alive for the first few days after they have been invested. And as to defensive preparations, I have reason to think that few after ones of consequence took place, but those of counteracting the effects of our battering guns.

I am, nevertheless, one of those who would like to see the attempt made at an intermediate period. Breaches certainly serve the important end of distracting the attention of the garrison, and leading them to neglect other assailable points; though, whenever they have the opportunity of retrenching them, as at Badajos, they are undoubtedly the strongest parts of the works. I should therefore carry on the siege in the usual manner until about the time the batteries began to come into operation; and as it might then be fairly presumed that the garrison, by the regular order of proceedings, would be lulled into a notion of temporary security, I should feel monstrously inclined to try my luck. If it turned up trumps, it might save valuable time and a thousand or two of valuable lives. If it failed, the loss would be in proportion; but it would neither lose time, nor compromise the result of the siege.

Colonel Jones, an able writer and an able fighter, in his particular department, would have had us do what his great guns ought to have done on that memorable night—namely, to have cleared away the defences on the top of the breach, which he affirms might have been done by the rush of a dense mass of troops. But had he been where I was he would have seen that there was no scarcity of rushes of dense masses of troops; but, independently of every other engine of destruction which human ingenuity could invent—they were each time met by a dense rush of balls, and it is the nature of man to bow before them. No dense mass of troops could reach the top of that breach.

Major (then Lieutenant) Johnston, of ours, who was peculiarly calculated for desperate enterprise, preceded the forlorn hope, in command of a party carrying ropes, prepared with nooses, to throw over the sword blades, as the most likely method of displacing, by dragging them down the breach; but he and his whole party were stricken down before one of them had sot within throwing distance.

When an officer, as I have already mentioned, with a presentiment of death upon him, resigned a safe duty to take a desperate one—when my own servant, rather than remain behind, gave up his situation and took his place in the ranks□when another man of ours (resolved to win or to die) thrust himself beneath the chained sword blades, and there suffered the enemy to dash his brains out with the ends of their muskets—these, I say, out of as many thousand instances of the kind which may be furnished, will show that there was no want of daring leaders or desperate followers.

The defences on the tops of the breaches ought to have been cleared away by our batteries before the assault commenced. But failing that, I cannot see why a couple of six-pounders (or half a dozen) might not have been run up along with the storming party, to the crest of the glacis.

Our battalion took post there, and lay about ten minutes unknown to the enemy, and had a few guns been sent along with us, I am confident that we could have taken them up with equal silence, and had them pointed at the right place—when, at the time that the storming party commenced operations, a single discharge from each, at that range of a few yards, would not only have disturbed the economy of the sword blades and sandbags, but astonished the wigs of those behind them. As it was, however, when I visited the breaches next rooming, instead of seeing the ruin of a place just carried by storm, the whole presented the order and regularity of one freshly prepared to meet it—not a sword blade deranged, nor a sandbag removed!

The advance of the Fourth Division had been delayed by some accident, and the head of their column did not reach the ditch until our first attack had been repulsed, and when considerable confusion, consequently, prevailed.

The Seventh Fusiliers came gallantly on, headed by Major ———, who, though a very little man, shouted with the lungs of a giant, for the way to be cleared, to "let the Royal Fusiliers advance!" Several of our officers assisted him in such a laudable undertaking; but, in the mean time, a musket-ball found its way into some sensitive part, and sent the gallant major trundling heels over head among the loose stones, shouting to a less heroic tune—while his distinguished corps went determinedly on, but with no better success than those who had just preceded them, for the thing was not to be done.

After we had withdrawn from the ditch and re-formed the division for a renewal of the attack, (it must have been then about two or three o'clock in the morning,) some of those on the lookout brought us information that the enemy were leaving the breaches, and our battalion was instantly moved forward to take possession.

We stole down into the ditch with the same silence which marked our first advance—an occasional explosion or a discharge of musketry continued to be heard in distant parts of the works; but in the awful charnel pit we were then traversing to reach the foot of the breach, the only sounds that disturbed the night were the moans of the dying, with an occasional screech from others suffering under acute agony; while a third class lying there disabled, and alive to passing events, on hearing the movement of troops, (though too dark to distinguish them,) began proclaiming their names and regiments, and appealing to individual officers and soldiers of the different corps, on whose friendly aid they seemed to feel that they could rely if they happened to be within hearing.

It was a heart-rending moment to be obliged to leave such appeals unheeded; but, though the fate of those around might have been ours the next instant, our common weal, our honour, and our country's, alike demanded that everything should be sacrificed to secure the prize which was now within our grasp; and our onward movement was therefore continued into the breach with measured tread and stern silence, leaving the unfortunate sufferers to doubt whether the stone walls around had not been their only listeners.

Once established within the walls we felt satisfied that the town was ours—and, profiting by his experience at Ciudad, our commandant (Colonel Cameron) took the necessary measures to keep his battalion together, so long as the safety of the place could in anyway be compromised—for, knowing the barbarous license which soldiers employed in that desperate ser- vice claim, and which they will not be denied, he addressed them, and promised that they should have the same indulgence as others, and that he should not insist upon keeping them together longer than was absolutely necessary; but he assured them that if any man quitted the ranks until he gave permission, he would cause him to be put to death on the spot.

That had the desired effect until between nine and ten o'clock in the morning, when, seeing that the whole of the late garrison had been secured and marched off to Elvas, he again addressed his battalion, and thanked them for their conduct throughout; he concluded with, "Now, my men, you may fall out and enjoy yourselves for the remainder of the day, but I shall expect to see you all in camp at the usual roll-call in the evening!"

When the evening came, however, in place of the usual tattoo report of all present; it was all absent, and it could have been wished that the irregularities had ended with that evening's report.

As soon as a glimpse of daylight permitted I went to take a look at the breach, and there saw a solitary figure, with a drawn sword, stalking over the ruins and the slain, which, in the gray dawn of morning appeared to my astonished eyes like a headless trunk, and concluded that it was the ghost of one of the departed come in search of his earthly remains. I cautiously approached to take a nearer survey, when I found that it was Captain M'Nair, of the 52nd, with his head wrapped in a red handkerchief.

He told me that he was looking for his cap and his scabbard, both of which had parted company from him in the storm, about that particular spot; but his search proved a forlorn hope. I congratulated him that his head had not gone in the cap, as had been the case with but too many of our mutual companions on that fatal night.

When our regiment had reformed after the assault we found a melancholy list of absent officers, ten of whom were doomed never to see it more, and it was not until our return to the camp that we learnt the fate of all.

The wounded had found their way or been removed to their own tents—the fallen filled a glorious grave on the spot where they fell.

The first tent that I entered was Johnston's, with his shattered arm bandaged; he was lying on his boat- cloak fast asleep; and, coupling his appearance with the recollection of the daring duty he had been called on to perform but a few hours before,- in front of the forlorn hope, I thought that I had never set my eyes on a nobler picture of a soldier. His whole appearance, even in sleep, showed exactly as it had been in the execution of that duty; his splendid figure was so disposed that it seemed as if he was taking the first step on the breach—his eyebrows were elevated—his nostrils still distended— and, altogether, he looked as if he would clutch the castle in his remaining hand. No one could have seen him at that moment without saying "There lies a hero!"

Of the doomed, who still survived, was poor Donald MacPherson, a gigantic highlander of about six feet and a half, as good a soul as ever lived; in peace a lamb—in war a lion. Donald feared for nothing either in this world or the next; he had been true to man and true to his God, and he looked his last hour in the face like a soldier and a Christian!

Donald's final departure from this life showed him a worthy specimen of his country, and his methodical arrangements, while they prove what I have stated, may, at the same time, serve as a model for Joe Hume himself, when he comes to cast up his last earthly accounts.

Donald had but an old mare and a portmanteau, with its contents, worth about £15, to leave behind him. He took a double inventory of the latter, sending one to the regiment by post, and giving the other in charge of his servant—and paying the said worthy his wages up to the probable day of his death; he gave him a conditional order on the paymaster for whatever more might be his due, should he survive beyond his time—and, if ever man did, he certainly quitted this world with a clear conscience.

Poor Donald! peace be to thy manes, for thou wert one whom memory loves to dwell on!

It is curious to remark the fatality which attends individual officers in warfare. In our regiment there were many fine young men who joined us, and fell in their first encounter with the enemy; but, amongst the old standing dishes, there were some who never, by any chance got hit; while others, again, never went into action without.

At the close of the war, when we returned to Eng- land, if our battalion did not show symptoms of its being a well-shot corps, it is very odd: nor was it to be wondered at if the camp-colours were not covered with that precision, nor the salute given with the grace usually expected from a reviewed body, when I furnish the following account of the officers commanding companies on the day of inspection, *viz.*

Beckwith with a cork-leg—Pemberton and Manners with a shot each in the knee, making them as stiff as the other's tree one—Loftus Gray with a gash in the lip, and minus a portion of one heel, which made him march to the tune of dot and go one—Smith with a shot in the ankle—Eeles minus a thumb—Johnston, in addition to other shot holes, a stiff elbow, which deprived him of the power of disturbing his friends as a scratcher of Scotch reels upon the violin—Percival with a shot through his lungs. Hope with a grape-shot lacerated leg—and George Simmons with his riddled body held together by a pair of stays, for his was no holyday waist, which naturally required such an appendage lest the burst of a sigh should snap it asunder; but one that appertained to a figure framed in nature's fittest mould to *brave the battle and the breeze!*

I know not to what particular circumstances British tailors were in the first instance indebted, for ranking them so low in the scale of humanity; but, as far as my knowledge extends, there never was a more traduced race. Those of our regiment I know were among the best soldiers in it, and more frequently hit than any, very much to our mortification; for the very limited allowance of an officer's campaigning baggage left him almost constantly at their mercy for the decoration of his outward man; but as the musket-balls showed no mercy to them, we could not of course expect them to extend it to us.

Our master-man having at this time got his third shot, we deemed it high time to place him on the shelf, by confining his operations in the field to the baggage guard. So long as we could preserve him in a condition to wield the scissors, we luckily discovered that there were minor thimble-plyers ready to rally round him, for we should otherwise have been driven sometimes to the extraordinary necessity of invading the nether garments of the ladies!

The last night at Badajos had been to the belligerents such as few had ever seen—the next to its devoted inhabitants was such as none would ever wish to see again; for there was no sanctuary within its walls.

I was conversing with a friend the day after, at the door of his tent, when we observed two ladies coming from the city, who made directly towards us; they seemed both young, and when they came near, the elder of the two threw back her *mantilla* to address us, showing a remarkably handsome figure, with fine features; but her sallow, sunburnt, and care-worn, though still youthful countenance, showed that in her, *The time for tender thoughts and soft endearments had fled away and gone.*

She at once addressed us in that confident heroic manner so characteristic of the high-bred Spanish maiden, told us who they were, the last of an ancient and honourable house, and referred to an officer high in rank in our army, who had been quartered there in the days of her prosperity, for the truth of her tale.

Her husband, she said, was a Spanish officer in a distant part of the kingdom; he might or he might not still be living. But yesterday, she and this her young sister were able to live in affluence and in a handsome house—today, they knew not where to lay their heads—where to get a change of raiment, or a morsel of bread. Her house, she said, was a wreck, and, to show the indignities to which they had been subjected, she pointed to where the blood was still trickling down their necks, caused by the wrenching of their ear-rings through the flesh, by the hands of worse than savages, who would not take the trouble to unclasp them!

For herself, she said, she cared not; but for the agitated, and almost unconscious maiden by her side, whom she had but lately received over from the hands of her conventual instructresses she was in despair, and knew not what to do; and that in the rapine and ruin which was at that moment desolating the city, she saw no security for her but the seemingly indelicate one she had adopted, of coming to the camp and throwing themselves upon the protection of any British officer who would afford it; and so great, she said, was her faith in our national character, that she knew the appeal would not be made in vain, nor the confidence abused. Nor was it made in vain, nor could it be abused, for she stood by the side of an angel!—A being more transcendently lovely I had never before seen—one more amiable I have never yet known!

Fourteen summers had not yet passed over her youthful countenance, which was of a delicate freshness, more English than Spanish—her face, though not perhaps rigidly beautiful, was nevertheless so remarkably handsome, and so irresistibly attractive, surmounting a figure cast in nature's fairest mould, that to look at her was to love her—and I did love her; but I never told my love, and in the meantime another, and a more impudent fellow stepped in and won her! but yet I was happy for in him she found such a one as her loveliness and her misfortunes claimed—a man of honour, and a husband in every way worthy of her!

That a being so young, so lovely, so interesting, just emancipated from the gloom of a convent, unknowing of the world and to the world unknown, should thus have been wrecked on a sea of troubles, and thrown on the mercy of strangers under circumstances so dreadful, so uncontrollable, and not to have sunk to rise no more, roust be the wonder of everyone. Yet from the moment she was thrown on her own resources, her star was in the ascendant.

Guided by a just sense of rectitude, an innate purity of mind, a singleness of purpose which defied malice, and a soul that soared above circumstances, she became alike the adored of the camp and of the drawing-room, and eventually the admired associate of princes. She yet lives, in the affections of her gallant husband in an elevated situation in life, a pattern to her sex, and the everybody's *beau ideal* of what a wife should be.

My reader will perhaps bear with me on this subject yet a little longer.

Thrown upon each other's acquaintance in a manner so interesting, it is not to be wondered at that she and I conceived a friendship for each other, which has proved as lasting as our lives—a friendship which was cemented by after circumstances so singularly romantic, that imagination may scarcely picture them! The friendship of man is one thing—the friendship of woman another; and those only who have been on the theatre of fierce warfare, and knowing that such a being was on the spot, watching with earnest and unceasing solicitude over his safety alike with those most dear to her, can fully appreciate the additional value which it gives to one's existence.

About a year after we became acquainted, I remember that our battalion was one day moving down to battle, and had occasion to pass by the lone country-house in which she had been lodged.

The situation was so near to the outposts, and a battle certain, I concluded that she must ere then have been removed to a place of greater security, and, big with the thought of coming events, I scarcely even looked at it as we rolled along; but just as I had passed the door, I found my hand suddenly grasped in hers—she gave it a gentle pressure, and without uttering a word had rushed back into the house again, almost before I could see to whom I was indebted for a kindness so unexpected and so gratifying.

My mind had the moment before been sternly occupied in calculating the difference which it makes in a man's future prospects—his killing or being killed, when *a change at once came o'er, the spirit of the dream*, and throughout the remainder of that long; and trying day, I felt a lightness of heart and buoyancy of spirit which, in such a situation, was no less new than delightful.

I never, until then, felt so forcibly the beautiful description of Fitz James's expression of feeling, after his leave-taking of Helen under somewhat similar circumstances:—

And after oft the knight would say,
That not when prize of festal day.
Was dealt him by the brightest fair
That e'er wore jewel in her hair,
So highly did his bosom swell,
As at that simple, mute, farewell.

Chapter 14

A Line Drawn Between Man and Beast

With discipline restored, Badajos secured, and the French relieving army gone to the right about, we found ourselves once more transferred to the North.

Marmont had, during our absence, thrown away much valuable time in cutting some unmeaning vagaries before the Portuguese militia, which, happily for us, he might have spent more profitably; and now that we approached him, he fell back upon Salamanca, leaving us to take quiet possession of our former cantonments.

Lord Wellington had thus, by a foresight almost superhuman, and by a rapidity of execution equal to the conception, succeeded in snatching the two frontier fortresses out of the enemy's hands in the face of their superior armies, it gave him a double set of keys for the security of rescued Portugal, and left his victorious army free and unfettered for the field.

We had been on the watch long enough, with the enemy before, beside, and around us; but it had now become their tarn to look out for squalls, and by and by they caught it—but in the mean while we were allowed to have some respite after the extraordinary fatigues of the past.

Spring had by that time furnished the face of nature with her annual suit of regimentals, (I wish it had done as much for us,) our pretty little village stood basking in the sunshine of the plain, while the surrounding forest courted the lovers of solitude to repose within its shady bosom. There the nightingale and the bee-bird made love to their mates—and there too the wolf made love to his meat, for which he preferred the hind-quarter of a living horse, but failing that, he did not despise a slice from a mule or a donkey.

Nature seemed to have intended that region as the abode of rural tranquillity, but man had doomed it otherwise. The white tent rearing its fiery top among the green leaves of the forest—the war-steed careering on the plains—the voice of the trumpet for the bleat of the lamb—and the sharp clans of the rifle with its thousand echoes reverberating from the rocks at target-practice, were none of them in keeping with the scene; so that the nightingale was fain to hush its melody, and the wolf his howl, until a change of circumstances should restore him to his former sinecure of head ranger.

The actors on that busy scene too continued to be wild and reckless as their occupation, their lives had been so long in perpetual jeopardy that they now held them of very little value. A rifleman one day in marking the target, went behind to fix it more steadily; another, who did not observe him go there, sent a ball through, which must have passed within a hair's breadth of the marker, but the only notice he took was to poke his head from behind, and thundering out, "Hilloah there, do you mean to shoot us?" went on with his work as if it had been nothing.

Whilst on the subject of rifle-shooting, and thinking of the late Indian exhibition of its nicety on the London stage, it reminds me that the late Colonel Wade, and one of the privates of our second battalion, were in the habit of holding the target for each other at the distance of 200 yards.

I cannot think of those days without reflecting on the mutability of human life, and the chances and changes which man is heir to. For, to think that I, who had so many years been the sleeping and waking companion of dead men's bones, and not only accustomed to hold them valueless, but often to curse the chance *which brought them between the wind and my nobility*; I say that, under such circumstances, to think I should e'er have stood the chance of dying the death of a body snatcher, is to me astonishing, and would show, even without any scriptural authority, *that in the midst of life we are in death*, for so it was.

Some years after, I was on my way from Ireland to Scotland, when I was taken seriously ill at Belfast. After being confined to bed several days in a hotel there, and not getting better, I became anxious to reach home, and had myself conveyed on board a steamboat which was on the point of sailing.

I had been but a few minutes in bed when I heard a confused noise about the boat; but I was in a low listless mood, dead to everything but a feeling of supreme misery, until my cabin-door was opened, and the ugly faces of several legal understrappers protruded themselves, and began to reconnoitre me with a strong sinister expression; I was dead even to that, but when they at length explained, that in searching the luggage of the passengers, they had found a defunct gentleman in one of the boxes, and as he belonged to nobody out of bed, he must naturally be the property of the only one in it, *viz*: myself! a very reasonable inference, at which I found it high time to stir myself, the more particularly as the intimation was accompanied by an invitation to visit the police-office.

My unshaved countenance worn down to a most cadaverous hue with several days' intense suffering, was but ill calculated to bear me out in assertions to the contrary; but having some documentary evidence to show who I was, and, seeing too that I was really the invalid which they thought I had only affected, they went away quite satisfied. Not so, however, the mob without, who insisted on being allowed to judge for themselves, so that the officers were obliged to return and beg of me to show myself at the cabin window to pacify them.

There is no doubt but I must at that time, have borne a much stronger resemblance to the gentleman in the box, than to the gentleman proprietor; but to show the justice and discrimination of mobites, I had no sooner exhibited my countenance such as it was, than half of them shouted that they knew me to be the man, and demanded that I should be handed over to them; and had there not been some of the family of the hotel fortunately on board seeing their friends off, who vouched for my authenticity, and for my having been in bed in their house ever since I came to town, there is little doubt but they would have made a subject of me.

Returning from this grave anecdote to the seat of war, I pass on to the assembling of the army in front of Ciudad Rodrigo, preparatory to the advance upon Salamanca.

Our last assemblage on the same spot was to visit the walls of that fortress with the thunder of our artillery, and having, by the force of such persuasive arguments, succeeded in converting them into friends, in whom, with confidence, we might rely in the hour of need we were now about to bid them and our peasant associates an adieu, with a fervent wish on our part that it might be a final one, while with joy we looked forward to the brightening prospect which seemed to promise us an opportunity of diving a little deeper into their land of romance than we had yet done.

Division after division of our iron framed warriors successively arrived, and took possession of the rugged banks of the Agueda, in gallant array and in gayer shape than formerly, for in our first campaigns the canopy of heaven had been our only covering, and our walking on two legs, clothed in rags, the only distinction between us and the wild beast of the forest —whereas, we were now indulged in the before unheard of luxury of a tent—three being allowed to the soldiers of each company, and one to the officers.

There is nothing on earth so splendid—nothing so amusing to a military soul as this assembling of an army for active service—to see fifty thousand men all actuated by one common spirit of enterprise, and the cause their country's! And to see the manner, too, in which it acts on the national characters enlisted in it—the grave-looking, but merry-hearted Englishman—the canny, cautious, and calculating Scotchman, and the devil-may-care nonchalance of the Irish.

I should always prefer to serve in a mixed corps, but I love to see a national one—for while the natives of the three amalgamate well, and make, generally speaking, the most steady, there is, nevertheless, an *esprit* about a national one which cannot fail to please.

Nothing occasions so much controversy in civil life as the comparative merits of those same corps—the Scotchman claiming every victory in behalf of his countrymen, and the Irishman being no less voracious—so that the unfortunate English regiments, who furnish more food for powder than both put together, are thus left to fight and die unhonoured.

Those who know no better, naturally enough award the greatest glory to the greatest sufferers; but that is no true criterion—for great loss in battle, in place of being a proof of superior valour and discipline, is not unfrequently occasioned by a want of the latter essential.

The proudest trophy which the commanding officer of a regiment can ever acquire is the credit of having done a brilliant deed with little loss—and although there are many instances in which they may justly boast of such misfortunes—witness the Fifty-Seventh at Albuera, the Twenty-Seventh at Waterloo, and a hundred similar cases, in which they nearly all perished on the spot they were ordered to defend, yet I am of opinion, that if the sentiments of old service officers could be gathered, it would be found among a majority, that their proudest regimental days were not those on which they had suffered most.

National regiments have, perhaps, a greater *esprit de corps* generally, than the majority of mixed ones; but in action they are more apt to be carried away by some sudden burst of undisciplined valour, as Napier would have it, to the great danger of themselves and others.

An Irishman, after the battle of Vimiera, in writing home to his friends, said, "We chained them over fifteen leagues of country, we never waited for the word of command, for we were all Irish!" And I think I could furnish a Highland anecdote or two of a similar tendency.

In the present day, the crack national regiments, officered as they are with their share of the elite of their country's youth, are not to be surpassed—but in war time I have never considered a crack national regiment equal to a cracked mixed one.

The Irishman seems sworn never to drink water when he can get whisky, unless he likes it better—the Scotch man, for a soldier, sometimes shows too much of the lawyer—the Englishman, too, has his besetting sin—but by mixing the three in due proportions, the evils are found to counteract each other. As regards personal bravery there is not a choice among them—and for the making of a perfect regiment, I should, therefore, prescribe one-half English, and of Irish and Scotch a quarter each. Yet, as I said before, I have to see a national corps, and hope never to see a British army without them.

With regard to officers, I think I mentioned before that in war we had but a slender sprinkling of the aristocracy among us. The reason I consider a very sensible one, for whatever may be the sins with which they have, at different times, been charged, the want of pluck has never been reckoned among the number. But as there never was any scarcity of officers for the field, and consequently their country did not demand the sacrifice—they may very conscientiously stand acquitted for not going abroad, to fight and be starved when they could live at home in peace and plenty.

I have often lamented, however, that a greater number had not been induced to try their fortunes on the tented field, for I have ever found that their presence and example tended to correct many existing evils. How it should have happened I leave to others, but I have rarely known one who was not beloved by those under him. They were not better officers, nor were they better or braver men than the soldiers of fortune,[1] with which they were mingled; but there was a degree of refinement in all their actions, even in mischief, which commanded the respect of the soldiers, while those who had been framed in rougher moulds, and left unpolished, were sometimes obliged

---
1. Meaning soldiers of no fortune.

to have recourse to harsh measures to enforce it. The example was, therefore, invaluable for its tendency to show that habitual severity was not a necessary ingredient in the art of governing—and, however individuals may affect to despise and condemn the higher orders, it is often because they feel that they sink in the comparison, and thus it is that they will ever have their cringers and imitators even among their abusers.

I have, without permission, taken the liberty of dedicating this volume to one of their number[2]—not because he is one of them, but that he is what I have found him—a nobleman! I dedicate it to him, because, though personally unacquainted, I knew and admired him in war, as one of the most able and splendid assistants of the illustrious chief with whom he served—and, *though poor the offering be*, I dedicate it to him in gratitude, that with no other recommendation than my public services, I have ever since the war experience at his hands a degree of consideration and kindness which none but a great and a good man could have known how to offer.

It may appear to my reader that I have no small share of personal vanity to gratify in making this announcement, and I own it. I am proud that 1 should have been thought deserving; of his lordship's notice, but I am still prouder that it is in my power to give myself as an example that men of rank in office are not all of them the heartless beings which many try to make them appear.

With the army assembled, and the baggage laden on a fine May morning, I shall place every infantry man on his legs, the dragoon in his saddle, and the followers on their donkeys, starting the whole cavalcade off on the high road to Salamanca, which, being a very uninteresting one, and without a shot to enliven the several days' march, I shall take advantage of the opportunity it affords to treat my young military readers to a dissertation on advanced guards—for we have been so long at peace that the customs of war in the like cases are liable to be forgotten, unless rubbed into existence from time to time by some such old

---

2. Major-General Lord Fitzroy Somerset.

foggy as I am, and for which posterity can never feel sufficiently thankful, as to see our army taking the field with the advanced guard on a plain, prescribed by the book of regulations, would bring every old soldier to what I for one am not prepared for—a premature end; as however well the said advanced guard may be calculated to find birds' nests in a barrack square or on a common parade, in the field it would worry an army to death.

In the first place, if a plain is an honest plain, it requires no advanced guard, for a man's eyes are not worth presenting if they cannot help him to see three or four miles all round about—but there is no such thing as a plain anywhere. Look at the plains of Salamanca, where you may fancy that you see fifty miles straight on end without so much as a wart on the face of nature, as big as a mole hill; yet within every league or two you find yourself descending into a ravine a couple of miles deep, taking half a day to regain the plain on the opposite side, within a couple of stones' throw of where you were.

In place of harassing the men with perpetual flank patrols, blistering their feet over the loose stones with shoes full of sand, and expending their valuable wind, which is so much wanted towards the end of the day, in scrambling over uneven ground, let me recommend the advanced guard to confine itself to the high road until patrolling becomes necessary, which, in a forest, will be from the time they enter until they leave it, unless they can trust to the information that the enemy are otherwise engaged.

And in the open country every officer commanding a regiment, troop, or company, who has got half a military eye in his head, will readily see when it is advisable to send a patrol to examine any particular ground; and in so doing; his best guide is to remember the amount of the force which he covers; for while he knows that the numbers necessary to surprise an army of fifty thousand men cannot be conveniently crammed within the compass of a nutshell, he must, on the other hand, remember that there are few countries which do not afford an ambuscade for five or ten thousand—*ergo*, if there be any truth in Cocker, the man covering five thousand men must look exactly ten times sharper than the man who covers fifty thousand.

With an army of rough and ready materials such as ours had now become, the usual precautions were scarcely necessary, except in the immediate vicinity of the foe, for they had by this time discovered that it was more easy to find than to get rid of us; but they ought, nevertheless, to be strictly observed at all times, unless there are good and sufficient reasons why they need not.

In an open country a few squadrons of dragoons shoved well to the front will procure every necessary information; but, in a close country, I hold the following to be the best advanced guard.

> 1st. A subaltern with twelve hussars, throwing two of them a hundred yards in front, and four at fifty.
>
> 2nd. A section of riflemen or light infantry at fifty yards.
>
> 3rd. The other three sections of the company at fifty yards.
>
> 4th. Four companies of light infantry at a hundred yards, with communicating files, and followed closely by two pieces of horse artillery, and a squadron of dragoons.

On falling in with the enemy, the advanced *videttes* will fire off their carabines to announce it, and if their opponents fall back they will continue their onward movement. If they do not, the intermediate four will join them, and try the result of a shot each; when, if the enemy still remain, it shows that they decline taking a civil hint, which, if they are infantry, they assuredly will; and dispositions must be made accordingly.

While the remaining hussars are, therefore, despatched to watch the flanks, the leading section of infantry will advance in skirmishing order, and take possession of the most favourable ground near the advanced *videttes*. The other three sections will close up to within fifty yards, one of them, if necessary to join the advanced one, but a subdivision must remain in reserve. The guns will remain on the road, and the dragoons and infantry composing the main body of the advanced guard will be formed on the flanks, in such manner as the ground will admit, so as to be best ready for either attack or defence; and in that disposition they will watt farther orders, presuming that the officer commanding the division will not be a hundred miles off.

The foregoing applies more particularly to the following of an enemy whom you have not lately thrashed, whereas, if following a beaten one, he ought never to be allowed a moment's respite so long as you have force enough of any kind up to shove him along. He ought to be bullied every inch of the way with dragoons and horse artillery, and the infantry brought to bear as often as possible.

However much additional celerity of movement on the part of the latter force may be desirable, I must impress upon the minds of all future comptrollers of knapsacks, that on no consideration should an infantry man ever be parted from his pack. He will not move a bit faster without than he does with it, nor do I think he can go a yard farther in a day's walking; they become so accustomed to the pace, and so inured to the load, that it makes little difference to them whether it is on or off,[3] while the leaving of them behind, leads, at all times, to serious loss, and to still more serious inconvenience.

The Rifles during the war were frequently, as an indulgence, made to fight without them, but on every occasion it proved a sacrifice, and a great one. For although they were carried for us by the dragoons, who followed after, yet as our skirmishing service took us off the road, the kit of every man who got wounded was sure to be lost, for while he was lying kicking on his back in the middle of a field, or behind a stone wall, impatiently waiting for assistance, his knapsack had passed on to the front, and was never heard of more, (for everyone has quite enough to do to take care or his own affairs on those occasions,) and the poor fellow was thus deprived of his comforts at a time when they

---

[3]. Lightly, however, as they felt the load at the time, it was one that told fearfully on the constitution, and I have seen many men discharged in consequence, as being worn out, at thirty-five years of age.

were most needed.

A dragoon, too, carrying several of them would sometimes get hit, and he of course took care of himself, and the unfortunate owners after their hard day's fighting were compelled to sleep in the open air for that and many succeeding nights, without the use of their blankets or necessaries. On one occasion I remember that they were left on the ground, and the battle rolled four miles beyond them, so that when it was over, and every one had already done enough, the soldiers were either obliged to go without, or to add eight or ten miles' walk to a harassing day's work.

The secretary at war eventually came in for his share of the trouble attendant on those movements, for many were the claims for compensation which poured in upon the War-Office in after years, by the poor fellows who had bled and lost their all upon those occasions, nor do I know whether they have ever yet been set at rest.

So much for advanced guards and people in a hurry, and as I happen to have a little leisure time and a vacant leaf or two to fill up, I shall employ it in taking a shot at field fortification; and in so doing, be it remarked, that I leave science in those matters to the scientific, for I am but a practical soldier.

The French showed themselves regular moles at field work, for they had no sooner taken post on a fresh position, than they were to be seen stirring up the ground in all directions. With us it was different. I have always understood that Lord Wellington had a dislike to them, and would rather receive his enemy in the open field than from behind a bank of mud. How far it was so I know not; but the report seemed to be verified by circumstances, for he rarely ever put us to the trouble of throwing up either redoubts or breast works, except at particular out- posts, where they were likely to be useful.

At Fuentes indeed he caused some holes to be dug on the right of the line, in which the enemy's cavalry might have comfortably broken their necks without hurting themselves much; but I do not recollect our ever disturbing the ground anywhere else—leaving the lines of Torres Vedras out of the question, as containing works of a different order.

If time and circumstances permitted common field works to be so constructed as to prevent an enemy from scrambling up the walls, they would indeed be a set of valuable pictures in the face of a position; but as with mud alone they never can, I, for one, hold them to be worse than nothing, and would rather go against one of them, than against the same number of men in the open field.

It is true that in such a place they will suffer less in the first instance, but if they do not repulse their assailants or make a speedy retreat, they are sure to be all netted in the long run, and the consequence is, that one rarely sees a work of that kind well Defended; for while its garrison is always prepared for a start, its fire is not so destructive as from the same number of men in the field; for in the field they will do their duty, but in the redoubt they will not, and half of their heads will be well sheltered under the ramparts, while they send the shot off at random. I know the fellows well, and it is only to swarm a body of light troops against the nearest angle, to get into the ditch as quickly as possible; to unkennel any garrison of that kind very cleverly, unless there be other obstacles than their bayonets to contend against.

From field works I return to our work in the field, to state that after several days' march under a broiling hot sun, and on roads of scorching dust, which makes good stiff broth in winter, we found ourselves on the banks of the Tormes, near the end of the bridge of Salamanca; but as the gatekeeper there required change for twenty-four pound shot; and we had none at the moment to give him, we were obliged to take to the stream.

I know not what sort of toes the Pope keeps for his friends to kiss, but I know that after a week's marching in summer I would not kiss those of the army for a trifle; however, I suppose that walking feet and kissing ones wear quite different pairs of shoes. The fording of the clear broad waters of the Tormes at all events proved a luxury in various ways, and considerably refreshed by that part of the ceremony, we found ourselves shortly after in the heart of that classical city where the first classics which we were called upon to study, were those of three forts, of a class of their own, which was well calculated to keep their neighbours in a constant supply of hot water. They were not field works such as I have been treating of in the last few pages, but town ones, with walls steep enough and ditches deep enough to hold the army, if packed like herrings. For ourselves we passed on to the front, leaving the Seventh Division to deal with them; and a hard bargain they drove for a time, though they finally brought them to terms.

I rode in from the outposts several times to visit them during the siege, and on one occasion finding an officer, stationed in a tower, overlooking the works and acting upon rather particular orders, it reminded me of an anecdote that occurred with us in the early part of the war. One of our majors had posted a subaltern with a party of riflemen in the tower of a church, and as the place was an important one, he ordered the officer, in the event of an attack, never to quit the place alive! In the course of the evening the commanding officer went to visit the picquet, and after satisfying himself on different points, he demanded of Lieutenant —— what dispositions he had made for retreat in the event of his post being forced—To which the other replied, "None."

"None, sir," said the commanding officer, "then let me tell you that you have neglected an important part of your duty."

"I beg your pardon," returned the officer, "but my orders are never to quit this spot alive, and, therefore, no arrangements for retreat can be necessary!"

It may be needless to add that a discretionary power was then extended to him in a midnight. visit which I paid to the same place in company with a staff friend, while the batteries were in full operation, we were admiring the splendour of the scene, the crash of the artillery, and the effect of the light and shade on the ruins around, caused by the perpetual flashes from the guns and fire-balls, when it recalled to his remembrance the siege of Copenhagen, where he described a similar scene which was enacted, but in a position so much more interesting.

The burying-grounds in the neighbourhood of that capital, were generally very tastefully laid out like shrubberies with beds of flowers, appropriate trees, &c., and intersected by winding gravel walks, neatly bordered with box. One of the prettiest of these cemeteries was that at the Lecton suburb, in which there was a profusion of white marble statues of men and women—many of them in loose flowing drapery, and also of various *quadrupeds*, erected in commemoration or in illustration of the habits and virtues of the dead. These status were generally overshadowed by cypress and other *lugubrious* trees.

Closely adjoining this beautiful cemetery, two heavy batteries were erected, one of ten-inch mortars, and the other of twenty-four pound battering guns.

In passing along through this receptacle of the dead, about the hour of midnight, the rapid flashes of the artillery seemed to call all these statues, men, women, and beasts, with all their dismal accompaniments, into a momentary and ghastly existence—and the immediate succession of the deep gloom of midnight produced an effect which, had it been visible to a congregation of Scotch nurses, would in their hands have thrown all the goblin tales of their ancestors into the shade, and generations of bairns yet unborn would have had to shudder at the midnight view of a churchyard.

Even among the stern hearts to whose view alone it was open, the spectacle was calculated to excite very interesting reflections. The crash of the artillery on both sides was enough to have awakened the dead, then came the round shot with its wholesale sweep, tearing up the ornamental trees and dashing statues into a thousand pieces,—next came the bursting shell sending its fragments chattering among the tombs and defacing everything it came in contact with.

These, all these came from the Danes themselves, and who knew but the hand that levelled the gun which destroyed that statue was not the same which had erected it to the memory of a beloved wife? Who knew but that the evergreens which had just been torn by a shot from a new-made grave, were planted there over the remains of an angelic daughter, and watered by the tears of the man who fired it? and who knew but that that exquisitely chiselled marble figure, which had its nose and eye defaced by a bursting shell, was not placed there to commemorate the decease of a beauteous and adored sweetheart, and valued more than existence by him who had caused its destruction! Ah, me! war, war! that

> *Snatching from the hand*
> *Of Time, the scythe of ruin, sits aloft,*
> *Or stalks in dreadful majesty abroad.*

I know not what sort of place Salamanca was on ordinary occasions, but at that time it was remarkably stupid. The inhabitants were yet too much at the mercy of circumstances to manifest any favourable disposition towards us, even if they felt so inclined, for it was far from decided whether the French, or we, were to have the supremacy, and, therefore, everyone who had the means betook himself elsewhere. Our position, too, in front of the town to cover the siege was anything but a comfortable one—totally unsheltered from the burning Spanish sun, and unprovided with either wood or water, so that it was with no small delight that we hailed the surrender of the forts already mentioned, and the consequent retreat of the French army, for in closing up to them, it brought us to a merry country on the banks of the Douro.

Mirth and duty there, however, were, as they often are, very much at variance. Our position was a ticklish one, and required half the division to sleep in the field in front of the town each night fully accoutred, so that while we had every alternate night to rejoice in quarters, the next was one of penance in the fields which would have been tolerably fair had they been measured by the same bushel, but it could not be, for while pleasure was the order of the evening we had only to close the window-shutters to make a summer's night as long as a winter's one—but in affairs of duty, stern duty, it told in an inverse ratio; for our vineyard beds on the alternate nights were not furnished with window-shutters, and if they had been, it would have made but little difference; for in defiance of sun, or stars, we were obliged to be on our legs an hour before daybreak, which in that climate and at that season, happened to be between one and two o'clock in the morning.

Our then brigadier. Sir O. Vandeleur, was rigorous on that point, and as our sleeping, bore no proportion to our waking moments, many officers would steal from the ranks to snatch a little repose under cover of the vines, and it became a highly amusing scene to see the general on horseback, threading up between the rows of bushes and ferreting put the sleepers. He netted a good number in the first cast or two, but they ultimately became too knowing for him, and had only to watch his passing up one row, to slip through the bushes into it, where they were perfectly secure for the next half hour.

I have already mentioned that Rueda was a capital wine country. Among many others there was a rough effervescent pure white wine, which I had never met with anywhere else, and which in warm weather was a most delicious beverage. Their wine cellars were all excavated in a sort of common, immediately outside the town; and though I am afraid to say the extent, they were of an amazing depth.

It is to be presumed that the natives were all strictly honest, for we found the different cellar, so indifferently provided with locks and keys, that our men, naturally inferring that good drinkers must have been the only characters in request, went to work most patriotically, without waiting to be pressed, and the cause being such a popular one, it was with no little difficulty that we kept them within bounds.

A man of ours, of the name of Taylor, wore a head so remarkably like Lord Wellington's, that he was dabbed " Sir Arthur" at the commencement of the war, and retained the name until the day of his death. At Rueda he was the servant of the good, the gallant Charley Eeles, who afterwards fell at Waterloo. Sir Arthur, in all his movements for twenty years, had been as regular as

Shrewsbury clock; he cleaned his master's clothes and boots, and paraded his traps in the morning, and in the evening he got blind drunk, unless the means were wanting.

In one so noted for regularity as he was, it is but reasonable to expect that his absence at toilet time should be missed and wondered at; he could not have gone over to the enemy, for he was too true blue for that He could not have gone to heaven without passing through the pains of death—he was too great a sinner for that. He could not have gone downwards without having passed the aforesaid ceremony, for nobody was ever known to do so but one man, to recover his wife, and as Sir Arthur had no wife, he had surely no inducement to go there; in short the cause of his disappearance remained clouded in mystery for twenty-five hours, but would have been cleared up in a tenth part of the time, had not the rifleman, who had been in the habit of sipping out of the same favourite cask, been on guard in the interim, but as soon as he was relieved, he went to pay his usual visit, and in stooping in the dark over the edge of the large headless butt to take his accustomed sip, his nose came in contact with that of poor Sir Arthur, which like that of his great prototype, was of no mean dimensions, and who was floating on the surface of his favourite liquid, into which he must have dived deeper than he intended and got swamped. Thus perished Sir Arthur, a little beyond the prime of life, but in what the soldiers considered, a prime death!

Our last day at Rueda furnished an instance so characteristic of the silence and secrecy with which the Duke of Wellington was in the habit of conducting his military movements, that I cannot help quoting it.

In my former volume I mentioned that when We were called to arms that evening, our officers had assembled for one of their usual dances. Our commanding officer, however, Colonel Cameron, had been invited to dine that day with his lordship, and in addition to the staff, the party consisted of several commanding officers of regiments and others. The conversation was lively and general, and no more allusion made to probable movements than if we were likely to be fixed there for years.

After having had a fair allowance of wine, Lord Wellington looked at his watch, and addressing himself to one of his staff, said, "Campbell, it is about time to be moving—order coffee." Coffee was accordingly introduced, and the guests, as usual, immediately after made their bow and retired. Our commandant, in passing out of the house, was rather surprised to see his lordship's baggage packed, and the mules at the door, saddled and ready to receive it, but his astonishment was still greater when he reached his own quarter, to find that his regiment was already under arms along with the rest of the troops, assembled on their alarm posts, and with baggage loaded in the act of moving off, we knew not whither!

We marched the whole of the night, and daylight next morning found us three or four leagues off, interposing ourselves between the enemy and their projected line of advance. It was the commencement of the brilliant series of movements which preceded tire battle of Salamanca. Pass we on, therefore, to that celebrated field.

It was late in the afternoon before it was decided whether that day's sun was to set on a battle or our farther retreat. The army all stood in position with the exception of the Third Division, which lay in reserve beyond the Tormes. Its commander. Sir Edward Packenham, along with the other generals of divisions, attended on the commander-in chief, who stood on an eminence which commanded a view of the enemy's movements.

The artillery on both sides was ploughing the ground in all directions, and making fearful gaps in the ranks exposed—the French were fast closing on and around our right—the different generals had received their instructions, and waited but the final order—a few minutes must decide whether there was to be a desperate battle or a bloody retreat; when, at length. Lord Wellington, who had been anxiously watching their movements with his spy-glass, called out, "Packenham, I can stand this no longer; now is your time!"

"Thank you," replied the gallant Packenham, "give me your

hand, my lord, and it shall be done!" Shaking hands accordingly, he vaulted into his saddle, and the result of his movement, as is well known, placed two eagles, several pieces of artillery, and four thousand prisoners in our possession.

Packenham afterwards told a friend of mine who was on his staff, that, while in the execution of that movement, he saw an opportunity in which, by a slight deviation from his original instructions, he might have cut off twenty thousand of the enemy, without greater risk to 'his own division than he was about to encounter; but he dreaded the possibility of its compromising the safety of some other portion of the army, and dared not to run the hazard.

I have, in the early part of this volume, in speaking of individual gallantry in general, given it as my opinion that if the merits of every victory that had been hotly contested could be traced to the proper, persons, it would be found to rest with a very few—for to those who know it not, it is inconceivable what may be effected in such situations by any individual ascending a little above mediocrity.

The day after the battle of Salamanca a brigade of heavy German dragoons, under the late Baron Bock, made one of the most brilliant charges recorded in history.

The enemy's rear guard, consisting of, I thinks three regiments of infantry, flanked by cavalry and artillery, were formed in squares on an abrupt eminence, the approach to which was fetlock deep in shingle. In short, it was a sort of position in which infantry generally think they have a right to consider themselves secure from horsemen.

The Baron was at the head of two splendid regiments, and, as some of the English prints, up to that period, had been very severe upon the employment of his countrymen in the British service, he was no doubt burning with the desire for an opportunity of removing the unjust attack that had been made upon them, and he could not have even dreamt of one more glorious than that alluded to.

Lord Wellington, who was up with the advanced guard, no

sooner observed the dispositions of the enemy than he sent an order for the Baron to charge them. They charged accordingly—broke through the squares, and took the whole of the infantry—the enemy's cavalry and artillery having fled.

Colonel May, of the British artillery, not satisfied with being the bearer of the order, gallantly headed the charge, and fell covered with wounds, from which, he eventually recovered; but Lord Wellington, however much he must have admired the action, cut him for a considerable time in consequence, by way of marking his disapproval of officers thrusting themselves into danger unnecessarily.

In an attempt so gallantly made—so gloriously executed—it would be invidious to exalt one individual above another, and yet I have every reason to believe that their success was in a great measure owing to the decisive conduct of one man.

Our battalion just rounded the hill in time to witness the end of it; and in conversing with one of the officers immediately after, he told me that their success was owing to the presence of mind of a captain commanding a squadron, who was ordered to charge the cavalry which covered a flank of the squares—that, while in full career, the enemy's horse in his front, without awaiting the shock, gave way, but, in place of pursuing them, he, with a decision calculated to turn the tide of any battle, at once brought up his outward flank, and went full tilt against a face of the square, which having until that moment been protected, was taken by surprise, and he bore down all before him!

My informant mentioned the name of the hero, but it was a severe German one, which died on the spot like an empty sound—nor have I ever since read or heard of it—so that one who ought to have filled a bright page in our history of that brilliant field, has, in all probability, passed—

> *Nor of his name or race*
> *Hath left a token or a trace,*

—save what I have here related.

The Baron, presuming that he had all the merit due to a

leader on that occasion, (for I knew him only by sight,) showed, in his own person, what we frequently see, that to be a bold man it is not necessary to be a big one. In stature he was under the middle size, slenderly made, and with a hump on one shoulder. He lived through many a bloody peninsular field to perish by shipwreck in returning to his native country.

Throughout our many hard-fought and invariably successful Peninsular fields, it used to be a subject of deep mortification for us to see the breasts of our numerous captives adorned with the different badges of the Legion of Honour, and to think that our country should never have thought their captors deserving, or some little mark of distinction, not only to commemorate the action, but to distinguish the man who fought, from him who did not—thereby leaving that strongest of all corps, the Belem Rangers, who had never seen a shot fired, to look as fierce and talk as big as the best.

Many officers, I see, by the periodicals, continue still to fight for such a distinction, but the day has gone by. No correct line could now be drawn, and the seeing of such a medal on the breast of a man who had no claim, would deprive it of its chief value in the eyes of him who had.

To show the importance attached to such distinctions in our service, I may remark that, though the Waterloo medal is intrinsically worth two or three shillings, and a soldier will sometimes be tempted to part with almost anything for drink, yet, during the fifteen years in which I remained with the rifles after Waterloo, I never knew a single instance of a medal being sold, and only one of its being pawned.

On that solitary occasion it was the property of a handsome, wild, rattling young fellow, named Roger Black. He, one night, at Cambray, when his last copper had gone, found the last glass of wine so good, that he could not resist the temptation of one bottle more, for which he left his medal in pledge with the *aubergiste*, for the value of ten *sous*. Roger's credit was low—a review day arrived, and he could not raise the wind to redeem the thing he gloried in, but, putting a bold face on it, he went to the holder, and telling him that he had come for the purpose of re-emption, he got it in his hands, and politely wished the landlord good morning, telling him, as he was marching off, that he would call and pay the *franc* out of the first money he received; but the arrangement did not suit mine host, who opposed his exit with all the strength of his establishment, consisting of his wife, two daughters, a well-frizzled waiter, and a club-footed hostler. Roger, however, painted the whole family group, ladies and all, with a set of beautiful black eyes, and then marched off triumphantly.

Poor Roger for that feat, was obliged to be paid in kind, very much against the grain of his judges, for his defence was an honest one—namely, that he had no intention of cheating the man, but he had no money, "and you know, gentlemen, I could never think of going to a review without my medal!"

Lightning Source UK Ltd.
Milton Keynes UK
05 January 2011

165211UK00001B/126/P